Visible and Invisible
Nuclear Energy, Shale Gas and Wind Power in the Polish Media Discourse

Visible and Invisible
Nuclear Energy, Shale Gas and Wind Power, in the Polish Media Discourse

Edited by
Aleksandra Wagner

Translated by
Benjamin Koschalka

Jagiellonian University Press

This book is the result of research project funded by Polish National Science Center (decision number 2011/03/D/HS6/05874).

REVIEWER
dr hab. Marian Niezgoda, em. prof. UJ

Originally published under the title *Widoczne i niewidoczne. Atom, łupki, wiatr w dyskursach medialnych wokół energetyki.*

COVER DESIGN
Andrzej Pilichowski-Ragno

ISBN 978-83-233-4229-8
ISBN 978-83-233-9585-0 (e-book)

www.wuj.pl

Jagiellonian University Press
Editorial Offices: Michałowskiego St. 9/2, 31-126 Cracow
Phone: +48 12 663 23 82, Fax: +48 12 663 23 83
Distribution: Phone: +48 12 631 01 97, Fax: +48 12 631 01 98
Cell Phone: +48 506 006 674, e-mail: sprzedaz@wuj.pl
Bank: PEKAO SA, IBAN PL 80 1240 4722 1111 0000 4856 3325

CONTENTS

INTRODUCTION   7

Aleksandra Wagner

THE MEDIA ENERGY DISCOURSE AS AN OBJECT OF SOCIOLOGICAL
REFLECTION – THE THEORETICAL AND METHODOLOGICAL
CONTEXT   11

Is energy a sociological topic?   11
A discursive approach to analysis of public policies. Deliberation and visibility
    in the public sphere   15
Situational analysis as a way of mapping the discursive media space   23
Conclusion   28

Aleksandra Wagner

ORGANISING THE RESEARCH   33

General information about the research   33
Research questions   35
Historical analyses of press discourses   37
Building a corpus of texts from the 1980s   38
Nuclear, shale, wind energy – the press discourse from 2007–2012   39
Building a corpus of texts from 2007–2012   40
Analysis of discourse from 2013–2014   42

Rafał Garpiel

NUCLEAR ENERGY IN THE POLISH MEDIA DISCOURSE   49

Nuclear energy from a CDA perspective   49
The discourse in the 1980s   51
The discourse in 2007–2012   64
The discourse in 2013 and 2014   84
Conclusion   102

Maria Świątkiewicz-Mośny

THE MEDIA DISCOURSE ON WIND ENERGY   105

Actors engaged in the wind discourse   107
Power – interests – knowledge   110
Diagnosis of communication strategies   113
Between quality of life and development   118
Democracy and participation   120
Conclusion   122

Aleksandra Wagner

SHALE GAS IN THE POLISH MEDIA DISCOURSE   125

Introduction   125
Economic conditions   126
Geopolitical conditions   127
Political conditions   128
Media discourses in the USA and European countries   130
The dynamic of the Polish shale gas discourse   132
Shale gas as a discursive construct   133
Language   136
Social worlds and arenas   138
Actors   141
Conflicts played out in arenas   144
Arena or agora?   147
Conceptualisations of risk   150
Law   152
The media as a space of deliberation: exclusion and inclusion mechanisms   153

Wit Hubert

REPRESENTATION OF SELECTED ENERGY TOPICS ON THE POLISH INTERNET   159

Introduction   159
Methods used in analyses   163
Study of expert internet discourse – method   164
Study of social media internet discourse – method   165
Expert internet energy discourse   166
The online/social media energy discourse   171
Conclusion   175

Aleksandra Wagner

THE MEDIA AS A SPACE OF DELIBERATION BASED ON THE EXAMPLE OF MEDIA DISCOURSE ON SELECTED ENERGY TOPICS – CONCLUSION   177

APPENDICES   187

INTRODUCTION

This book came about as the result of research encompassing a period from the 1980s (archival research) until 2014. Various media forms and diverse channels of mass communication were analysed in the selected time periods, which allowed us to gather material that on the one hand was abundant and differentiated and on the other illustrated the dynamic of changes based on consistent tracking of the fields of nuclear and wind policy and shale gas. It was no coincidence that these types of energy were chosen, while the most obvious one in Poland, coal, was left out. When the research began, they were (all in their own way) innovative technologies. Nuclear energy – perhaps the hardest to define in this way (as many actors treat it as a technology of the past) – is still to be implemented in Poland. For several years, though, it has again begun to be considered as a solution that might satisfy the future demands of energy policy, assuring a stable energy supply, increasing the country's energy independence and leading to reduced CO_2 emissions. In this sense (as a new solution), it is an innovative approach for the Polish energy system.

Wind energy is the most popular renewable energy source (RES) in Poland, as well as the most recognisable and the one most readily associated with environmental friendliness. As a result, although it has been around since the 1990s, and in recent years has even undergone a marked increase in generating capacity (albeit remaining relatively low in comparison to leading European countries), it is treated as an alternative to "hard" yet "dirty" energy technologies based on fossil fuels (including uranium).

Shale gas is a new subject that appeared in the media discourse just two years before the beginning of the study, during which it became a hot topic in the media. Unlike the remaining two energy types, saddled with a certain history of discourses around which specific epistemic communities had developed and narrative tracks, types of argument and symbolic representations had formed, the selection of the topic of shale gas permitted an ongoing observation of all these processes. New media representations need to in some way be anchored in the world of already existing meanings, which meant that it was also possible to track the networks with connections to foreign discourses or the traditions of the Polish gas industry. A further significant consideration was the positioning of shale gas compared to other energy sources, actors and their various interests.

Let us stress from the outset that the aim of the analyses was not to assess the usefulness or risk of a given energy technology, but rather to reconstruct their media representations in the context of dynamically developing discourses. As such, the selected energy topics, concerning all citizens as well as their descendants, thus determine the future not only of their immediate environment, but also that of the region and the world. In terms of their relations to the key economic interests of various groups and entities, meanwhile, they become peculiar case studies of the way in which media discourses function in the contemporary public sphere. The main question is therefore about the way in which public policies are formed, presented and discussed in the media space, with particular attention given to the participation (and /or lack thereof) of diverse social actors in these processes.

There are two main parts to this book. The purpose of first part, comprising the first two chapters, is to present the theoretical and methodological foundations. It shows the results of the conceptualisation work and explains how the research was organised. Owing to the diversity of this research, conducted in a number of stages using various methods, it is impossible to include all the analytical tools and detailed interim reports (analysing a given topic in a specific media type) in the book. This presentation of the theoretical-methodological framework and essential approach to thinking about media discourses developed over the last three years is therefore especially important.

Second part includes individual analyses of specific topics, and is more diverse. It begins with Chapter 3, Rafał Garpiel's analysis of the nuclear energy discourse, followed by Chapter 4, in which Maria Świątkiewicz-Mośny examines the discourse on wind energy, and Chapter 5, in which Aleksandra Wagner tackles media discourses on shale gas.

The logic in Chapter 6 is somewhat different. Wit Hubert uses data provided by the SentiOne group to analyse the specific nature of discourses developed in social media. Rather than simply presenting a subject discourse, then, the author concentrates on the medium – and specifically the discourses developed in the communication space constituted by new media. Our reasoning for this was that the initially planned analyses of the internet discourse and the accepted criterion of its visibility led to the conclusion that the sources are mostly institutional. We therefore decided to expand the spectrum of analyses to allow us to take into account discourses that were dispersed and therefore less visible, yet no less significant for the developing argumentative structures and dynamically related to the expert discourse of professional websites and blogs.

All the authors, as members of the research team, worked within an agreed-upon theoretical conception, employing a joint conceptual frame-work and common categories, yet remained independent, and the individual chapters are the result of their incisive observation, individual astuteness and creative interpretation. The analysis is based on the materials generated over the course of the research. We ought to point out that, to keep the qualitative analyses as intersubjective as possible, the researchers exchanged interim reports, analytical notes, conceptual and location maps, discussing and consulting their findings and conclusions together. And this is as good as place as any to thank them for this.

As the editor of this book and head of the research project, I thank Maria Świątkiewicz-Mośny, Rafał Garpiel and Wit Hubert for accompanying me on this fascinating journey and offering their support in the form of advice and ideas, for their hard work and commitment. My thanks also to all who participated in the project for their painstaking coding, piloting the research methods and their valuable comments. I am hugely grateful to Jacek Bednarz, Ewa Niezgoda, Katarzyna Rabiej-Sienicka, Magdalena Stawicka and Aleksandra Latko, as well as to the Press Service and SentiOne teams, who furnished us with high-quality data. I thank Professor Marian Niezgoda for his meticulous reading and review of the book, as well as his kind support throughout the project. His enormous technical knowledge meant that we were able to steer clear of many errors; we ourselves are to blame for any that we failed to avoid.

I also thank Alicja Franaszek, whose kindness and experience helped our team through organisational difficulties, and the Polish National Science Centre, for funding the research.

Lastly, I am grateful to the editors of the Jagiellonian University Press for their diligent work and assistance.

Aleksandra Wagner

Aleksandra Wagner

THE MEDIA ENERGY DISCOURSE AS AN OBJECT OF SOCIOLOGICAL REFLECTION — THE THEORETICAL AND METHODOLOGICAL CONTEXT

Is energy a sociological topic?

Questions concerning acquisition, storage and use of energy crop up in diverse contexts associated with how societies operate at various levels: from micro (household and individuals' practices), via meso (when energy issues are considered in the context of the functioning of cities, municipalities or regions), to macro (referring to state policies, the workings of transnational organisations, and global markets and geopolitical systems). We can also identify the global level, when the operation of the energy industries is discussed in the context of the future of the planet, climate, reduction of greenhouse gas emissions and responsible management of resources on a global scale. Energy policy as a type of public policy is generating increased interest among diverse social actors, coinciding with calls for civic empowerment and participatory development of these policies.[1] These demands

---

1   With reference to the five stages of the process of managing public policies (Jann, Wegrich 2007; cf. Palumbo, Maynard-Moody 1991; Dye 2013; Górniak, Żmuda, Prokopowicz 2015), the process of civic deliberation is usually applied in the first stage, i.e. "agenda setting," or paying attention to a given issue requiring state intervention, and the third one, acquiring legitimation for specific proposals for action. This fits into the Habermasian conception of dialogue between the authorities and society, in which the civil society is a space for forming demands and the political system is supposed to respond to them (cf. Habermas 1992; Hess 2013). Yet public deliberation in the sense of procedures of governance can also play an

are associated with a growing popularity of the concepts of deliberative and participatory democracy (Habermas 1996; Dryzek 1990, 2000, 2010; Fishkin, Laslett 2003), and involve consideration of the reflexive public opinion (Fishkin 2009) and civic engagement, for example in the concept of "multilane governance" (Sroka 2009). They are gaining in importance as the needs for transformations of the current energy systems are expressed increasingly clearly in transnational (scientific, political, economic) discourses. These transformations would aim to find new, innovative solutions to allow humanity to respond to the increasing energy requirements of contemporary civilisations, as well as responding to threats related to climate, the environment and limited supplies of fossil fuels. Social protests are no longer interpreted solely in terms of a lack of knowledge or irrational fears of technology (Stankiewicz 2009) and the NIMBY ("Not in my back yard") syndrome, too frequently reduced to people's egoistic aversion to investments (which they otherwise view as justified) being realised in their neighbourhood (Wolsink 2006; Devine-Wright 2009b). Instead, they are increasingly regarded as a dramatic voice in the public sphere resulting from exclusion or marginalisation of some actors[2] (cf. Bell, Grey, Haggett 2005). Some argue that the industrial revolution and its model of energy culture[3] founded on coal, oil and gas created an era of modernisation whose potential in its original form is coming to its limit (Giddens, Lash, Beck 1994). The world is in need of a new paradigm, as illustrated by changes in the organisation of the global economy, lifestyle patterns, values and objectives and the corresponding narratives of crisis: of democracy, capitalism, finances, family, religion, migration etc. A need is emerging to define a new energy basis for further civilisational growth. Among those today writing of a new order with a key role for change in energy policies in the world economy are Jeremy Rifkin (2013), Nico Stehr (2015) and John Urry (2014). Also important is the perception of knowledge as social constructs generated according to new models beyond the university or research laboratory (Gross 2015) and of ignorance that is sometimes no simple gap of knowledge, but rather also a social construct that is an additional source of uncertainty and risk (Fischer, Gottweis 2012; Gross 2015), and frequently a resource employed strategically (McGoey 2012).

With all this in mind, social scientists' growing interest in energy issues in recent decades comes as no surprise. This interest is linked to a comprehensive understanding of energy systems as socio-technological wholes,

---

important role in the remaining stages – i.e. developing specific policies, making decisions and implementing them – on condition that the administrative/technocratic model of public policy administration is done away with in favour of a participatory model (cf. also the argumentative model of public policy analysis [Majone 1989]).

2   A separate issue is that of self-exclusion, which has a cultural basis (cf. Sroka 2009).

3   We understand the concept of energy culture following Łucki, Misiak (2011).

and therefore not only in categories of natural resources (what can we use?) and technologies (how can we use it?), but rather as cultural and individual models of defining the social practices, values and norms that regulate them (Stirling 2014). With this comes the belief that "since the domestication of fire, energy revolutions and cultural shifts have stood in a relationship of mutual interdependency" (Sarrica et al. 2015). It remains a challenge how to overcome the dichotomy between the technological and human aspects of energy, and further, between their social and individual dimensions (Sarrica et al. 2015; Bergmans et al. 2014). The discourses emerging in energy issues conceptualise the problems, challenges and solutions. They organise the symbolic resources both for creating new, innovative paths of development and for consolidating the status quo and preserving the existing balance of power and cultural models. They are a space for forming coalitions and oppositions, and legitimise and delegitimise competing values and visions. They constitute a space for defining social situations, and therefore – if we consider the accepted definitions to be dispositions for these actions to work or be abandoned – forming the future of humanity. This is also the area in which we define the undefined, generate and negotiate ways of dealing with the unknown, and discuss strategies for acting in the face of risk and uncertainty. It is therefore impossible to analyse or plan energy transformations in isolation from the accompanying discourses, as it is they that are the product of this, but at the same time comprise a metanarrative focusing the attention of the existing epistemic communities (Fischer, Gottweis 2012; Cotton, Rattle, Alstine 2014) on the issues of change.

Something that remains a separate issue is the visibility of these discourses in the public sphere – where social problems are determined and the public policies in response to them are legitimised. Among the most important spaces of this visibility is media communication (Dobek-Ostrowska 2007; Hess 2013; Adut 2012). This means both the mass media, i.e. television, radio and press, and the internet space. In the latter, despite the lower entry barriers for social actors, as well as what would appear to be unlimited possibilities of articulation, visibility remains a pressing, and even crucial problem. Some critically oriented researchers of the internet, working from an optimistic and normative vision of the virtual space that emphasises equality and freedom, highlight the dominant position of global corporations and their influence on the access to contents offered to users (cf. Juza 2016; Fuchs 2014). Mediatised discourses on public policies – in this case energy policy – are therefore irrevocably linked to the working of social life in all its aspects: power, violence, knowledge and ignorance, competition, ideologies, interests, statuses, inequalities, etc.

The empowerment of citizens advanced in theories of democracy involves their participation in decision processes and treats the media as an important source of knowledge about the world. It also demands the ability to critically analyse the discourses that are taking place and to discern their constructivist nature. Awareness of discursive mechanisms supports transparency of the public sphere and increases the chances for it to be open to new actors and alternative arguments. This is one of the most important tasks of discursive analyses of public policies.

Social scientists in Poland are only just starting to become interested in energy issues. Whereas for years economic aspects and questions of legislation, and more recently energy security from a political science perspective, have been the subject of research and analyses, thus far it has been rare to take a sociological approach. One of the few attempts to outline the field of interests of sociology of energy is Łucki and Misiak's important monograph *Energetyka a społeczeństwo* (*Energy and Society*, Łucki, Misiak 2011). Numerous public opinion polls on subjects related to the issues of energy policy often boil down to discussing the support, or lack thereof, for a given investment project. These tend to be more journalistic and political than scientific. Against this background, Piotr Stankiewicz and Aleksandra Lis's (2012) sociological study on the knowledge, attitudes and interest of Poles about nuclear energy, as well as the monograph *Social Science and Energy Issues* edited by Sylwia Mrozowska (2016), stand out. Further, separate attention is merited by books on aspects of civic participation and decision processes referring to various problems of energy – from the perception and evaluation of new technologies (Stankiewicz 2008), to the creation of conditions for participation (Stankiewicz 2013; Stankiewicz, Stasik, Suchomska 2015). Both Polish and international authors explore Polish discourses on energy issues (Wagner, Grobelski, Harembski 2016; Upham et al. 2015; Jaspal, Nerlich, Lemańczyk 2014; Wagner 2014; Świątkiewcz-Mośny, Wagner 2012; Mrozowska, Kijowska 2016).

It would also appear that a large section of society do not pay attention to energy policy issues. Less than 18% declare that they follow such topics in the media, while 66.5% admit to a lack of interest in such contents (TNS OBOP 2015). Opinion polls on shale gas illustrate the knowledge deficit among Poles, especially regarding threats (CBOS 2013, 2011), although the respondents themselves describe their knowledge of shale gas as sufficient. They also sometimes fail to discern a need for knowledge even on such practical issues as the level of electricity bills (25% do not know how much they pay, and do not view this knowledge as necessary – TNS OBOP 2015). Energy issues are often presented in the media in a very abstract fashion, conceptualised at the macro level of social life; this means that media communications operate between systems (e.g. mediatised information exchange between economic and political institutions), rather than taking place between the authorities and citizens (cf. Świątkiewicz--Mośny, Wagner 2012). As a result, citizens tend to become spectators in a show that presents specific directions of energy policy, rather than direct or even actually represented participants. Therefore, the visibility of problems and discussions in the media is fundamental to the formation of the social agenda, which then becomes a reference point for systems generating certain solutions within the public policy.

A discursive approach
to analysis of public policies.
Deliberation and visibility in the public sphere

The objective of the research presented in this book was to answer the question of the deliberative potential of the Polish information media. We understand deliberation as collective consideration on matters of importance to a given community (Fishkin 2009). By differentiating deliberation from the concept of civic participation, understood as active participation of citizens in the processes of making political decisions, we also refer to the meaning of deliberation as dialogical exchange and development of arguments. We accept normative assumptions on the exchange of arguments by the participants in deliberation, their readiness to change opinion, capacity to refer to the arguments of others and to produce criteria for judging which of these arguments to further develop. In referring to conceptions of deliberative decision making, acknowledging its influence and significance for contemporary theories of democracy and appreciating the forms of direct democracy, we also observe an underestimation in the subject literature of the potential of mediatisation of deliberation and the significance of media activity for the operation of this process in the public sphere.[4]

By defining the public sphere through its communicative dimension (cf. Ferree et al. 2002), we therefore wish to reflect critically on whether the information media support social deliberation, both by creating a space for debate and by informing citizens on the processes of dialogue taking place and mobilising them to take active part in then. The essential questions here are: who participates in the debate in the information media; what events

---

4   Numerous authors discuss (often critically) the issue of the role of media in deliberation processes, including Ben Page (1996), Simone Chambers and Anne N. Costain (2000), Maarten Wolsink (2006), along with many articles to which we refer in this book. In most works, however, the authors ask about the role of the media (their practices, media representations, etc.) in deliberation processes. Conceptualisation of the media as a space where a process of deliberation can occur (present, for example, in Hess 2013) is a rarity in the subject literature.

and topics determine its dynamic; what values and principles organise the discourses that exist in the media space; how do these discourses reflect specific epistemic communities and how do these communities create coalitions and oppositions; finally, which symbolic resources do actors employ to legitimise their positions, and according to which mechanisms are they used? The question of whether the media space is a space of deliberation, and if so in what way, in fact turns out to be a question on the vision of the public sphere accepted by communicatively active actors, as well one as on the visibility and invisibility of the discourses in this mediatised reality.

We treated the media themselves here as a communicative space, and therefore a symbolic dimension of the public sphere, examined on two levels – as a space of communication between government and society, and within civil society (a space in which the actors of this society make themselves visible, become empowered, and shape and negotiate among themselves definitions of a situation). This corresponds to the Habermasian understanding of a political public sphere (in which public opinion identifies and thematises problems, so that the political system can then respond to them), and of the civic public sphere, where the actors of civil society become visible to each other (cf. Habermas 1996; Hess 2013). We assumed that this is a space of organised, intentional, yet dispersed communicative actions. These produce images of reality within the limits they construct, to which actors, including the media themselves as collective actors, refer as if to external reality. Following Niklas Luhman (2000), it is important to stress that we are not denying the existence of this reality per se, but merely emphasising that the actors of communicative actions do not refer to it directly, but rather through the constructions of reality they produce. When we speak of the media, it is to this communicative space that we shall be referring, whereas when discussing media institutions as actants,[5] we shall use the term "broadcaster," or, for individual actors, "journalists."

This understanding of a communicative space therefore comprises a set of institutional spaces and discursive rules which as a result form public opinion (Habermas 1996). Yet these spaces go beyond the media, and not only are dispersed, but also have no centre; they might be invisible, self-referential and isolated from each other, though they can also merge and connect together. The problem of semiotic visibility of discourse therefore seems important.[6]

---

5   We borrow the notion of the "actant" from the tradition of the ideas of Bruno Latour (2007), and refer to non-human acting entities, here institutions working as networks that encompass not only individuals, but also technologies, models and norms of their operation, interactions between the various elements and media institutions.

6   The categories of semiotic visibility of actors in the context of their sensual accessibility and physical presence in the public sphere, as well as publicity, are discussed by Ari Adut (2012). Here we modify his definitions of visibility, relating it to generally sensually and cognitively accessible discourses recognised as sets of communicative actions of communicatively determined groups of actors.

This visibility goes beyond the social niches that these discourses formed. This condition is crucial for confronting them, regardless of whether it is to lead to mutual understanding and create accord for the common good, or to competition and the struggle for hegemony.

The category of visibility was introduced and discussed by Ari Adut (2012) as something of a counterproposal to normative concepts of the public sphere, which linked the notion with civic engagement and the intention to serve the common good. Semiotic visibility therefore refers mostly to individuals appearing in the public sphere, irrespective of their intentions, accessible to the remaining individuals (spectators) as non-engaged others. The fundamental resource in the public sphere is therefore the attention of the audience, which can then be converted into other capitals, for example economic or political. The spectators themselves refer to those who appear using simplifications and typifications (Adut 2012). However, the category of visibility can be related not only to actors, as Adut suggests, but also to discourses themselves. According to this conception, the discourses produced by epistemic communities need a space where they can potentially be accessible to everybody (thus satisfying the condition of a generally accessible public sphere), and their potential for attracting the attention of the audience is an important factor – albeit not the only one – affecting their capacity to create social definitions of situations. At the same time, these discourses themselves undergo typification and simplification reflexively. Adut emphasises the significance of publicity, and notes that the asymmetry that occurs between the audience and the actor does not deprive the former of its significant power understood as the capacity to form groups around that which is watched – by the very fact of sharing participation in the watching (Adut 2012). Yet it is hard to agree with this. The sociology of mass communication has described the characteristics of various types of audiences. The act of participation in an audience alone – be it a diffuse mass audience or one concentrated in one place – is not a sufficient group-forming factor. We can speak of this kind of bond only in reference to the type of public described by Gabriel Tarde (1898). Yet the visibility of discourses in the generally accessible public sphere – here the media space – is significant, as it is here that coalitions of epistemic communities generating the various discourses (as well as the oppositions of these discourses) visible for the wider audience can emerge. Examples might be the support of expert economists for the discourse of the government administration or of environmental scientists for social activists.

The thematic discourses analysed in this book refer to energy policy. This is in turn part of public policies, meaning rationalised and comprehensive actions of society undertaken with the aim of solving socially important problems or attending to society's needs. The discursive approach, which studies argumentative structures in the narratives of members of society, occupies an important place among the various ways of analysing public policies. The strategies are produced by the aforementioned epistemic communities, which are understood as informal, often dispersed networks generating knowledge and constructing specific definitions, which can in turn exert influence on political actors on a micro scale (O'Riordan, Jordan 1996: 87[7]). These communities are capable of mobilising around specific discourses (Cotton, Rattle, Alstine 2014). And the discourses provide a framework for them, defining who is entitled to speak on behalf of the given community and on what basis (Fisher, Forester 1993). Furthermore, these discourses produce sets of rules that determine which subjects are permissible as well as pointing to the symbolic resources that may be used: knowledge and ignorance, values and anti-values. They are immersed in external contexts, but simultaneously shift these into themselves, defining situations in a certain way and thus transforming the external circumstances into internal elements of the situation (cf. Clarke 2005).

The discursive turn in analysis of public policies, dated to the beginning of the 1990s, entailed facing the dominant way of treating public policies as neutral in terms of the values of technical products (Fisher, Forester 1993). Public policy, it was stressed, is not and cannot be a simple application of scientific methods; without denying the importance of empirical data, a relationship was sought between these data and normative guidelines. The most significant thing became how these relations are constructed in communicative processes. What therefore proved to be the consequence was the opening of the field to qualitative and interpretive analyses, which contrasted with the technocratic and positivistic approach to analysis of public policies (Fischer, Gottweis 2012).

In discursive analyses of public policies from around the turn of the 21st century, an important dimension was language perceived as a medium and tool for organising thinking about selected problems. This is the basis for the proposal for critical analysis of language, reproducing and understanding meanings as support for the deliberation process concerning various actors – politicians, administration, citizens (Lindblom, Cohen 1979; Fischer, Gottweis 2012: 2).

What we therefore find in the discursive approach is an orientation towards civic participation and deliberation – a process during which various actors can strive to create a common solution. We are therefore dealing with

---

7   Here we depart from the definitions of epistemic communities as communities of professionals proposed by Hass (1992), for example. The criteria he proposes – shared rules, norms and values organising knowledge and providing the foundations for assessing the rationality of social actions and public policies – would seem to also encompass actors who cannot be defined as "professional experts," e.g. activists, members of communities and informal neighbourhood groups – in short, all those engaged in matters of individuals.

a normative ideal of deliberation that derives from the ideas of Habermas and Rawls, and a procedural view of it that opens the field for developing the methodology of participation. What is also stressed is the uncertainty of the times and variability of reality, in which even science and the resultant knowledge do not provide a guarantee of finding optimal solutions, and science itself often becomes a source of uncertainty and risk. As a result, deliberation as a process of collectively agreeing on knowledge, integrating its various resources and accepting its various sources, as well as searching for innovative solutions through rational exchange and evaluation of arguments becomes a way of coping with risk and uncertainty, and with even more clarity emphasises how distinct it is from the expert/governmental model of forming public policies.

In the introduction to their edited volume on this subject, however, Fischer and Gottweis (2012) report that in practice social actors compete with each other, presenting various argumentative strategies and representing diverse, often contradictory interests. Discourse analyses are therefore supposed to make it possible to recognise the mechanism according to which they construct these competing narratives and within which they deal with the problems of risk and uncertainty. The authors argue that a constructivist understanding of discourses and argumentation leads to a deliberative finding of a consensus and public solution of problems (in the process of deliberation) (Fischer, Gottweis 2012). As demonstrated by Hemant Ojha, John Cameron and Chetan Kumar (2012) in their analysis of the order of forest management in Nepal, supplementing the normative approach with an analysis of the deep structures of power and symbolic violence permits a multidimensional understanding of the dynamic of this process. Following Habermas's ideas does not mean that categories of alternative analytical approaches cannot be employed; in the case of the cited work this meant the critical sociology of Pierre Bourdieu (albeit bearing the fundamental differences of these approaches in mind). Deliberation as a normative ideal can therefore be important for opening closed fields and changing the doxa. Introducing new narratives of knowledge to the public sphere (Ojha, Cameron, Kumar 2012) as a result supports the process of change in the area of public policies and increases the flexibility of reacting to turbulent reality.

Despite the obvious references to the ideas of Habermas, the discursive approach proposed by Fischer and Gottweis appears at the operational level to be characterised rather by a different vision of the public sphere. They emphasise the existence within and between discourses of inalienable conflicts, pointing out moreover that a rational discourse does not exhaust argumentative possibilities, and that it is also necessary to take into account irrational discourses, emotional engagement and the resultant differing means of communication. They also stress the relations of knowledge and power, noting the constructivist nature of knowledge and its diverse types: expert, popular and practical knowledge. To this we should also add ignorance, which most researchers today interpret as being more than a simple opposition to knowledge – as the lack thereof – and its various types and variants (Gross, McGoey 2015).

What is important here, however, is to mobilise resources in the form of values and to construct collective agreement within discursive communities as to their meaning and significance. As Fischer and Gottweis (2012) rightly note, it was agreement on values and ideas that propelled social movements in making significant steps in the development of democracy in Western societies, such as the abolition of slavery, granting the vote to women and focusing attention on environmental issues. Yet they also claim that today the criterion of rationality of a debate is often reduced to economic rationality; although their observation refers to the realities of liberal capitalism in the USA, it also seems to fit the public sphere in Poland. The criterion of economic profitability is extremely common in the analysed discourses.

Since the discursive approach assumes that public communication is strategic in nature, in the research we emphasised the reconstruction of argumentative strategies, which consequently means that the rhetorical aspects of the narrative need to be taken into account. An argument itself is understood as a statement about reality based on a rhetorical device fulfilling a persuasive function (Majone 1989). An analysis must therefore also consider this level of communication.

All this leads us to understand discourse in the context of the relationship of knowledge and power, exerting influence and competition for media visibility. As a result, we adopt the operational procedures of critical discourse analysis (CDA) – on the one hand stressing the significance of rhetoric (as an extremely important aspect of argumentative analysis) and language, and thus using semiotic and linguistic tools, and on the other critical consideration of the discursive practices rooted in the economic, political and cultural contexts that condition the way in which the media work. We shall therefore utilise the discourse theories of Norman Fairclough (2012) and Teun van Dijk (1991) to seek the hidden relations of power, supported by the concepts of Michel Foucault (1990), and following Pierre Bourdieu (1991) in analysing the construction of the power of arguments.

It will be extremely important to analyse the interactions between the actors of the discourse. The optimum solution, which combines the interactive approach with critical reconstruction of the discursive structures of knowledge, power, human and non-human components, appears to be provided by the situational analysis of Adele Clarke (2005), which treats external contexts as internal components of the situation created in the progress of the discourse. This therefore makes it possible to analyse the contexts significant in the tradition of CDA (social, historical, etc.) as internal elements in discursive maps, while simultaneously observing actors and their actions in various configurations. This method is based on discerning discourses from the point of view of their capacity "to map the things that can be thought, said and done in many aspects of life" (Salskov-Iversen, Krause Hansen 2008: 409). All this was the inspiration for creating procedures for the research at the stage of analysis of media sources.

The analyses also took account of the approaches to discourse analysis at the opposite end of the spectrum: the normative premises of Habermas's conception (cf. Czyżewski 2013), and especially those referring to self-description of discursive communities. This led to questions on the rhetorical power of their impact, and the vision of the public sphere adopted by its visible actors. At present, the rhetoric of deliberation and participation (not necessarily reflected in procedures actually in place) that political actors often take up determines the guidelines for defining the public sphere, and these conceptions frequently also become a component of the self-descriptions of the political systems of contemporary democracies. Yet the calls for greater inclusiveness in the public sphere, exchange of arguments and arriving at a consensus that are viewed as autotelic values can themselves become tools of symbolic violence. Marek Czyżewski (2013) observes that they can be an element of the rhetoric game between competing actors who legitimise their discourses by invoking this ideal of deliberation, while also showing that alternative or rival discourses do not satisfy these criteria. They are thus less civic and non-public. Also interesting is the question of how much this deliberative ideal becomes an element of the self-description of the media space, legitimising it as a modern agora (or forum) – a space of inclusion of social actors and an area in which the mechanisms of translatability of perspectives operate. Therefore, if we take the metaphor of media as a system of communication (Luhmann 2000), we experience two levels here – that of self-description shaping a system's identity, and that of actual operations (cf. Wagner 2010). The question we shall try to answer is therefore the following: in what way does the media space favour striving for a normative ideal of deliberation and realising deliberative democracy? Does it satisfy the demands of inclusiveness, mapping diverse discourses, stimulating their dialogical nature and promoting the pursuit of agreement, or does it rather correspond to a critical vision of the public sphere as an agonistic space in which competing interests are reflected in alternative discourses struggling for hegemony in the public sphere? It remains a separate question whether even a pluralistic – meaning that various discourses are visible – public sphere generates questions that receive a real answer in the form of influence on formation of public policies – here the state's energy policy. In other words: are the problems defined by these discourses taken into account in the processes of designing and/or implementing public policies? Discourse analyses in other countries show that this is not necessarily the case (Cotton, Rattle, Alstine 2014).

In the case of discourses focused on energy issues in Poland, one can notice references to the ideas of dialogue and deliberation by the representatives of marginalised discourses – in particular the environmental one, which makes protection of nature the main value and criterion of evaluating actions undertaken within public policies. They question the dominant discourses as non-civic, at the same time fighting for acknowledgement of their own presence in the mediatised public sphere. A frequent response to this in the media space is other mechanisms of exclusion, for example referring to deprecation of competing ideas in the following ways: questioning their rationality (referring to the logical order, and criteria of economic assessment of costs and profits), labelling the proposed solutions as naive and utopian (invoking practical reason), stressing the emotional nature of statements, in contrast to the sober expert verdicts ("clinical reason"), and finally ignoring certain actors and limiting their access to the media space (e.g. according to the rule of representativeness, which favours the representatives of the largest groups in access to the media). With all this in mind, we operationalise the "visibility" of discourses through the mechanisms of inclusion and exclusion of actors and evaluating arguments (e.g. through claims of importance or assessment of rationality).

The consequence of adopting these theoretical premises is that we conceptualise the media space as a public sphere in which, within the existing discourses,[8] knowledge and ignorance as well as values and norms are constructed, while specific individual and collective actors are defined as visible (and invisible), the status of the situation is characterised and its definitions negotiated, and the equally important areas of what is concealed are formed. This in turn determined the methodology that was used and the way in which the research was organised, as laid out in the next chapter.

---

8   The concept of discourse is defined in diverse ways by various theoretical currents, and often used without precise definition. With this in mind, we accept an operational definition of discourse as a collection of texts thematically focused around specific issues (cf. Czyżewski 1997) within a given timeframe. At the same time, we do not lose sight of the understanding of discourse as acting with the aid of words in a specific social and cultural context, accompanied by awareness of the forms of use of language (formal structure) and its cognitive component within a system of concepts and values (van Dijk 1997). We also assume that textual strategies will be realised in the analysed discourses (Duszak 1998).

Situational analysis as a way of mapping the discursive media space

Our analyses of the press discourse – and media discourse in the final stage – encompassed quantitative analyses allowing us to categorise the elements of the discourse, analyses of vocabulary (frequency lists) and links between concepts (cluster analyses) as well as fundamental qualitative analyses designed to describe the various discourses within a framework set by the above research questions. Owing to the theoretical tensions within discourse theory (cf. Czyżewski 2013; Jabłońska 2012) and the numerous conceptual categories identified during the quantitative stages, it proved to be a challenge to find an analysis track that would make it possible to deal with the chaos, contradictions and "disorder" of the research material, while at the same time discerning the subtle relations between key categories and the dynamic of changes within the discourses. These needs were met by the three-stage working method proposed by the situational analysis – drawing up situational maps, maps of worlds/arenas and positional maps (Clarke 2005) (as well as its interactive nature and inspiration from cartographic methods, in keeping with the accepted notion of the media "space"). In spite of certain theoretical weaknesses (cf. Mathar 2008; Kacperczyk 2007) and limitations caused by the researcher's interpretive subjectivism (hence the suggestion of constant awareness of one's own input to the analysed material), this method permitted creative and systemic work with the material, as well as allowing the researchers to be restrained in making authoritative claims and analytically ready to "be surprised" by their observations until the end of the project. This awareness of the relativity of the analysed discourses is especially valuable in response to the charges sometimes levelled at researchers who lose sight of this epistemological requirement, which is fundamental to the discursive approach (cf. Salskov-Iversen, Krause Hansen 2008; Czyżewski 2013).

By combining inspirations from CDA and situational analysis, we were faced with the challenge of specifying the category of context. According to van Dijk, the context is a set of external circumstances influencing the way in which we interpret contents. In a situational analysis, the context as an internalised construct of the discourse itself is significant inasmuch as it has been introduced into the field called the situation. As for the situation itself, which is left as a concept that is undefined but rooted in specific theoretical traditions (cf. Kacperczyk 2007), we understand it as a brief moment when various actors meet and negotiate, confront meanings, but also reproduce and process them (cf. Mathar 2008). All resources, including knowledge and ignorance, are therefore open in nature, defined by somebody and for somebody in a given moment. Tom Mathar (2008), following the ideas of Donna Haraway, underlines the situational meaning of knowledge as produced by various, not only expert groups, and utilised and reproduced by actors from various networks. In a similar, situational way, within the discourse values, symbols, and metaphors are processed, but also the actors and actants themselves, the interpretations of their actions, the framework of social practices etc. This approach refers strongly to the classical understanding of the definition of a situation as an interactive and subjective way of defining reality by the members of a given cultural group (Thomas, Znaniecki 1996; Hałas 1991). It assumes that there are multiple social worlds and demonstrates their interaction – the dynamic of variable actions of actors occupying various positions and constructing different definitions of that to which they refer.

A separate paragraph is needed for the power–knowledge relationship, which plays a very important role in energy issues. In the Habermasian view, power is redistributed in a process of uninterrupted communication by the primacy of the better argument. This important connection creating normative foundations for the concept of deliberation must therefore become the starting point for a project seeking to diagnose the media space as an area of deliberation. In media communication, though, apart from the level of normative self-description of the media, it is hard to find an uninterrupted communication situation. Therefore, accepting the key category of argument, we operationalise power in two dimensions: structural, employing Foucault's ideas; and cultural, following Bourdieu's conception of power in communication. We treat structural power as permeating all relations, dynamically manifested in discourse and characterising all practices of its actors. Power in communication is therefore manifested by admitting somebody (others – an actor or discourse) to the process of communication (or excluding somebody from this process) and/or by recognising or challenging this input to the dialogue. This brings us to the process of producing and regulating discourses of truth (Foucault 1990). We therefore see that also significant is internal power understood as the capacity of argument for emerging as the better one in the discourse – the key question is "Which arguments win in practice?" (Pellizioni 2001). The cultural capital owned by specific groups defines the criteria for appraising an argument. The dominant discourses will therefore determine the knowledge that is acknowledged, repelling (or not admitting) competing narratives. We shall understand knowledge itself as theoretical knowledge founded in science and legitimised by its institutional authority (produced at universities and research centres and cited by scientists). This is contrasted with the categories of techne – technical, practical knowledge – and doxa, meaning knowledge understood in terms of social consciousness, beliefs and opinions (cf. Ziółkowski 2002), often within a given field treated as a set of assumptions accepted "in themselves," unquestioned and regarded as a certainty (Bourdieu 2010). The media have the power to exhibit and disseminate arguments, and this can lead to their reproduction in non-media discourses (as in certain unreflexive responses given in surveys; cf. Wagner 2010), or to a false consensus (excessive and unauthorised emphasis of the agreement and equality of resources of actors participating in a discourse) (Bohman 1996). The way in which a deliberation process (resulting from participation) is designed, conducted, but also presented can also result in forming and imposing practices in a similar fashion to expert decisions (Stirling 2005). We define an argument here as a complex structure combining specific knowledge and information, a subjective judgement and a certain rhetorical device (Majone 1989). Arguments are confronted, exchanged and developed, which means that the argumentation itself develops. We assume that this also occurs in the media space.

Our search for the mechanisms of the "power of an argument" by using the symbolic resources available in specific fields of social action leads us to make use of Bourdieu's theory emphasising the importance of cultural factors. If we treat deliberation as a way of searching for new solutions, including those which were initially inaccessible to the actors joining the debate and which can come from outside of the field of knowledge regarded as the valid one, deliberation can be seen as a mechanism that opens a closed field of dogmatic knowledge – doxa (cf. Ojha et al. 2012).

The type of work that results from a situational analysis allows us to make use of these diverse sources. The cartographic metaphor dovetails with our perception of media discourse as above all a communicative space, and subsequently as actants defining themselves in this space. Just as a map is a conventional interpretation of external space (Luhmann 2000[9]), discursive maps are a dual interpretation, as they represent the subjective interpretation of the researcher, who draws conclusions on the interpretation made by actors. This means that we can treat the key categories of knowledge very flexibly, taking into account the construction of areas of ignorance (in its numerous types) and uncertainty, which sometimes takes the form of risk defined in such various ways. The main section will comprise a sociologically orientated discourse analysis emphasising dynamics and interactivity (Pawliszak, Rancew-Sikora 2012) – important categories when we construe deliberation as a process. A situational analysis assumes that, as Anna Kacperczyk writes in reference to Clarke's work, the study "should conduct a detailed description, presentation and explanation of the individual, collective, organisational institutional, temporal, geographical, material, discursive, cultural, symbolic, visual and historical aspects of a situation" (Kacperczyk 2007: 5). This means that we can not only reconstruct subjective visions of the problems

---

9   Our use of Luhmann's metaphor is mostly confined to the constructivist dimension of his ideas, and does not apply his systemic theory of media.

and solutions of actors defined and legitimised by individual discourse, but also consider the human and non-human factors of the situation. Owing to the temporal, variable and complex nature of the situation, its conception appears ideal for studying media representations, as this method allows us to go beyond the level of representations and consider the significance of formal language structures and their dynamic variability (see Figure 1).

The maps drawn up to support the researcher's subjective interpretation are meant not for construction of models based on analytical simplifications, but to reveal the complexity of the situation, and all its various elements, in order to then identify and explain both the models reconstructed and the process of change. In keeping with the research procedure recommended by Clarke, the analysis incorporated the following dimensions:

1) human, nonhuman, and discursive elements of the situation
2) social worlds and arenas
3) the positions taken by subjects in discourses or controversial discussions.

1) The dimension of the human, nonhuman (material) and discursive elements of the situation was drawn up during the quantitative analysis. Such maps were sketched separately for each title in this study. We also drew up integrated maps for the entire analysed material. These became the basis for an in-depth, qualitative discourse analysis which aimed to "understand the complexity and heterogeneity of individual and collective situations, discourses and interpretations of the situation" (Kacperczyk 2007: 10). Once prepared and regulated, the maps become the foundation of a relational analysis – exploring the links between the various categories and elements.

2) The analysis of social worlds and arenas takes as its unit of analysis the "social world" understood as subjects of discourse, the community producing meanings and taking certain collective actions. This step involved drawing up maps to test the collective engagement of actors and to examine the connections between them and the areas of the actions carried out.

3) The final phase of the research is production of positional maps serving to illustrate the possible positions articulated in the discourse. Importantly, these are not necessarily attributed to a given actor – an individual, group or institution – but rather reflect argumentative strategies. This approach makes it possible to treat all strategies – including rarer and even marginal ones – as equally important for understanding the complexity of a situation. The central categories here are not just the articulated topics, but also the areas which are not discussed.

Figure 1 summarises these reflections illustrating the guidelines adopted for the analysis, which in the final stage of the research considers the discourse described as "current," yet at the same time referring to the results of the analyses carried out in the previous stages.

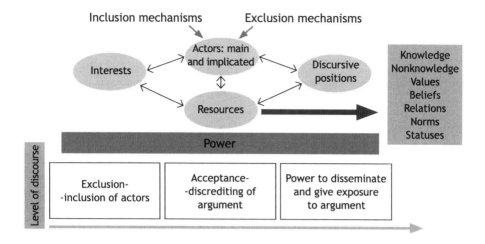

Figure 1. Outline of discourse analysis in individual thematic topics
Source: own elaboration.

In accordance with the principles of CDA, the research incorporated analysis of the level of the linguistic organisation of the material. Three dimensions were taken into account: semantic (focusing on the construction of arguments; the component of knowledge and of subjective judgement); formal (analysing the figurativeness of the language, with particular consideration for the style of the statement and the modality as a transmitted status created in the statement of reality, i.e. presenting reality as desired, objectively existing or supposed to exist in a given time); and finally that of the linguistic dynamic (including the dimension of dialogicality and intertextuality in the accepted understanding (see Chapter 2: Research Organisation).

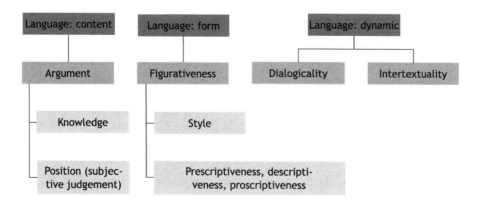

Figure 2. Overview of sociolinguistic analyses
Source: own elaboration.

Conclusion

The theoretical and methodological context outlined in this chapter defines the fundamental research problem explored in this book. This is the role and meaning of media discourses for a wide-ranging social debate on topics that are important for this society. Energy here is an example, a kind of case study that illustrates the specific mechanisms of inclusion and exclusion of actors and arguments, and thus constructing that which becomes visible in the public sphere and might be a reference point for both institutional and group or individual decisions and actions. In this sense, media discourses are an important dimension of social practices whose consequences measurably determine the future.

Bibliography

Adut, A. (2012), "A Theory of the Public Sphere," *Sociological Theory*, 30 (4), pp. 238–62.

Bell, D., Grey, T., Haggett, C. (2005), "Policy, Participation and the Social Gap in Wind Farm Siting Decisions," *Environmental Politics*, vol. 14, no. 4, pp. 460–70.

Bergmans, A., Sundkvist, G., Kos, D., Simons, P. (2014), "The Participatory Turn in Radioactive Waste Management. Deliberation and the Social-Technical Divide," *Journal of Risk Research*, 18 (3), November.

Bohman, J. (1996), *Public Deliberation, Pluralism and Complexity*, Cambridge, MA.

Bourdieu, P. (1991), *Language and Symbolic Power*, Cambridge, MA.

Bourdieu, P. (2010), "Conclusion: Classes and Classifications" [in:] P. Bourdieu, *Distinction: A Social Critique of the Judgement of Taste*, trans. R. Nice, Abingdon, pp. 468–86.

CBOS (2011), *Wydobywać? Polacy o gazie łupkowym*, BS/112/2011, Warszawa.

CBOS (2013), *Społeczny stosunek do gazu łupkowego*, BS/76/2013, Warszawa.

Chambers, S., Costain, A. (eds.) (2000), *Deliberation, Democracy and Media*, Lanham.

Clarke, A. E. (2003), "Situational Analyses: Grounded Theory Mapping after the Postmodern Turn," *Symbolic Interaction*, vol. 26 (4), pp. 553–76.

Clarke, A. (2005), *Situational Analysis: Grounded Theory after the Postmodern Turn*, Thousand Oaks, CA.

Cotton, M., Rattle, I., Alstine, J. V. (2014), "Shale Gas Policy in the United Kingdom. An Argumentative Discourse Analysis," *Energy Policy*, 73, pp. 427–38.

Czyżewski, M. (1997), "Trzy rodzaje dyskursu" [in:] M. Czyżewski, A. Piotrowski, S. Kowalski (eds.), *Rytualny chaos*, Kraków, pp. 10–22.

Czyżewski, M. (2013), "Teorie dyskursu i dyskursy teorii," *Kultura i Społeczeństwo*, no. 2.

Dijk, T. van (1991), "The Interdisciplinary Study of News as Discourse" [in:] K. B. Jensen, N. W. Jankowski (eds.), *A Handbook of Qualitative Methodologies for Mass Communication Research*, London, pp. 108–20.

Dijk, T. (ed.) (1997), *Discourse as a Structure and Proccess*, Sage London–Thousand Oaks–New Delhi.

Devine-Wright, P. (2009a), "Public Engagement with Renewables Energy: Introduction" [in:] *Renewable Energy and the Public: From NIMBY to Participation*, London–Washington.

Devine-Wright, P. (2009b), "Rethinking Nimbyism: The Role of Place Attachment and Place Identity in Explaining Place Protective Action," *Journal of Community and Applied Social Psychology*, vol. 19, no. 6, pp. 426–41.

Dobek-Ostrowska, B. (2007), *Komunikowanie polityczne i publiczne*, Warszawa.

Dryzek, J. S. (1990), *Discursive Democracy: Politics, Policy and Political Science*, Cambridge.

Dryzek, J. S. (2000), *Deliberative Democracy and Beyond: Liberals, Critics, Contestations*, Oxford.

Dryzek, J. S. (2010), *Foundations and Frontiers of Deliberative Governance*, Oxford–New York.

Duszak, A. (1998), *Tekst, dyskurs, komunikacja*, Warszawa.

Duszak, A., Fairclough, N. (eds.) (2008), *Krytyczna analiza dyskursu. Interdyscyplinarne podejście do komunikacji społecznej*, Kraków.

Dye, T. R. (2013), *Understanding Public Policy*, Upper Saddle River, NJ.

Fairclough, N. (2011), *Media Discourse*, London–New York.

Fairclough, N. (2012), *Discourse and Social Change*, Cambridge, MA.

Ferree, M. M., Gamson, W. A., Gerhards, J., Rucht, D. (2002), "Four Models of the Public Sphere in Modern Democracies," *Theory & Society*, 31 (3), pp. 289–324.

Fisher, F., Forester, J. (1993), "Introduction" [in:] *The Argumentative Turn in Policy Analysis and Planning*, Durham, NC.

Fischer, F., Gottweis, H. (2012), "Introduction" [in:] F. Fischer, H. Gottweis (eds.), *The Argumentative Turn Revisited Public Policy as Communicative Practice*, Durham–London.

Fishkin, J. S. (2009), *When the People Speak: Deliberative Democracy and Public Consultation*, Oxford.

Fishkin, J. S., Laslett, P. (eds.) (2003), *Debating Deliberative Democracy*, Malden, MA.

Foucault, M. (1990), *The History of Sexuality*, New York.

Fuchs, C. (2014), *Social Media: A Critical Introduction*, London.

Giddens, A., Lash, S., Beck, U. (1994), *Reflexive Modernization: Politics, Tradition and Aesthetics in the Modern Social Order*, Stanford.

Górniak, J., Żmuda, G., Prokopowicz, P. (2015), "Ocena wpływu w kontekście polityk publicznych" [in:] J. Górniak (ed.), *Ocena wpływu oparta na dowodach*, Warszawa.

Gross, M. (2015), "Give Me an Experiment and I Will Raise a Laboratory," *Science, Technology, & Human Values*, pp. 1–22.

Gross, M., McGoey, L. (eds.) (2015), *Routledge International Handbook of Ignorance Studies*, London.

Habermas, J. (1992), *Faktizität und Geltung: Beiträge zur Diskurstheorie des Rechts und des demokratischen Rechtsstaats*, Frankfurt.

Habermas, J. (1996), *Between Facts and Norms: Contributions to a Discourse Theory of Law and Democracy*, Cambridge, MA.

Hałas, E. (1991), *Znaczenia i wartości społeczne. O socjologii Floriana Znanieckiego*, Lublin.

Hass, P. M. (1992), "Epistemic Communities and International Policy Coordination," *International Organization*, 46 (1), pp. 1–35.

Hess, A. (2013), *Społeczni uczestnicy medialnego dyskursu społecznego w Polsce. Mediatyzacja i strategie komunikacyjne organizacji pozarządowych w Polsce*, Kraków.

Jabłońska, B. (2012), "Władza i wiedza w krytycznych studiach nad dyskursem – szkic teoretyczny," *Studia Socjologiczne*, 204, pp. 75–92.

Jaspal, R., Nerlich, B., Lemańczyk, S. (2014), "Fracking in the Polish Press: Geopolitics and National Identity," *Energy Policy*, vol. 74, November, pp. 253–61.

Jann, W., Wegrich, K. (2007), "Theories of the Policy Cycle" [in:] F. Fischer, G. Miller, M. S. Sidney (eds.), *Handbook of Public Policy Analysis: Theory, Politics and Methods*, Boca Raton–London–New York, pp. 43–62.

Juza, M. (2016), "Dwadzieścia lat obecności internetu w życiu społecznym – nadzieje, obawy, krytyka," *Studia Socjologiczne*, 1.

Kacperczyk, A. (2007), "Badacz i jego poszukiwania w świetle 'Analizy sytuacyjnej' Adele E. Clarke," *Przegląd Socjologii Jakościowej*, vol. 3, no. 2.

Latour, B. (2007), *Reassembling the Social: An Introduction to Actor-Network Theory*, Oxford.

Lindblom, C. E., Cohen, D. K. (1979), *Usable Knowledge: Social Science and Social Problem Solving*, New Haven.

Luhmann, N. (2000), *The Reality of the Mass Media*, Cambridge.

Łucki, Z., Misiak, W. (2011), *Energetyka a społeczeństwo. Aspekty socjologiczne*, Warszawa.

Majone, G. (1989), *Evidence, Argument and Persuasion in the Policy Process*, New Haven–London.

Mathar, T. (2008), "Making a Mess with Situational Analysis?," *Forum. Qualitative Social Research*, vol. 9, no. 2, May.

McGoey, L. (2012), "The Logic of Strategic Ignorance," *The British Journal of Sociology*, vol. 63, issue 3, pp. 533–76.

Mrozowska, S. (2016), *Social Sciences and Energy Issues*, Kraków.

Mrozowska, S., Kijowska, B. (2016), "Public Understanding of Nuclear Energy: Polish Case Study" [in:] S. Mrozowska, *Social Sciences and Energy Issues*, Kraków, pp. 69–87.

Ojha, H. R., Cameron, J., Kumar, C. (2012), "Deliberation or Symbolic Violence? The Governance of Community Forestry in Nepal," *Forest Policy and Economics*, 11 (5), pp. 365–74.

O'Riordan, T., Jordan, A. (1996), "Social Institution and Climate Change" [in:] T. O'Riordan, J. Jager (eds.), *Politics of Climate Change: A European Perspective*, London.

Page, B. (1996), *Who Deliberates? Mass Media in Modern Democracy*, Chicago.

Palumbo, D. J., Maynard-Moody S. (1991), *Contemporary Public Administration*, New York.

Pawliszak, P., Rancew-Sikora, D. (2012), "Wprowadzenie do SAD," *Studia Socjologiczne*, 1 (204), pp. 5–15.

Pellizioni, L. (2001), "The Myth of the Best Argument: Power, Deliberation and Reason," *The British Journal of Sociology*, vol. 52, no. 1, March, pp. 59–86.

Rifkin, J. (2013), *Digital Leadership – Interview with Jeremy Rifikin*, https://www.capgemini-consulting.com/resource-file-access/resource/pdf/jeremy_rifkin_14_06_2013.pdf (access: 26 December 2014).

Salskov-Iversen, D., Krause Hansen, H. (2008), "Momenty dyskursywne. Zarządzanie modernizacją sektora publicznego" [in:] R. Wodak, M. Krzyżanowski (eds.), *Jakościowa analiza dyskursu w naukach społecznych*, Kraków.

Sarrica, M., Brondi, S., Cottone, P., Mazzara, B. (2015), "One, no One, One Hundred Thousand Energy Transitions in Europe: The Quest for a Cultural Approach," *Energy Research and Social Science*.

Sroka, J. (2009), *Deliberacja i rządzenie wielopasmowe. Teoria i praktyka*, Wrocław.

Stankiewicz, P. (2009), "The Role of Risks and Uncertainties in Technological Conflicts: Three Strategies of Constructing Ignorance Innovation," *The European Journal of Social Science Research*, 22 (1), pp. 105–24.

Stankiewicz, P. (2013), "'Razem o łupkach': czyli jak prowadzić dialog publiczny przy poszukiwaniu i wydobyciu gazu z łupków," *Przegląd Geologiczny*, 61 (6), pp. 374–80.

Stankiewicz, P. (2014), "Zbudujemy wam elektrownię (atomową!). Praktyka oceny technologii przy rozwoju energetyki jądrowej w Polsce," *Studia Socjologiczne*, 1, pp. 77–107.

Stankiewicz, P., Lis, A. (2012), "Dla kogo elektrownia jądrowa? Wyniki badań opinii publicznej" [in:] K. Jeleń, Z. Rau (eds.), *Energetyka jądrowa w Polsce*, Warszawa, pp. 1019–62.

Stankiewicz, P., Stasik, A., Suchomska, J. (2015), "Od informowania do współdecydowania i z powrotem. Prototypowanie technologicznej demokracji," *Studia Socjologiczne*, 3 (218), pp. 65–101.

Steenbergen, M., Bächtiger, A., Spörndli, M., Steiner, J. (2003), "Measuring Political Deliberation: A Discourse Quality Index," *Comparative European Politics*, vol. 1, pp. 21–48.

Stehr, N. (2015), *Our Changing Climate: Democracy and Knowledge*, lecture held in Kraków (3.11) and made available by the author in written form as a synopsis, http://www.socjologia.uj.edu.pl/documents/15033991/48db455f-62a4-4297-9bd1-ed6b-80b76ab6 (access: 26 December 2015).

Stirling, A. (2005), "Opening up or Closing Down: Analysis, Participation and Power in the Social Appraisal of Technology" [in:] M. Leach, I. Scoones, and B. Wynne (eds.), *Science and Citizens: Globalization and the Challenge of Engagement*, London, pp. 218–31.

Stirling, A. (2014), "Transforming Power: Social Science and the Politics of Energy Choices," *Energy Research & Social Science*, 1, pp. 83–95.

Świątkiewicz-Mośny, M., Wagner, A. (2012), "How Much Energy in Energy Policy? The Media on Energy Problems in Developing Countries (with the Example of Poland)," *Energy Policy*, 50, pp. 383–90.

Tarde, G. (1969), "The Public and the Crowd," trans. T. Clark [in:] *On Communication and Social Influence*, Chicago, pp. 277–96.

Thomas, W., Znaniecki, F. (1996), *The Polish Peasant in Europe and America*, Urbana.

TNS OBOP (2015), *Co Polacy sądzą o rynku energii*, Warszawa, http://www.rwe.pl/pl/dla-mediow/aktualnosci/co-polacy-sadza-o-rynku-energii (access: 8 December 2015).

Upham, P., Lis, A., Riesch, H., Stankiewicz, P. (2014), "Addressing Social Representations in Socio-Technical Transitions with the Case of Shale Gas," *Environmental Innovation and Societal Transitions*.

Urry, J. (2014), "The Problem of Energy," *Theory, Culture & Society*, July 1.

Wagner, A. (2010), *Zaufać mediom? Analiza mechanizmów samoopisu prasy w sytuacjach kryzysowych*, Kraków.

Wagner, A. (2014), "Shale Gas. Energy Innovation in a (non-)Knowledge Society: A Press Discourse Analysis," *Science and Public Policy*, 7 August.

Wagner, A., Grobelski, T., Harembski, M. (2016), "Is Energy Policy a Public Issue? Nuclear Power in Poland and Implications for Energy Transitions in Central and East Europe," *Energy Research and Social Science*.

Wodak, R., Krzyżanowski, M. (eds.) (2011), *Jakościowa analiza dyskursu w naukach społecznych*, trans. D. Przepiórkowska, Warszawa.

Wolsink, M. (2006), "Invalid Theory Impedes Our Understanding: A Critique on a Persistence of the Language of a NIMBY," *Transactions of the Institute of British Geographers*, vol. 31, no. 1, pp. 85–91.

Ziółkowski, M. (2002), "Wiedza" [in:] *Encyklopedia socjologii*, Warszawa.

Aleksandra Wagner

ORGANISING THE RESEARCH

General information about the research

The objective of the research was to ascertain whether the media space – conceived as the communicative dimension of the public sphere in Poland – is favourable to deliberation. Therefore, the first thing to be analysed was the way in which public discourses concerning the given topic exist or do not exist in the media. In the case of the current ones, their internal structure and dynamic was analysed, as well as the mechanisms that dictate their media visibility. Secondly, apart from analysing the media space, we also examined the role of the media themselves as actants in the field of promoting the ideas of deliberation and participation, creating certain representations of these concepts, as well as the function of mobilising citizens to participate in them and providing information on their progress.

The material selected for exploring how these mechanisms worked comprised topics linked to energy policy as an area of policy that is on the one hand presented as strategic for the country and extremely important for its citizens' quality of life, and on the other as complicated, difficult and demanding particular competences. Three subject areas were chosen from the related areas. In 2011, at the research planning stage, two of these were so-called "hot topics" that were capturing the media's attention – nuclear energy and shale gas. We also chose the topic of wind energy, as the form of alternative energy based on renewable energy sources that was the most recognised and most common in the Polish media. The initial exploratory research showed that wind energy tended to be treated as something of a counterpoint for the remaining two energy sources.

The main load of the analyses concerns current discourses, anchored "here and now," meaning in practice systematic monitoring of the media for 12 months. We then conducted a qualitative analysis of the contents of the sources in selected periods from this time, permitting us to observe the continuity of the discourses, and thus the process of how the arguments used developed, topics were continued, actors were included and excluded as the discourses developed, the scenes of events were constructed, and specific definitions of the situation created and negotiated. Thanks to continual monitoring, the researchers were able to refer to the current socio-political situation.

As we accepted the premises of intertextual[1] continuity of topics and subjects in the sphere of media communication, we had to broaden the scope of the research, especially when current discourses referred to the past, forming points of anchoring in specific symbols, metaphors or historical constructions. We therefore also included historical press analyses. In the case of nuclear energy this concerned the time when the discourse on this subject appeared in the information media and then disappeared, i.e. the 1980s, and subsequently the five years immediately preceding the period of the current analyses, 2007–2012.

In the other two cases – shale gas and wind energy – we looked at press publications from the same period (2007–2012); the first publications on shale gas only appeared in late 2009, however. The selection of the same time period for the historical analyses for all three topics was intentional, as we assumed that the same actors would appear in different discourses, entering coalitions, forming resources and assuming positions towards various problems and values. The same period of analysis therefore made it possible to create a list of actors, resources and rules valid for the given time. It was assumed that these could be an important point of reference for analysing the mechanisms of development of the current discourses. In the press materials selected using key words we therefore picked a sample of texts which then underwent quantitative and qualitative analysis, the results of which became the point of reference for critical analysis of the media discourse for 2013–2014.

---

1   We cite the notion of intertextuality here following Mikhail Bakhtin (1975) to refer to the idea of dialogicality and polyphony of texts, moving beyond novels and applying this concept to what the author calls verbal-ideological reality and we construe in operational terms as a collection of texts (in the broad sense of a cultural text) accessible to its users within the existing contexts. Dialogicality here means that no statement exists in isolation, but it always refers to the contexts in which it existed previously or to which it can refer. Polyphony therefore, just as in a novel it means the existence of many voices expressing many worldviews of characters often polemical towards each other and not subject to the author's overriding consciousness, in the public sphere refers to the multitude of voices of various discourses all expressing their own judgements on the world and not subject to an overriding interpretation of the truth, but rather to the integrating-centralising tendencies created by these discourses, which Bakhtin calls cultural tendencies (cf. also Fairclough 2011).

To conclude, the research procedure encompassed three stages of analysis:
- Analysis of the 1980s press discourse on the subject of nuclear energy
- Analysis of the press discourse from 2007–2012 on wind energy, shale gas and nuclear energy
- Analysis of the media discourse (television, press, radio, internet) from deliberately selected periods between April 2013 and April 2014.

In addition, for the period from April 2013 to April 2014 we conducted a quantitative analysis of the contents of discussions concerning subject areas in social media using algorithms developed by the company SentiOne. The detailed methodological premises of this research are discussed in Chapter, which focuses on analysis of social media (Wit Hubert, "Representations of Selected Energy Topics on the Polish Internet").

Computer software was used for all the analyses on which this study is based. Analysis of the press and internet publications made use of the QDA Miner program, whereas ATLAS.ti was used for analysis of video and audio sources.

Research questions

The authors of the articles in this collection, discussing in turn the media discourses on nuclear energy, shale gas and wind energy, essentially try to answer the following research questions:
- Do the media create conditions for public deliberation, and how is this understood? Do the media create a bridge between deliberation at the micro and macro levels? Do they promote civic participation?
- Which mechanisms of inclusion and exclusion of actors are observed in the media discourses?
- How are power relations manifested? Can participatory discourse be (and is it) a space of domination?

The specific questions concern:
a) *Inclusiveness.* Who are the actors in the discourses, and what gives them their media visibility and status accorded in the communication? In what roles do they appear? What are the mechanisms of *inclusion* of actors? Can we observe any *counteracting of exclusion* – reference to missing actors, drawing attention to groups omitted in the discussion, diagnosis of the problems related to participation in the discussion?
b) *Ways of communicating.* What forms of communication are preferred in the discourse (e.g. emotional vs. rational approach)?
c) *Interests.* Which interests are articulated in the discussion, and which are assigned to actors? Are these entitled to claims for validity? Are

individual (group) interests expressed in the discourse, or the common interest – if so, how is this constituted? Are interests negotiated (something for something else) or agreed upon (persuasion), or are they accompanied by the search for a new solution? What are the mechanisms for legitimising interests (e.g. through the common good – defined how, and by whom?)? What are the mechanisms of delegitimisation of interests?

d) *Dialogicality.* Are the media discourses within a given topic polyphonic? What are the universal values accepted by the actors as foundations of the debate and of shaping energy policy? What anti-values are attributed to actors? Can we observe mechanisms of the "translatability of perspectives," and which ones? What are the mechanisms of establishing and developing arguments: discourse as interaction? What are the mechanisms of demonstrating respect?

Dialogicality at the discourse level is defined in reference to the idea of intertextuality (according to the presented understanding of it), and also refers to the level of the statements of actors, making use of the discourse quality index, initially designed for evaluation of parliamentary debates (Steenbergen 2003).

The dimensions of dialogicality here, then, are:

- *Participation* – the role of diverse actors in the debate, active participation in the media
- *Level of justification* – expressing one's own position, referring to opponents' position and counterarguments, referring to opponents' position and depreciating it or group of opponents without using counterarguments
- *Content of justification* – addressing group interests or common good (how is the common good defined – e.g. as the good of the majority or as a solution improving the position of the less privileged in the social structure?)
- *Respect accorded* – expressed in the statement
- *Capacity to change one's mind.*

e) *Objectives and forms of debate.* Can we observe attempts to reach a consensus (addressing the common good, searching for a new solution), or rather mapping of positions and differences (as a normative aim), striving for compromise (focus on negotiations) or imposing solutions (dominations)? Are forms of deliberation identified and promoted? Which ones (councils, advisory/consulting bodies, etc.)?

For the authors of the various chapters, the above questions provide a compass marking the direction of analytical reflection on the discourses focused on energy topics visible in the media space. At the same time, they critically discuss the aspects that are invisible in this space: omitted arguments, absent actors, indicated areas of ignorance and the unpredictable, as well as how the public communication space deals with areas of the invisible and unspecified.

Historical analyses of press discourses

The history of discourses on nuclear energy stretches back to the period after the Second World War. A number of analyses carried out by social researchers throughout the world have shown not only that these discourses vary markedly, but also that they have a high degree of internal consolidation, and developed symbolic means, including iconic representations and a tendency towards polarisation of the groups organising themselves around these discourses (cf. Gamson, Modigliani 1989).

In Poland, to a large extent this discourse began to appear in the information media in 1985, as a result of the announcement of the intention to construct a reactor in the country. The Chernobyl disaster left its mark on nuclear discourses across the world, and the dynamic of the Polish discourse was no exception. The socio-political transformations that followed soon afterwards, and the decision to abandon the construction plans, meant that the discourse was put on hold for some years afterwards. Despite the fundamental differences in the functioning, role and importance of the media in the 1980s and today, what is surprising about comparing the nuclear discourses is firstly the persistence of certain structures of argumentation, but secondly the differing mechanisms used to legitimise these arguments. Retaining key concepts while changing their semantic scope – for example the understanding of risk – means that it is easier to visualise the dynamic of the development of the discourse and the mechanism of generating its internal rules.

The analysis of press material was a two-stage process. During the first stage, we carried out a quantitative analysis of selected content of publications. The analysis focuses on the frequency of coded categories and their mutual relations. The description contained:

- formal characteristics: title of newspaper, date of publication, nature of text (an opinion piece, i.e. statement including elements of judgement and interpretation, or news – a statement with a predominantly informative function, giving facts)
- characteristics of content: main subjects coded according to an open procedure, therefore based on the presence of specific events and issues which were then grouped into more general categories (e.g. con-

struction of nuclear power station, description of nuclear technology, Chernobyl accident – dealing with the fallout of the disaster, description of the events, preventive action, description of social tensions and conflicts, political tensions and conflicts, energy crisis, economic/civilisational development), and differing perspectives on them (domestic politics, international politics, economy, technology, environment).

The analyses also covered: the statement's context, the type of actors (individual/collective), judgements, language used (formal elements), elements of persuasion (semantic elements).

The research was carried out using a coding system method. The coding was performed in a partially closed way using the QDA Miner program. The coding involved taking general code categories, and then, based on the coded excerpts, disregarding code subcategories from the content. For example, we took the category of "persuasion" (from the aim of the statement), then from those passages classed as persuasive identified the persuasive mechanisms employed in the texts. This type of coding not only allowed us to use codes embedded in the texts, but also made it easier to work consistently during the second, qualitative stage of the research.

We should add that during the research we decided not to use separable coding, as codes overlapped (e.g. a particular person appeared in one article as both an expert and a politician). The piloting of the methods was performed independently by three people on the same textual material. Only the version remaining after discussion and modifications was used as the basis for the final research.

In the second stage of the study we used situational analysis methodology as described by Adele Clarke (cf. Kacperczyk 2007) – the categories resulting from the first stage were used to draw up maps illustrating the relations between them. To this end we carried out an analysis of situational maps and an analysis of social worlds and arenas. This method is discussed in detail below.

Building a corpus of texts from the 1980s

The selection of texts was based on the National Library of Poland's Index of the Content of Periodicals. This demonstrated a significant increase in the number of articles on energy issues in the general press in 1986. We took as the culmination point in the 1980s the nuclear power station disaster in Chernobyl. In 1985, the planned construction of the power station in Poland led to a marked increase in the frequency of references to nuclear energy in the Polish press compared to previous years, when it had been mentioned almost solely in the technical trade press. After 1986 and until the end of the 1980s, the subject of nuclear energy cropped up increasingly rarely.

After drawing up a list of the articles published in the general information press from 1985 to 1989 recorded by the Index of the Content of Periodicals, we omitted from further analysis those titles in which articles were published only sporadically (one-two articles per year), instead focusing on analysis of those which permitted a certain continuity of the discourse.

From the initial corpus, we therefore excluded the following titles: *Pobrzeże, Przegląd Techniczny, Tygodnik Demokratyczny, Przegląd Tygodniowy, Energetyka, Zeszyty Naukowe, Nauka Polska, Życie Gospodarcze*, and *Państwo i Prawo*. This left the initial corpus of texts, which is presented in detail in Appendix 1.

After the initial selection of material (in terms of the actual thematic fit), 63 articles published from January 1985 to December 1989 qualified for the analysis. The analysed titles are described in brief in Appendix 2.

Nuclear, shale, wind energy – the press discourse from 2007–2012

As with the analysis of 1980s press discourse, there were two stages to the research. These were a *quantitative analysis of the content of selected periodicals and a qualitative situational analysis of press texts*. The aim of the quantitative research was to produce a list of the elements that appeared in the discourses, which were then analysed in terms of the relations linking them. The main categories used in the method from the previous stage were again applied, including:

- formal characteristics: title of newspaper, date of publication, nature of text (an opinion piece, i.e. statement including elements of judgement and interpretation, or news – a statement with a predominantly informative function, giving facts, interview)
- characteristics of content: main subjects (construction of nuclear power station in Poland, the workings of nuclear power stations in the world, description of nuclear technologies, alternative energy sources, energy crisis, energy security, environmental issues (other than sources), increase in energy costs, economic situation, energy balance in the country, events, international cooperation, law, others), and perspectives on them (political-administrative, political-economic, economic, technological, educational, environmental, "lifeworld," others)

- functions of the text: context of statement, individual actors, collective actors, judgements, language of statement (formal elements), elements of persuasion (semantic aspects), discursive constructs, such as conflict, contemporary and past experiences, visions of the future, numerical data – statistics, dimensions etc., key events, solutions and proposals) categorised using the coding system.

We also made use of vocabulary analysis. To do this, we conducted a word frequency analysis, which was then used to identify the key words and vocabulary construction with QDA Miner software. Cluster analyses allowed us to identify the concentration of key words (designated in advance on the basis of the frequency analysis) according to the Jaccard index (*Provalis Research* 2009) (an article was deemed to be one unit of analysis). We were able to use these images of the concentrations of key words to model the dominant elements of description of energy topics (e.g. concepts from economics, politics, ecology, technology, everyday life, etc.).[2]

Building a corpus of texts from 2007–2012

The logic of the construction of a corpus of texts was analogous for all three energy topics. The selection of texts was based on collecting all the articles containing key words defined in a given topic, published between 2007 and 2012 in the daily newspapers *Gazeta Wyborcza* and its local supplements, *Rzeczpospolita* and its thematic supplements, and *Fakt*, and the weeklies *Newsweek, Polityka* and *Wprost*.

Nuclear energy

The texts included in the set were those that contained one of the key phrases in all grammatical cases. For nuclear energy these were variations of "nuclear/atomic power station/plant" and "nuclear/atomic energy/power (production)" (*elektrownia jądrowa, elektrownia atomowa, energetyka jądrowa, energetyka atomowa, energetyka nuklearna, energia jądrowa, energia atomowa, energia nuklearna, siłownia jądrowa, siłownia atomowa*).

From this frame, comprising 1252 articles, we eliminated repeat texts, illegible ones, or those making analysis impossible, thus ending up with a

---

2   Further examples of this type of analysis are Wagner (2010), and Świątkiewicz-Mośny and Wagner (2012).

set of 990 press articles. We then drew a representative sample (assuming a confidence level of 0.95 and an error of 0.05%), taking into account the proportion of texts published in given years. Texts of television programmes and summaries of feature films containing the key phrases were eliminated from the analysis.

The structure of the sample is presented in Table 1.

Table 1. Articles on nuclear energy – structure of sample

	2012	2011	2010	2009	2008	2007	TOTAL
Number of articles in frame	248	266	133	171	71	101	990
Number of articles in sample	74	76	40	47	21	34	292

Source: own elaboration.

Wind energy

For wind energy, the key words were the following: "wind energy (production)" (*energetyka wiatrowa, energia wiatrowa*, "wind power station" (*elektrownia wiatrowa*), "wind farm" (*farma wiatrowa*). Searching the press archives for occurrences of the key phrases resulted in 1103 texts. Of these, using the same logic of sample selection described above, we chose 286. The corpus of texts built in this way thus comprised 286 articles. Table 2 presents their breakdown into specific titles.

Table 2. Articles on wind energy – structure of sample

	2012	2011	2010	2009	2008	2007	TOTAL
Number of articles in frame	196	257	228	173	146	103	1103
Number of articles in sample	51	66	58	45	28	27	275

Source: own elaboration.

Given that information concerning local supplements was also recorded, it is possible to draw up a press wind map of Poland. Most texts appeared in the Tri-City local supplement (29), followed by Poznań and Szczecin (12). The spatial distribution of texts coincides with the areas with most wind turbines. These are also the areas with the best potential as sites for wind farms owing to the strength of the wind.

Shale gas

For shale gas the following key phrases were used: "shale gas" (*gaz łupkowy*), "unconventional gas" (*gaz niekonwencjalny*), "shale" (*łupki*); in the last case texts not addressing shale gas were discarded manually. The sampling logic applied for wind and nuclear energy was again retained, as was the publication period. In practice, however, the analysis covered texts published from 2010 to 2012, as in 2007–2008 no single article containing the key phrase was recorded, and in 2009 just two articles.

From the resultant frame, comprising 1738 articles, we removed repeat texts, illegible ones, or those making analysis impossible, thus ending up with a set of 1713 press articles. We then drew a representative sample (assuming a confidence level of 0.95 and an error of 0.05%), taking into account the proportion of texts published in given years. Table 3 depicts the structure of the sample.

Table 3. Articles on shale gas – structure of sample

	2012	2011	2010	2009	2008	2007	RAZEM
Number of articles in frame	861	643	207	2	0	0	1713
Number of articles in sample	164	120	40	0	0	0	324

Source: own elaboration.

The dynamic increase in the number of articles published in 2010–2012 particularly applies to *Rzeczpospolita* daily. This clear numerical supremacy (more than 50% of the analysed articles) affects the nature of the discourse on shale gas owing to this newspaper's distinct profile as a legal-economic daily. However, the overrepresentation of texts published in this newspaper also influences the visibility of a specific type of discourse in the public sphere, and points to a clear indication of perception of shale gas in the context of economic and legal issues.

Analysis of discourse from 2013–2014

The third stage of the data analysis was a comprehensive analysis of the national and local information media, conducted in three selected two-week periods over a 12-month period between April 2013 and April 2014.

The analysis of the material took place separately for each type of media – press, internet, radio and television – with the last two being joined together as radio/TV, taking into account the differences between the two media. The shift from the subject matter to the type of medium as the criterion of the analysis was intended to permit a comparative analysis within a given form of media. Although the various topics were coded separately, this allowed the researchers to work in a more comprehensive and flexible manner with the material, reconstructing the links between given energy sources in the discursive strategies of a given group of actors as well as forming coalitions of sorts between them. The same subjects often referred to various energy sources simultaneously depending on the situation, treating them as competing or complementing each other on the energy market. Within each medium we separated the discourse focused on a given topic.

The starting media material was monitored for 12 months – from 1 April 2013 to 31 March 2014 – by a company called Press Service. The following media outlets were monitored:

- Television: TVP1, TVP2, TVN, Polsat and TVP Szczecin, TVP Łódź, TVP Katowice, TVP Lublin, TVP Gdańsk, TVP Białystok, TVP Katowice, TVP Poznań
- Radio: RMF, Radio Zet, PR1, PR3 and Polskie Radio: Lublin, Gdańsk, Szczecin, Białystok, Katowice, Łódź, Poznań
- Press: national and local editions of *Gazeta Wyborcza*, *Rzeczpospolita* and *Dziennik Polski*, as well as local media: *Polska – Głos Wielkopolski* (Greater Poland), *Kurier Szczeciński* (West Pomerania), *Polska – Dziennik Bałtycki* (Pomerania), *Gazeta Olsztyńska* (Warmia-Masuria), *Gazeta Współczesna* (Podlasie), *Dziennik Wschodni* (Lublin), *Super Nowości* (Subcarpathia), *Dziennik Polski* (Kraków) (Lesser Poland/Małopolska), *Echo Dnia* – (Holy Cross/Świętokrzyskie), *Polska – Dziennik Zachodni* (Silesia), *Nowa Trybuna Opolska* (Opole), *Polska – Gazeta Wrocławska* (Lower Silesia), *Gazeta Lubuska* (Gorzów) – Lubuskie, *Gazeta Pomorska* (Bydgoszcz) (Kuyavia-Pomerania), *Polska – Dziennik Łódzki* (Łódź)
- Media with an information/economic profile: *Parkiet*, *Puls Biznesu*
- Opinion weeklies: *Wprost*, *Polityka*, *Newsweek*, *Gość Niedzielny*
- Internet: 50 websites (portals) chosen for their content and scope (the average number of hits was taken into account).

A detailed breakdown of the sources we analysed is provided in Appendix 3. Furthermore, in addition to the internet analysis, the intensification of the discourse on social media for the three subject areas according to the key words given above was studied. This research was carried out by the company SentiOne, whose methodology is described in detail by Wit Hubert in "Representation of selected energy topics on the polish internet". At this point we should stress that the internet was treated as a public sphere, and thus the analysis covered those areas of it that fulfil the condition of open access. Private profiles closed to the general public, meant for circles of friends, or selected members of groups, were outside the scope of the study. The focus on those websites and social media with the largest number of users complies with our criterion of visibility. In Poland the most popular way of finding information is using the Google search engine – 80% of web users do so. Moreover, most of them make use of pages that Google displays on the first page of search results. Among the factors taken into account by the search mechanism is the number of hits to a page, its description (whether it is connected to the user's enquiry), links to other pages linking to it and the user's search history (for more on page ranking see http://infolab. stanford.edu/~backrub/google.html). A page's visibility on the internet, understood as the extent to which users notice it among the plethora of contents, makes it easier to search for it, which in turn increases its visibility. For users without any special interests, searching for basic contents, this is the most important category, as it decides on the sources of information that they find (note that active, and therefore expensive, promotion of contents also leads to an increase in their visibility). Users with an already specified profile of interests have a good chance of arriving at a certain type of profile, i.e. remaining closed in a certain information niche (cf. Juza 2016; Fuchs 2014). The year-long media monitoring allowed us to produce an extensive starting material base containing texts, audio and video recordings, as well as photographs. The total amounts obtained were:

- Radio/TV material: nuclear – 759, shale gas – 1080, wind – 411, total – 2250 recordings
- Press material: nuclear – 1387, shale gas – 1627, wind – 1105, total – 4119 press texts
- Internet: nuclear – 3753, shale gas – 5064, wind – 2847, total – 11,664 internet publications.

This gives a total of 18,033 units of analysis.

It was necessary to reduce the material before conducting qualitative analyses. We wished to preserve the subject continuity and assumed connections between the various media, and therefore opted for a deliberate sample of the periods characterised by the highest intensity of publication of contents linked to a given topic. The method used to designate these periods was inspired by methodology for identifying trends (Murphy 1999). Since 70% of the radio/TV material comprised brief news bulletins, and the internet was characterised by a high degree of repetitiveness of contents, the most suitable way of measuring the intensity of discourse was deemed to be the number of press publications in a given period. We therefore compiled a breakdown of the frequency of publications from a daily perspective for 12 months for each subject area. Two 2-week periods and one 1-week period were chosen, each of them showing a trend for a growing number of publications up to a culmination point, and then a reduction of this intensity to a lower number than that observed at the start of the increase.

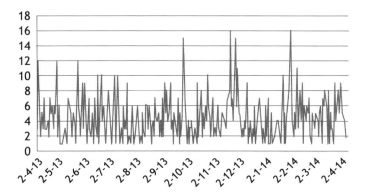

Chart 1. Frequency of press publications on nuclear energy
Source: own elaboration.

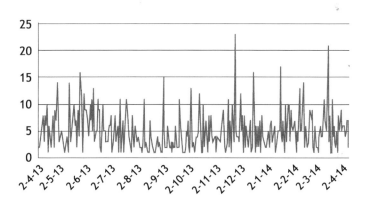

Chart 2. Frequency of publications on shale gas
Source: own elaboration.

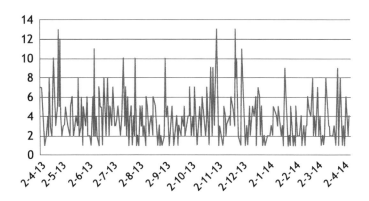

Chart 3. Frequency of publications on wind energy
Source: own elaboration.

This resulted in three periods being selected for each subject area (see Table 4).

Table 4. Periods of publication of texts and radio/TV programmes included in the analysis

Nuclear	25 Nov–7 Dec 2013	27 Jan–8 Feb 2014	24–29 Mar 2014
Shale gas	17–30 Nov 2013	6–20 Jan 2014	10–16 Mar 2014
Wind	15–29 Apr 2013	20 Oct–2 Nov 2013	20–26 Mar 2014

Source: own elaboration.

There are certain limitations to the chosen method of material selection. Firstly, when analysing the discourses during their largest media intensity it is important to remember that the dynamic of this discourse will be set by events that propel the interest in a given subject. Given the nature of mainstream media, these are most likely to be political and economic events, conflicts or scandals.

One can therefore assume that at times when the visibility of a specific topic increases in the public sphere, there will be diverse groups mobilising their resources to have a presence in the media space. Yet their chances will certainly prove to be unequal. Marginalised discourses, which are weaker in terms of visibility, have greater opportunities to gain media interest at times lacking in spectacular events. As a result, however, they receive less social attention. Since 65% of people declare a lack of interest in energy issues, additional stimulation is required to attract public attention. The objective of the third stage of the research was to characterise the communication and media space of a given type of media as a space of the public sphere and a place of deliberation on the main issues of energy. Constructing discursive maps for a specific type of medium and within a given subject area was the basis of the next step – a discourse meta-analysis conducted by the researchers on the basis of all reports and databases as well as maps, notes and working materials that had been produced. The framework of this analytical work was demarcated by a critical discourse analysis whose core was inspired by the approach of Fairclough (2011), taking into account not only the sociolinguistic level but also the intertextual dynamics and socio-cultural references.

Bibliography

Bakhtin, M. (1975), *Questions of Literature and Aesthetics* (Russian), Moscow.

Bakhtin, M. (1982), *The Dialogical Imagination*, Austin.

Clarke, A. E. (2003), "Situational Analyses. Grounded Theory Mapping after the Postmodern Turn," *Symbolic Interaction*, vol. 26, vol. 4, pp. 553–76.

Clarke, A. (2005), *Situational Analysis. Grounded Theory after the Postmodern Turn*, Thousand Oaks, CA.

Czyżewski, M. (2013), "Teorie dyskursu i dyskursy teorii," *Kultura i Społeczeństwo*, no. 2.

Fairclough, N. (2011), *Media Discourse*, London–New York.

Fairclough, N. (2012), *Discourse and Social Change*, Cambridge, MA.

Fuchs, C. (2014), *Social Media. A Critical Introduction*, London.

Gamson, A. W., Modigliani, A. (1989), "Media Discourse and Public Opinion on Nuclear Power: A consructionist Approach," *American Journal of Sociology*, vol. 95, no. 1, p. 1–37.

Juza, M. (2016), "Dwadzieścia lat obecności internetu w życiu społecznym – nadzieje, obawy, krytyka," *Studia Socjologiczne*.

Kacperczyk, A. (2007), "Badacz i jego poszukiwania w świetle 'Analizy Sytuacyjnej' Adele E. Clarke," *Przegląd Socjologii Jakościowej*, vol. 3, no. 2.

Mathar, T. (2008), "Making a Mess with Situational Analysis?," *Forum. Qualitative Social Research*, vol. 9, no. 2.

Murphy, J. (1999), *Technical Analysis of the Financial Markets*, Paramus, NJ.

Ojha, H. R., Cameron, J., Kumar, C. (2012), "Deliberation or Symbolic Violence? The Governance of Community Forestry in Nepal," *Forest Policy and Economics*, 11 (5), pp. 365–74.

Provalis Research Handbook, Jaccard's Index, http://www.provalisresearch.com/Documents/QDAMiner32.pdf (access: 28 December 2015).

Steenbergen, M. R., Bächtinger, A., Spörnolli, M., Steiner, J. (2003), "Measuring Political Deliberation: A Discourse Quality Index," *Comparative European Politics*, 1, p. 21–48.

Świątkiewicz-Mośny, M., Wagner, A. (2012), "How Much Energy in Energy Policy? The Media on Energy Problems in Developing Countries (with the Example of Poland)," *Energy Policy*, 50, pp. 383–90.

Wagner, A. (2010), *Zaufać mediom? Analiza mechanizmów samoopisu prasy w sytuacjach kryzysowych*, Kraków.

Rafał Garpiel

NUCLEAR ENERGY
IN THE POLISH MEDIA DISCOURSE

Nuclear energy from a CDA perspective

Looking at nuclear discourse from the point of view of the analytical paradigms that constitute critical discourse analysis (CDA) as presented by Norman Fairclough (see Wagner, Chapter 1: "The Media Energy Discourse as an Object of Sociological Reflection – the Theoretical and Methodological Context"), we intend to concentrate on the relations within a triad of key notions: power – interests – knowledge. If we follow Michel Foucault (1995: 27) in assuming that "power and knowledge directly imply one another; that there is no power relation without the correlative constitution of a field of knowledge, nor any knowledge that does not presuppose and constitute at the same time power relations," then at the splice of this dyad we will find interests closely correlated to them, and behind these interests stand concrete – individual or collective – actors, striving to realise these interests. Interests are therefore closely related to centres of knowledge, and translate into specific, teleologically oriented strategies for management of knowledge, which we can understand by studying media discourse. Something of importance for both Foucault (Horwarth 2000) and Fairclough is the impact of social exclusion – including exclusion from participation in processes of decision making in public affairs – on discourse, and indirectly, on society. In critical discourse analysis, the asymmetries of power, exploitation, manipulation and structural inequalities are essential to the analyses that are carried out. Here too this is our perspective (Bulcaen 2000: 450–451), as we examine both the active actors in the discourse and the great absentees, meaning actors whom we perceive to be legitimate participants in the discourse owing to its subject matter, yet whose role is either very limited or even imperceptible.

Discussing Fairclough's ideas, Adam Warzecha writes, "discourse is an element of social life which is dialectically interconnected with other elements, and may have constructive and transformative effects on them" (Warzecha 2014: 166). Following this premise, and treating discourse as a tool for forming and transforming the material world, we therefore also accept that the social, political and economic aspects of the way in which nuclear energy functions as a field of human actions depend on the form and content of the discourse, as well as its specific characteristics, dynamic, internal diversity and thematic specialisation, and on the mosaic of actors who shape it. In Fairclough's view, discourse analyses are part of the standards of critical realism: "unlike the structuralist determinism visible, for example, in Derrida, he acknowledges the autonomy of social reality (the material world, participants in discourse), and does not reduce it to discourse, which he conceives dialectically – as constituting (social reality) and constituted (by this reality)" (Warzecha 2014: 172). We accept this perspective, and treat the discourse on nuclear energy as, on the one hand, the representation of human actions and the social structure in which they are realised, and on the other, as a factor that conditions and constitutes the identity of actors, interpersonal relations and the social structure in areas associated with energy.

In attributing to discourses a creationist causative power towards the social world, let us bear in mind that this influence can lead to three fundamental, independent (in the sense of the possibility of existing together or separately) results:

- Discourses being played out as forms of action and interaction – this can be subject to institutionalisation
- Individual and collective social actors adopting them as the matter of identity
- Their materialisation in the features of the physical world (Fairclough, Duszak 2008).

Let us return to the internal differentiation of discourse. On the one hand, this chapter considers various orders of the discourse, but on the other it concentrates on those that are dominant, and thus potentially have the strongest impact on the social environment. Warzecha writes that "there is usually one dominant aspect of this ordering – certain ways of producing a meaning dominate or lead in a specific order of discourse, while others are marginalised or treated as oppositional or 'alternative'" (Warzecha 2014: 180). It is these "model," frequently appearing, versions of discourse that we will particularly stress. This does not mean explanatory neglect of the blank spaces in nuclear discourse, as these too will be indicated and their significance stressed.

This analysis explores the ways in which previously defined interest groups appropriate the public discourse and the results of this process, and underlines the models of using knowledge to legitimise one's own interests and delegitimise those of others. The analysis reveals a model of the public sphere constitutive for the analysed media discourse. It also identifies the bilateral relations between the discourse taking place and social, economic, cultural and political changes.[1]

The discourse in the 1980s

The contemporary media discourse on nuclear energy in Poland has long historic roots stretching back to the 1980s. This sets it apart from the other discourses taking place, on shale gas and renewable energy sources. It was in this decade that the scale of the presence of nuclear energy in media content was much larger not only than it had been previously, but also than it would be in the 1990s or the first decade of the 21st century. The media discourse became much denser in the mid-1980s, with an increase in the number and frequency of mainstream media articles focusing on nuclear energy or those on other subjects making reference to it. As we shall see in the next parts of this chapter, this concentration was linked to the strong anchoring of the issue in current affairs, yet the intensity of the discourse also certainly had a strong, reflexive influence on the agenda of public affairs and the increased media visibility of nuclear energy issues.

Main topics

The researchers treated the media discourse of the 1980s, whose central meta-issue was nuclear energy, as an intertextual context of the contemporary discourse on nuclear energy, and therefore as having an impact on the shape of its now popularised social representations. Two facts that were important from the perspective of public opinion in Poland had a direct impact on the density of the media discourse in the mid-1980s: the plan to build the first Polish nuclear power station and the Chernobyl disaster. Taking these circumstances into account, we analyse the content published in the daily and weekly newspa-

---

1   In addition to the source material, the analysis whose results are presented here was based on the interim reports produced during the research project "The Media as a Space of Deliberation" by Maria Świątkiewicz-Mośny, Aleksandra Wagner and Wit Hubert – See Appendix 3.

pers and magazines that constituted this discourse and gave it continuity over time: *Polityka, Tygodnika Powszechny, Rzeczpospolita, Trybuna Ludu* and *Życie Warszawy*. In total, we analysed 68 articles from 1985–1989 (by a long way the most, 41, came from 1986). Over 86% of the pieces were opinion columns, and, notably, only 29 of them were advertised on the front pages.

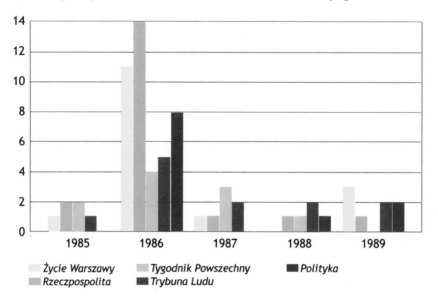

Figure 1. Number of articles, divided by publication and date

Source: A. Wagner, *Energetyka jądrowa w dyskursie prasowym lat 80. Analiza zawartości wybranych tytułów prasowych. Raport z badań*, p. 12.

Two currents of media discourse coexisted: one developmental, associated with the plans to create a new sector of nuclear energy in Poland; the other catastrophic, marked by discussions on the causes and consequences of the Chernobyl disaster. Together, these shaped the discourse and the priorities on the map of topics that were tackled.

We should add, however, that the dynamic, situational, catastrophic strand of discourse motivated by concrete events was by no means dominant. The majority of sources, occurring more frequently, were part of a more static (in terms of manner of communication), sober developmental strand, encompassing discourse on the prospects and directions of the development of energy. So the more optimistic strand, based on categories of development of civilisation, defeated its counterpart concerning current events, despite the magnitude and far-reaching consequences of the latter. Economic development was therefore the most frequent context in which nuclear energy was discussed in the 1980s; other popular thematic frameworks were dealing with the consequences of Chernobyl, a topic rooted very much in the here and now, as well as the safety of nuclear energy in general. The nuclear accident itself was usually presented as the result of human error in the face of technology working properly, i.e. as an incidental case of well-designed and well-built machinery functioning badly.

Relatively popular thematic contexts also included the preventive action carried out in Poland as a reaction to the Chernobyl disaster, as well as reports on the progress in the construction of the nuclear power station in Poland. Issues of management of the waste ensuing from the working of the power station and references to social conflicts caused by Poland's plans to invest in nuclear energy or to political conflicts resulting from the Chernobyl disaster were confined to the side-lines of the media discourse, and reflections on the global energy crisis, the risk associated with building power stations or the technological aspects of the construction and utilising this kind of plant were almost entirely marginalised.

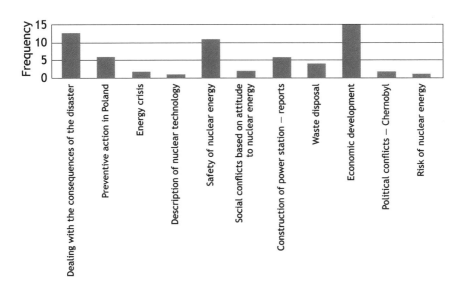

Figure 2. Subjects covered in the press discourse in 1985–1989

Source: A. Wagner, *Energetyka jądrowa w dyskursie prasowym lat 80. Analiza zawartości wybranych tytułów prasowych. Raport z badań*, p. 15.

Notably, there were significant differences in the breakdown of the dominant topics between the various publications that we analysed.

In *Życie Warszawy*, most attention was paid to dealing with the consequences of Chernobyl and the safety of nuclear energy (34%), and less on nuclear energy as a determinant of economic development (22%). In *Rzeczpospolita*, reports on the building of the power station in Poland were equally important as information on the preventive action and reflections on safety

(15%). Yet it was the current and emotional issue of dealing with the effects of the disaster that proved to be dominant. In *Tygodnik Powszechny*, economic development centred around nuclear energy (63%) (and to a lesser extent, the topic of radioactive waste disposal –18%, unpopular in other publications) dominated the discourse. In *Polityka*, three topics were equally popular (33%): dealing with the consequences of the disaster, the preventive action and safety of nuclear energy. In *Trybuna Ludu*, examination of economic development based on development of nuclear energy was dominant (25%), ahead of other topics that were also often covered – dealing with the consequences of the accident and safety of development of nuclear energy (16%).

The major contexts

All of the analysed material reflecting the course of discourse on nuclear energy that can be found in the press published in Poland in the 1980s is placed in several main contexts. We can understand these as sets of external determinants of the progress of the discourse that shape its concentration on a specific point of view on nuclear energy; the contexts therefore reflect the discourse's inclination towards one of the perspectives considered by the researchers: technological, economic, political-administrative, lifeworld, environmental, economic-political and educational. The last of these contextual perspectives was not reflected in the analysed material, while the remainder are arranged below according to the frequency of their occurrence.

Technological economic

political-administrative lifeworld environmental economic-political

educational

Figure 3. Frequency of occurrence of codes in the category "contexts"

Source: A. Wagner, *Energetyka jądrowa w dyskursie prasowym lat 80. Analiza zawartości wybranych tytułów prasowych. Raport z badań*, p. 22.

The technological context was by far the most frequent perspective for viewing nuclear energy. It allowed the authors of the material to move in a space of discourse constructed by specialists representing an impenetrable area of knowledge, considerably limiting the number of fully fledged participants in the discourse. Economic and political-administrative topics were in second place and still prominent in the discourse, while those of lifeworld as well as environmental and economic-political issues were in third, owing to the relatively low level of impenetrability of the reflections within the semantic boundaries of these categories. Topics that could make the discourse relatively and potentially more egalitarian could not be excluded from its progression, but could be – and were – controlled by managing the communication in an unthreatening way not questioning the authorities or positions of the most important actors in the discourse, listed below.

Actors

Irrespective of the most important subject area in a given text, most of them were dominated by a specialist tone represented by a number of experts with a positive approach to the prospects of development of nuclear energy in Poland. The optimistic and rational view of the development of this sector of energy was contrasted with the emotional – and therefore lacking rational causes – fear-based layman's approach to the issue. The cult of technological progress, connected to the more general cult of civilisational development, easily overcame (at least in terms of the impression constructed among consumers of the media) the communicatively accentuated characteristics of irrationality and dilettantism that were attributed to the representatives of circles sceptical towards development of nuclear energy in Poland. Any knowledge that was not technological and did not concern advanced nuclear technology solutions was therefore treated as an area of ignorance, a competence gap, contrasting with the advanced research-backed knowledge of experts, and, especially importantly in this context, the authority of representatives of the scientific and research communities.

We can view the mid-1980s media discourse on nuclear energy as having been appropriated by experts whose authority was communicatively strengthened by displaying their academic titles (professors, lecturers) and positions as heads of research centres or their roles (authors of publications and analyses), and sometimes also their administrative functions. Over 63% of statements of individual actors in the sources came from experts, a fifth from Polish or Soviet politicians, and only a little over 7% from officials. Residents appeared in the role of actors in discourse in less than 5% of statements, while representatives of businesses and journalists were barely discernible in the margins of the discourse.

It is worth pointing out that the politicians in question were, in the case of the USSR, top-ranking ones (Mikhail Gorbachev, Deputy Chairman of the Council of Ministers Ivan Silayev), but less so where Polish ones were concerned (Józef Kozioł, Minister for Protection of the Environment and Natural Resources; Adam Dunalewicz, director of the government's press office). The most important players on the Polish political scene – Wojciech Jaruzelski, Zbigniew Messner, Mieczysław Rakowski – did not take part in the discourse.

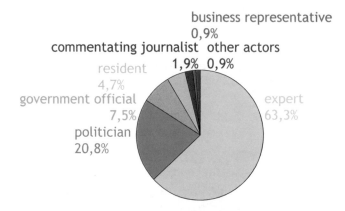

Figure 4. Percentage of codes in the "individual actors" category

Source: A. Wagner, *Energetyka jądrowa w dyskursie prasowym lat 80. Analiza zawartości wybranych tytułów prasowych. Raport z badań*, p. 17.

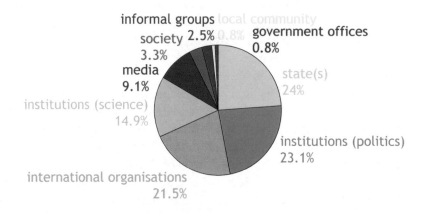

Figure 5. Percentage of codes in the "collective actors" category

Source: A. Wagner, *Energetyka jądrowa w dyskursie prasowym lat 80. Analiza zawartości wybranych tytułów prasowych. Raport z badań*, p. 21.

As for the collective actors participating in the discourse, the most frequent were states (24% of occurrences of collective actors), followed by national political institutions and international organisations (slightly over 23% and 21% respectively). Scientific institutions comprised 15% of such cases, the media 9%, and society and informal groups a little over 3% and 2% respectively. Local communities were on the margins of the discourse – appearing in only 1% of analysed cases.

"State actors" refers in particular to the Soviet Union, COMECON countries, the USA, France, Japan and Sweden. Among the political institutions of importance for the progression of the discourse we should highlight the

Government Committee for Assessing Radiation Levels and Preventive Actions, regional sanitary-epidemiological stations, the Council of Ministers, the Ministry of Health and Social Welfare, the Ministry of Internal Affairs, and the National Atomic Energy Agency. In an international context, the main actor of note is the Politburo of the Communist Party of the Soviet Union.

Actors not participating in the discourse were the Central Committee of the Polish United Workers' Party, the Ministry of Foreign Affairs and the Ministry of National Defence. State-actors were invoked in our material as foreign reference points for the investments planned in Poland; as we can see, both socialist and capitalist countries were included in the field of reference, although of course with differing judgements of their energy policies, in favour of the countries of the Eastern Bloc.

The technological context, which received the greatest exposure in the discourse, was the cause of actors in most cases – scientific institutions, individual experts and international organisations – concentrating on the possibilities of efficient utilisation of the available resources and technical solutions, as well as on the numbers reflecting the optimal solutions. The constitutive values of development and civilisational progress occurred against the background of this type of discourse. In addition, where the technological context was emphasised this often came together with the political-administrative context and the appearance of such actors as politicians, political institutions and states.

The largest difference between the sub-discourses taking place in the various periodicals was recorded in the political-administrative context. Here, individual politicians and political institutions appeared much less in *Tygodnik Powszechny* compared to the other media, reflecting this publication's thematic and axiological profile at the time.

Appraisal and methods of argument

The analysed material was very much dominated by statements presenting nuclear energy in a positive light; sceptical opinions were less common.

Table 1. Appraisal in press texts

	Życie Warszawy	Rzecz-pospolita	Tygodnik Powszechny	Trybuna Ludu	Polityka
Positive appraisal	53.80%	70.70%	18.80%	57.10%	36.36%
Negative appraisal	46.20%	29.30%	81.20%	42.90%	63.63%

Source: A. Wagner, *Energetyka jądrowa w dyskursie prasowym lat 80. Analiza zawartości wybranych tytułów prasowych. Raport z badań.*

The publication that was most positive towards the subject of the research was *Rzeczpospolita* (particularly regarding administrative-political decisions). *Tygodnik Powszechny*, on the other hand, contained the most material featuring negative appraisal, especially concerning the lack of knowledge, understood as ignorance, attributed to opponents of nuclear energy in general, including those averse to its development in Poland. The articles published during this period in *Tygodnik Powszechny* therefore formed a picture of an island of long-term thinking, imagining Poland's situation in the distant future, closely related to the current (1980s) events and decisions of those responsible for running the country. *Trybuna Ludu* depicted a global conflict on an East–West line, with a polarisation between positive and negative appraisals appearing in the text resulting from this political-ideological dichotomy. This was in accordance with the mainstream press propaganda of the time, devoted to painting a black-and-white picture of the relations between capitalist and socialist countries.

Table 2. Persuasive elements used in the arguments of press articles

	Życie Warszawy	*Rzecz-pospolita*	*Tygodnik Powszechny*	*Trybuna Ludu*	*Polityka*
Stereotypes	6.70%	0.00%	12.50%	3.60%	9.00%
Visions of the future	13.30%	5.60%	31.30%	17.90%	45.00%
Conflict	6.70%	5.60%	6.30%	14.30%	9.00%
Numbers	46.70%	44.40%	25.00%	42.90%	18.00%
Experiences	6.70%	38.90%	18.80%	14.30%	32.00%
Solutions /proposals	20.00%	5.60%	6.30%	7.10%	15.40%

Source: A. Wagner, *Energetyka jądrowa w dyskursie prasowym lat 80. Analiza zawartości wybranych tytułów prasowych. Raport z badań*

The persuasive methods used to reinforce the positions varied according to the publications. *Życie Warszawy* made extensive use of figures as well as solutions and proposals as responses to the objectively existing problems and challenges (civilisational progress, dealing with the results of the accident), and also featured a large percentage of arguments based on a vision of the future (positive, on condition of implementation of a vision for development of nuclear energy). *Rzeczpospolita* also most frequently cited numbers, and slightly less often referred to the experiences of other countries, while *Tygodnik Powszechny* mostly presented visions of the future supported by figures and references to the experiences of others. In *Trybuna Ludu* there was a preponderance of numbers in arguments in favour of nuclear energy, alongside references to the experiences of other countries, but here the East–West conflict was also often presented. Stereotypes and visions of the future were used in arguments most commonly in *Tygodnik Powszechny*, conflicts based on nuclear energy in *Trybuna Ludu*, and numerical data with a similar intensity in *Życie Warszawy*, *Rzeczpospolita* and *Trybuna Ludu*, and relatively less often in *Tygodnik Powszechny*. References to the experiences of other countries proved to be the domain of *Rzeczpospolita*, while presentation of solutions and proposals was characteristic of the discourse in *Życie Warszawy*.

This description of the differing models of discourse presented in the various press titles shows that on the one hand the mosaic of perspectives on nuclear energy was extremely diverse, but on the other it was subject to several fundamental communicative trends that are described above. These included the omnipotence of experts, domination of the technological discourse type and a concentration on categories of development and progress.

Dynamic of discourse

Different categories of actors gained in importance at different moments, as a direct result of the variable intensity of topics connected to the planned building of the nuclear power station in Poland and the reverberations of the Chernobyl disaster on the discourse. The objectively major significance of these two subjects meant that state actors and international institutions dictated the tone of the debate on nuclear energy in 1985, before gradually (international organisations) or suddenly (states) losing their relative importance in the course of the discussion in 1986. The reason for this drop in relative significance was not so much a decrease in the exposure of these actors as the greater diversification of the network of actors, and thus the larger exposure of other categories of actors of the discourse in 1986, including an active presence of the media, and above all political and scientific institutions.

In 1987, states, scientific institutions and political ones shared a balanced amount of exposure, followed in 1988 by far-reaching balanced exposure of most groups of collective actors. The following year scientific institutions held an increasingly strong position, dominating in terms of exposure, compared to other groups of collective actors; this was against the background of a drastic drop in the temperature of the nuclear discourse in general.

Among individual actors in 1985–1989, experts constantly dominated, demarcating paths for presentation of nuclear energy that mostly exhibited technological subjects. The second most common category of individual actors was politicians, who reached the highest level of relative exposure in 1986 and 1988. The latter year was unique (in terms of the relative balance of discourse) when it comes to the proportions of exposure of the various categories of individual actors, as in this time the role of experts temporarily

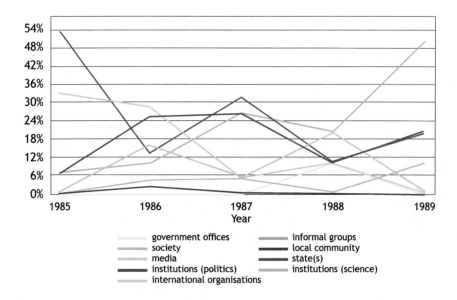

Figure 6. Dynamic of changes in media exposure of collective actors over time – percentage

Source: A. Wagner, *Energetyka jądrowa w dyskursie prasowym lat 80. Analiza zawartości wybranych tytułów prasowych. Raport z badań*, p. 32.

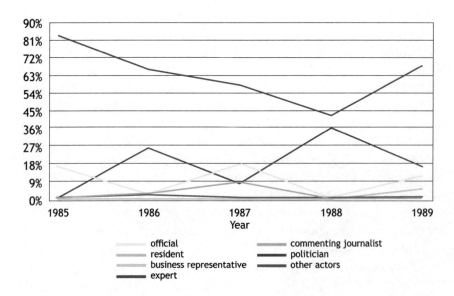

Figure 7. Dynamic of changes in media exposure of individual actors over time – percentage

Source: A. Wagner, *Energetyka jądrowa w dyskursie prasowym lat 80. Analiza zawartości wybranych tytułów prasowych. Raport z badań*, p. 33.

decreased, while that of politicians increased markedly, and, less obvious-
ly, the role of the usually entirely marginalised category of residents grew
relatively. Both politicians and residents lost their prominent positions in
communication in 1989, at the costs of experts, who constantly retained the
greatest exposure at the forefront of the discourse.

Changes over time were also recorded in the case of the aforementioned
specific contexts that affected the direction of the discourse. In 1985 the
political-administrative and economic contexts were dominant, and the
temperature of the discourse was low. In 1986, though, the dynamic of the
discourse exploded, and was appropriated by contextual technological categories, the cause of which was doubtless the intensification of the discourse
on the Chernobyl disaster and plans to construct a nuclear power station in
Poland. At the same time, political-administrative and economic contexts
developed almost equally sharply.

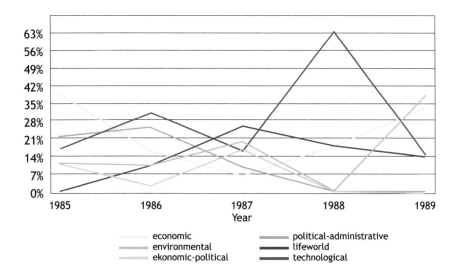

Figure 8. Dynamic of changes in media exposure of contexts over time – percentage
Source: A. Wagner, *Energetyka jądrowa w dyskursie prasowym lat 80. Analiza zawartości wybranych
tytułów prasowych. Raport z badań*, p. 34.

The lifeworld, the context closest to the average person, received relative exposure only in 1986 and 1987, while in 1988, with the fall in the
temperature of discourse, the technological context again became relatively
significant. In 1989, the environmental context had the greatest exposure
compared to other contexts.

Critical discourse analysis — 1980s

Analysis of the discourse on nuclear energy from the mid-1980s to the end of that decade leads to unequivocal conclusions concerning the relations within the triad of key concepts: power, knowledge and interests. The discourse in question was extremely exclusive in character, in terms of both its active participants, i.e. the individual and collective actors of the discourse, and the audience of the media discourse. The specialist terminology used by actors participating in the discourse (mostly by experts) and the dominance of its technological context automatically restricted the numbers of those who could fully participate in it, as well as, to an equal extent, the numbers of conscious, passive recipients of the discourse.

Politicians, political institutions and international organisations were also active participants in the discourse, and apart from the strong presence of the technological context, the economic and political-administrative contexts were also relatively common. All these characteristics – the dominant categories of collective and individual actors and the most frequently and intensively activated contexts – only sustained the exclusive character of the discourse on nuclear energy in Poland. In the central field of media communication, the activity of the two strongest communities – political-organisational (responsible for decisions and actions) and academic-expert (responsible for legitimising, proving the validity of positions, decisions and actions communicated by politicians and representative of political organisations) came together.

The two main topics of the nuclear discourse – the accident at Chernobyl and the plans to build the first Polish nuclear power station in Żarnowiec – appeared almost simultaneously, to the detriment of the politicians of the Polish People's Republic, as it proved impossible to separate them fully, tactically, for propaganda purposes. Clearly, whereas the gradual introduction of information on the plans to construct and operate the first Polish nuclear power station into the media discourse represented the realisation of a certain wider plan of action (encompassing public communication), media communication referring to Chernobyl was inevitably an unplanned, only partially controlled reaction to unfavourable political-economic circumstances. Owing to their temporal coexistence, the two topics began not only to appear together in the same periodicals and the same articles, but also to affect each other and intersect semantically. This must have led the major actors to adopt a strategy of isolating the discourse, making it inaccessible to the masses in terms of cognitive factors and arguments used. Allowing even a relatively open discussion (for the conditions in which the media operated in Poland in the mid-1980s) on the plans to build a power plant in Żarnowiec, in the context of the very fresh reports on the Chernobyl accident, would carry the risk that the two issues could become irreversibly connected cognitively. In fact, it proved impossible to prevent this effect entirely, but the damage was limited by maintaining the discourse on a consistently expert level, concentrating largely on the technological aspect of nuclear energy. There were far fewer actors potentially participating in the discourse capable of polemicising using calculations, analyses, reports and expert appraisals than there were potential discussants of the desired directions of development of energy in Poland following the tragic events of Chernobyl.

It was no coincidence that emotional, fearful reactions to the events beyond Poland's eastern border were discredited as positions that showed the people expressing them in a bad light, contrasted with the analytical, balanced and fact-based positions of experts and politicians, presented as absolutely more valuable.

Especially interesting, however, is the fact that Polish politicians did not take part in the discourse, although in the planned economy it was they who had an overwhelming influence on the strategic decisions concerning energy development in Poland, and were the most important people in the country. We can surmise that the policy makers wanted to avoid excessive emphasis on strategic and political issues, finding the technological and economic contexts much safer, as they permitted communication based on categories of objective justice or even inevitability, as opposed to the will of the policy makers themselves, which was subjective, even if intersubjective (as the object of the mutual consideration of Polish and Soviet politicians and experts supporting them).

Given the circumstances of the discourse on nuclear energy in the second half of the 1980s in Poland, it is no surprise that local communities, informal groups and residents of a given area were excluded. Firstly, at this time thinking in terms of civil society and empowerment and participation of the citizens of a state or town/city was not yet common even in most democratic countries, let alone the states of the Eastern Bloc, where decision makers operated in almost complete isolation from society and local communities. Secondly, the realisation of the plan for development of energy in Poland to include the construction and utilisation of nuclear power stations and far-reaching political, economic and technological cooperation with the USSR was endangered by the extremely stark example of the negative consequences of the Chernobyl disaster. It was therefore in the policy makers' interest to mould the discourse appropriately and intentionally by activating individual and collective actors speaking in positive terms about this direction of development.

The planned economy, as well as, undoubtedly, the large influence of politicians on the tone of the media discourse, are not the only factors that allowed the discourse to be appropriated by experts assuming the role of living, cognitive shields protecting politicians and justifying the steps they took. What also made it much easier to guide the discourse was the monopolisation of sources of expert knowledge (to which not everybody had access at the time), and simultaneously either the discrediting of potential alternative source of knowledge, or – in most cases – denying them access to the discourse, treated as being legitimised by positions and functions and the attributes of expert status (academic titles and affiliations, etc.).

Since the sources of alternative knowledge (to the expert-political brand) were denied access to the media discourse of the 1980s, the arguments of non-institutional actors were also largely absent. The discourse was forged by the activity of institutions and among their representatives; non-institutional actors were not invited to participate, or even admitted. Where the press did show signs of any activity of representatives of local communities, this was presented as contestation, often unthinking, not targeted at achieving any important goal for the state and society, but only on destroying what the participants in the discourse regarded as right and proper – building a nuclear power station in Poland.

We can regard the map of the major issues covered in the nuclear discourse in the 1980s and the main contextual and argumentative lines that appeared at the time as the essential (albeit not only) source of the later versions of the discourse, discussed below. While we do not suggest that the form and content of the discourse in each of the analysed periods were homogeneous, there is no doubt that the emotional, decisive and only partially controlled (as mentioned above) introduction of nuclear energy into public communication could not fail to leave a mark on every subsequent instalment of the nuclear discourse, despite the changed communication priorities and partial reallocation of the major categories of actors. What remained a constitutive topic was the prospect of development of nuclear energy, albeit perceived from a somewhat different perspective. The analysis in the following paragraphs of this chapter makes this clear.

The discourse in 2007–2012

We can track the media discourse taking place over the course of six years in the dailies *Gazeta Wyborcza* and its local supplements, *Rzeczpospolita* and its thematic supplements and *Fakt*, as well as the weeklies *Newsweek*, *Polityka* and *Wprost*, on the basis of an analysis of articles comprising a representative sample (taking into account the proportions of texts published in given years) of 292 texts selected from an initial set of 990 press articles in which the phrase "nuclear power station" appeared in the singular or plural. Owing to the density of the discourse in 2011 and 2012, half of the texts from the six years of the analysis (from 2007 to 2012) come from these two years. The least intensive discourse we observed was in 2008.

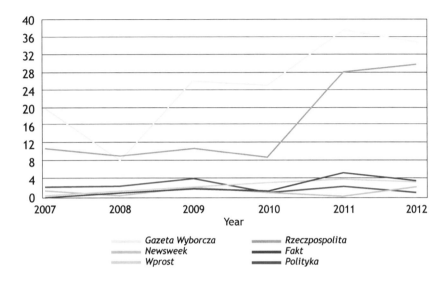

Figure 9. Graph showing the number of articles, divided by years of publication

Source: A. Wagner, *Energetyka jądrowa w dyskursie prasowym lat 2007–2012. Analiza zawartości wybranych tytułów prasowych. Raport z badań*, p. 8.

Main subjects

The media discourse of the years 2007–2012 was dominated by one distinct, and once again (following the mid-1980s) current topic – the prospect of construction of a nuclear power station in Poland, which was an issue addressed by 46% of the articles analysed. Over 8% of texts discussed the subject of alternative energy sources, and over 6% concerned nuclear power plants operating in various parts of the world. The remaining topics – somewhat less popular, with approx. 5% of articles, but still discernible in the discourse – were international cooperation in the context of building and utilisation of nuclear stations, and the economic situation of global companies from the nuclear sector. The main subject from the 1980s discourse – issues of technologies used for building and utilising nuclear power stations – appeared in just 3.4% of the texts from 2007–2012. Interestingly, despite the considerable density of the discourse on nuclear energy, against the background of the wider theme of development of energy as a whole – strategic and global topics connected with the country's energy security, energy balance or energy crisis proved to be of only marginal interest (each was covered in only approx. 2% of articles). The plans to build a Polish nuclear station are thus presented in strictly autotelic terms, without the need for in-depth presentation of its impact on Poland's functioning in the international economic-political context.

Word frequency lists

We acquired interesting information by analysing frequency lists of verbs, nouns and adjectives appearing in the texts. By compiling lists of the words that occur most frequently, we can draw cautious conclusions regarding the dominant perspective on nuclear energy as a subject tackled in the press from 2007 to 2012.

The fact that the word "say" (*mówić*) appears most frequently in the texts should not be treated as a particularly significant; the word in second place in the frequency list, however, is interesting. The word used is "arrive" (*powstać*), to refer indirectly to the construction ("arrival") of the power station, as opposed to the more concrete "build" (or "be built") (*budować*). The fact that the arrival of the power station is spoken of, rather than its building (this word occurs five times more frequently) suggests a desubjectification and depersonalisation of this developmental perspective, which is treated as the emanation of trends independent of the acts of this or another category of actors, and therefore the result of the actions of an unspecified higher power. We should also not underestimate the frequency of the verbs "can"/"be able to" (*móc*) and "must"/"have to" (*musieć*) and their derivatives, which are important and occupy high positions both in the analysed material and in generally available corpora of the Polish language.[2] Whereas the verb "can" appears in the National Corpus of the Polish Language around five times more frequently than "must," in our analysed material these proportions are reversed: "must" and "it is necessary to" (*trzeba*) together occur much more frequently than "can," which indirectly indicates the media view of the construction of the nuclear power station more in terms of necessity (and consequently not subject to debate) than as something that can possibly be realised, and thus whose pros and cons need to be considered. The next popular verbs in our material – "convince" (*przekonać*), "think" (*myśleć*), "change" (*zmienić*), have strongly persuasive and dynamic connotations, demonstrating a departure from the status quo in views and opinions, but also actions.

---

2   http://www.nkjp.uni.lodz.pl (access: 5 November 2015).

Table 3. Frequency list: most frequently used verbs

	FREQUENCY	NO. CASES
SAY (*MOWIĆ*)	382	151
ARRIVE (*POWSTAĆ*)	264	124
CAN (*MÓC*)	228	112
IT IS NECESSARY TO (*TRZEBA*)	206	98
MUST (*MUSIEĆ*)	159	90
CONVINCE (*PRZEKONAĆ*)	134	89
THINK (*MYŚLEĆ*)	112	66
CHANGE (*ZMIENIĆ*)	111	63
STAND (*STANĄĆ*)	108	76
WORK (*PRACOWAĆ*)	103	65
PLAN (*PLANOWAĆ*)	101	81
ASSURE (*ZAPEWNIAĆ*)	87	66
USE (*KORZYSTAĆ*)	86	51
INCREASE (*ZWIĘKSZYĆ*)	76	47
EXPLOIT (*WYKORZYSTAĆ*)	72	37
DEMAND (*WYMAGAĆ*)	68	51
PRODUCE (*WYTWARZAĆ*)	67	45
DECREASE (*ZMNIEJSZYĆ*)	63	40
LOOK FOR (*SZUKAĆ*)	56	39
BUILD (*BUDOWAĆ*)	53	46
COST (*KOSZTOWAĆ*)	48	33
SEE (*ZOBACZYĆ*)	46	19
BELIEVE (*WIERZYĆ*)	41	26
ANSWER (*ODPOWIADAĆ*)	39	34
START (*STARTOWAĆ*)	39	13
ESTIMATE (*SZACOWAĆ*)	38	36
SUFFICE (*WYSTARCZYĆ*)	36	31
CLAIM (*STWIERDZIĆ*)	36	30
FEAR (*OBAWIAĆ_SIĘ*)	36	26
EMIT (*EMITOWAĆ*)	36	21
SAY (*POWIEDZIEĆ*)	35	28
ISSUE (*WYDAWAĆ*)	31	30
ORGANISE (*ORGANIZOWAĆ*)	31	29
DEFEND (*BRONIĆ*)	31	23
SELL (*SPRZEDAWAĆ*)	29	26

LOOK/APPEAR (*WYGLĄDAĆ*)	29	21
BUY (*KUPOWAĆ*)	28	24
PARTICIPATE (*UCZESTNICZYĆ*)	27	24
GET TO (*DOJŚĆ*)	27	23
BE AFRAID OF (*BAĆ_SIĘ*)	27	23
CONSTRUCT (*WYBUDOWAĆ*)	26	21
LIE (*LEŻEĆ*)	25	20
UNDERSTAND (*ROZUMIEĆ*)	25	14
DEVELOP (*ROZWIJAĆ_SIĘ*)	23	20
INTEND (*ZAMIERZAĆ*)	22	22
ANNOUNCE (*ZAPOWIEDZIEĆ*)	22	20
PRODUCE (*PRODUKOWAĆ*)	20	17
PAY (*PŁACIĆ*)	20	15
GROW (*WZROSNĄĆ*)	19	16
DECLARE (*DEKLAROWAĆ*)	18	18
ALLOW (*POZWOLIĆ*)	17	14

Source: A. Wagner, *Energetyka jądrowa w dyskursie prasowym lat 2007–2012. Analiza zawartości wybranych tytułów prasowych. Raport z badań.*

The articles also frequently refer to "standing" (in the sense of appearing or being built), "working" in various contexts (referring to the power station, but also to the people to be employed there," "planning" (usually the construction of the power station), as well as "assuring," "using," "exploiting" and "increasing." The four last verbs have strongly economic connotations, and indirectly indicate the importance of this perspective in the texts. It is interesting to note that the frequency of the verb "cost," with unambiguously economic connotations, is only average, and more than five times less than that of "arrive" and almost three times less than "convince." "Cost" occurs slightly more often than "believe," which derives from an entirely different, non-economic and non-rational order. Verbs that indirectly indicate distance to the prospect of development of nuclear energy or even an aversion to it – "fear," "be afraid of," "defend"– were infrequent (almost ten times less common than "arrive," for example, and thus on the margins of the nuclear discourse from 2007–2012.

As for nouns, among the most frequent in the texts are "power station" and "energy" (*energia*). "Power station" in fact occurs twice as frequently as the next two most common nouns: "construction" – reflecting the plan connected to the power station – and "Poland" – as the planned site of the construction. High positions on the frequency list are also occupied by such nouns as "year" – indicating the importance attached to the timetable for the preparations, and then building of the power station, "country" – again defining the place, "energy (production)" (*energetyka*) – as a thematic background, and also "government," "company" and "investment" – representing the subjective and functional context of the planned venture. Of note is the relatively high position of the word "coal," in 14th place in the frequency list, ahead of such words as "state" and "decision." We also noted a relatively high frequency of occurrence of the noun "water," which appears more often than "atom" (*atom* – used as shorthand for "nuclear energy") and "technology," but also considerably more frequently than "development" and "market." This indirectly points to the significance of issues of cooling reactors and potential threats to drinking water reserves.

Nouns with negative connotations do not occupy high positions on the list: the most common was "problem," which occurred ten times less frequently than "power station." We encounter others – "protest," "waste," "accident," "risk," "crisis," "opponents" and "disaster" – twenty or more times more rarely than "power station."

Table 4. Frequency list: most frequently used nouns

	FREQUENCY	NO. CASES
POWER STATION (*ELEKTROWNIA*)	1324	280
CONSTRUCTION (*BUDOWA*)	652	199
POLAND (*POLSKA*)	686	197
ENERGY (*ENERGIA*)	912	188
YEAR (*ROK*)	510	164
COUNTRY (*KRAJ*)	473	162
ENERGY (PRODUCTION) (*ENERGETYKA*)	421	153
GOVERNMENT (*RZĄD*)	423	149
COMPANY (*FIRMA*)	484	134
INVESTMENT (*INWESTYCJA*)	378	131
ISSUE (*SPRAWA*)	288	119
PROJECT (*PROJEKT*)	316	118
WORK (*PRACA*)	267	114
COAL (*WĘGIEL*)	298	101
RESULT (*WYNIK*)	177	101
STATE (COUNTRY) (*PAŃSTWO*)	238	98
YEARS (*LATA*)	170	95
SOURCE (*ŹRÓDŁO*)	241	94
TIME (*CZAS*)	178	94
DECISION (*DECYZJA*)	168	94
WATER (*WODA*)	235	90

POWER (*MOC*)	196	90
ECONOMY (*GOSPODARKA*)	170	89
GROUP (*GRUPA*)	171	88
WORLD (*ŚWIAT*)	201	87
COST (*KOSZT*)	195	86
COMPANY (*SPÓŁKA*)	292	85
EUROPE (*EUROPA*)	232	85
ATOM (~NUCLEAR ENERGY) (*ATOM*)	149	84
PLANS (*PLANY*)	129	84
REACTOR (*REAKTOR*)	298	83
TECHNOLOGY (*TECHNOLOGIA*)	196	83
PLACE (*MIEJSCE*)	143	81
DEVELOPMENT (*ROZWÓJ*)	192	79
AGREEMENT (*ZGODA*)	113	78
GERMANY (*NIEMCY*)	211	77
PRESIDENT (CHAIR) (*PREZES*)	181	77
TRUTH (*PRAWDA*)	121	77
ELECTRICITY (*PRĄD*)	191	76
ENVIRONMENT(*ŚRODOWISKO*)	159	76
END (*KONIEC*)	111	76
BLOCK (*BLOK*)	144	75
OBLIGATION (*POWINNOŚĆ*)	123	75
PARTICIPATION (*UDZIAŁ*)	141	74
BOSS (*SZEF*)	122	74
MARKET (*RYNEK*)	184	73
MINISTER (*MINISTER*)	143	73
SITUATION (*SYTUACJA*)	131	70

Source: A. Wagner, *Energetyka jądrowa w dyskursie prasowym lat 2007–2012. Analiza zawartości wybranych tytułów prasowych. Raport z badań.*

When analysing the noun frequency list, it is worth taking a separate look at the exposure of the various nouns indicating appearance of the subjects in the discourse, collective or individual and indirectly or directly participating in the discourse on nuclear issues. But it is important not to confuse this list, based on frequency lists, with the analysis of the frequency of appearance of various subcategories of actors, to which a separate paragraph is devoted (below). The actors who dominate these references are certainly collective ones, especially state and institutional actors, including business. Among non-institutional and non-state collective actors, we relatively frequently (and much less often than institutional or state ones) encounter the nouns "residents," "people," "Poles," "employees," "opponents," and "children." The nouns showing traces of individual actors include "politician," "prime minister," "professor," "president," (Donald) "Tusk," "person," "director," "member of parliament," "commune head," "vice-president," "analyst," (Jarosław) "Kaczyński," (Witold) "Drożdż" (the CEO of PGE EJ1 in 2010–2012), and (Waldemar) "Pawlak." These were again mostly representatives of state, political and economic institutions, and to a lesser extent independent experts (professor, analyst). The only actor not representing an institution in this case is the anonymous "person."

The dominant adjectives in the discourse are words that supplement and specify the meaning of the most popular noun – power station ("nuclear" and its synonym "atomic," but also "energy" used adjectivally. Among the other popular words are obvious ones suggested by the analysis of nouns and verbs presented above, such as "Polish," "new," "European," "renewable" (in the context of rival energy sources to nuclear energy, often discussed by way of contrast), "EU," and "wind." There are also less obvious ones providing a value judgement, such as "good," "necessary," "safe," "key," "cheaper" or "modern," thus indirectly demonstrating a positive axiological direction of the analysed articles. This therefore at the same time constitutes a coherent lexical supplement to the trend demonstrated in the perspective of development of nuclear energy in Poland as necessary, and therefore not subject to or requiring discussion.

Table 5. Frequency list: most frequently used adjectives

	FREQUENCY	NO. CASES
NUCLEAR (*JĄDROWY*)	808	263
ENERGY (*ENERGETYCZNY*)	391	151
ATOMIC (*ATOMOWY*)	462	144
POLISH (*POLSKI*)	418	138
NEW (*NOWY*)	327	128
GOOD (*DOBRY*)	179	91
EUROPEAN (*EUROPEJSKI*)	188	79
SOCIAL/CIVIC (*SPOŁECZNY*)	136	57
RENEWABLE (*ODNAWIALNY*)	110	53
NECESSARY (*POTRZEBNY*)	57	48
EU (*UNIJNY*)	79	47
SAFE (*BEZPIECZNY*)	52	42
MARINE (*MORSKI*)	58	37
WIND (*WIATROWY*)	90	36

KEY (*KLUCZOWY*)	42	36
INVESTMENT (*INWESTYCYJNY*)	52	35
ENVIRONMENTAL (*EKOLOGICZNY*)	51	35
AMERICAN (*AMERYKAŃSKI*)	46	34
FOREIGN (*ZAGRANICZNY*)	61	33
POMERANIAN (*POMORSKI*)	54	33
SHALE (*ŁUPKOWY*)	117	31
CHEAPER (*TAŃSZY*)	37	31
NUCLEAR (*NUKLEARNY*)	54	30
MODERN (*NOWOCZESNY*)	47	28
GLOBAL (*GLOBALNY*)	52	27
WARSAW-BASED (*WARSZAWSKI*)	52	25
RADIOACTIVE (*RADIOAKTYWNY*)	50	22
PUBLIC (*PUBLICZNY*)	31	22
PRIVATE (*PRYWATNY*)	30	22
GEOLOGICAL(*GEOLOGICZNY*)	28	21
DANGEROUS (*NIEBEZPIECZNY*)	24	18
RUSSIAN (*ROSYJSKI*)	24	18
SCIENTIFIC (*NAUKOWY*)	45	17
BROWN (*BRUNATNY*)	26	16
PROBABLE (*PRAWDOPODOBNY*)	17	16
CONTEMPORARY (*WSPÓŁCZESNY*)	43	14
EFFICIENT (*EFEKTYWNY*)	15	13
NATURAL (GAS) (*ZIEMNY*)	15	10
FUTURE (*PRZYSZŁY*)	11	10

Source: A. Wagner, *Energetyka jądrowa w dyskursie prasowym lat 2007–2012. Analiza zawartości wybranych tytułów prasowych. Raport z badań.*

Adjectives with negative connotations, reflecting the fears of opponents of nuclear energy – "radioactive" (*radioaktywny*), "dangerous" (*niebezpieczny*) – were in peripheral positions in the discourse.

Cluster analysis

Taking a closer look at the hundred words that occurred most frequently in the analysed texts and their co-occurrence, we identified several clusters that were the most important for this analysis. Among these, we can particularly highlight the complicated, multi-level cluster with the nuclear power

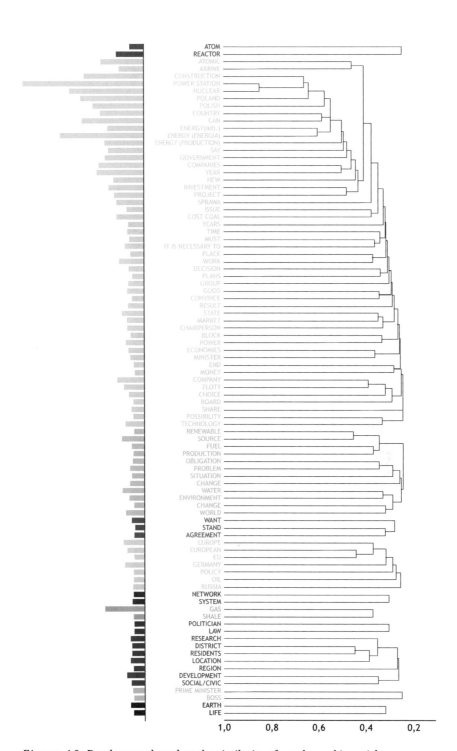

Figure 10. Dendrogram based on the similarity of words used in articles

Source: A. Wagner, *Energetyka jądrowa w dyskursie prasowym lat 2007–2012. Analiza zawartości wybranych tytułów prasowych. Raport z badań*, p. 22.

station as a metathematic cement, surrounded by topics linked to: change, development and progress ("arrive," "construction," "investment," "plans," "new," "year," "time," "end"; making decisions and completing tasks ("can," "must," "it is necessary to," "choice," "possibility," "project," "issue," "decision," "plans"), subjectivity and politics ("government," "company (*firma*)," "Poland," "Polish," "country," "state," "minister," "company" (*spółka*); economics ("cost," "result," "market," "money," "economy"), and sector ("energy" (*energetyczny*, *energia, energetyka*), "coal," "power"). This cluster also contained one value judgement ("good") and one explicitly persuasive connotation ("convince"). With this in mind, for the use of this analysis we can take into account a simplified argumentation model directed towards arguing that the building (or "appearance") of the nuclear power station in Poland is simply good for the country, just as the economic and political circumstances are good, meaning beneficial, and the whole venture leads inevitably, according to the cluster analysis, to the development of the country owing to decisions made and treated as being obvious, or even essential ones.

The remaining clusters are characterised by lesser horizontal and vertical complexity (they comprise fewer mutually related words, and these words form a smaller number of layered connections). Among these we can distinguish a cluster referring to alternative solutions (to nuclear energy) in the context of their positive and desirable impact on the natural environment ("renewable," "source," "fuel," "obligation," "problem," "water," "environment," "change" (noun), "change" (verb), "world") (here we should note that it is obligation, not necessity, that is being discussed), as well as relating to the international context ("Europe," "European," "EU," "Germany," "policy," "oil," "Russia"), and finally – and importantly – one referring to local issues ("research," "district," "residents," "location," "region," "development" and "social/civic"), which indicates the margins, rather than the main thread of the discourse.

Most important contexts

The discourse in the press published in 2007–2012 reveals a fundamentally different map of contexts defining its subject orientation from that observed in the 1980s. The media communication in the period was almost entirely dominated by the economic context, while other discernible contexts included the economic-political and environmental ones (with a similar percentage of occurrence), lifeworld (encompassing the popular perspective) and the political-administrative context. The remaining contexts – educational and technological – had little impact on the progress of the discourse. Compared to the 1980s, therefore, we can observe a radical drop in the significance of the technological context, a marked rise in the importance of environmental concerns, and the appearance of discernible, albeit few, instances of the educational context. The economic context decidedly shifted towards a central position in the discourse, although it was also constitutive in the 1980s discourse (at the time overshadowed by the technological discourse).

Table 6. Frequency of codes – contexts

Category	Code	Count	% Codes	Cases	% Cases
Context	Economic	160	4.50%	96	32.90%
Context	Political-administrative	11	0.30%	9	3.10%
Context	Environmental	34	1.00%	23	7.90%
Context	Lifeworld	17	0.50%	11	3.80%
Context	Economic-political	43	1.20%	25	8.60%
Context	Educational	6	0.20%	5	1.70%
Context	Technological	5	0.10%	5	1.70%
Context	Other	1	0.00%	1	0.30%

Source: A. Wagner, *Energetyka jądrowa w dyskursie prasowym lat 2007–2012. Analiza zawartości wybranych tytułów prasowych. Raport z badań.*

The context linking two orders (economic-political) became much more visible, whereas in the 1980s another hybrid context, political-administrative, had been more common, without any evident references to the world of economics. The lifeworld context, which was not very visible in the 1980s discourse, became even less important. The increased importance of the economic-political context over the previously exposed political-administrative context is a direct reflection of the changes in the political system, which radically redefined the map of decision-making and expert institutions.

Actors

Looking at the map of actors participating in the press discourse between 2007 and 2012, we can observe a clear preponderance in the frequency with which politicians appear as individual actors (almost half of all recorded appearances of individual actors) over experts (one fifth of cases of individual actors). We therefore see a reversal in positions: the dominant role of experts was assumed by politicians, with the former being relegated to a secondary role (although not even second place, as we shall see). Yet this change in positions is not the most symptomatic manifestation of the evolution of discourse in this period.

Rather, what is especially notable is that it is residents as individual actors who appeared in second place. Considering the fact that in the 1980s their role in the discourse was at its outer margins, their position post-2007 points to a radical change within the structure of actors, as well as a fundamental redefinition, of the discourse; people who did not represent either the authorities or the expert community, but simply lived in the area being considered as the location of a nuclear power station, were noticed, and appeared in the discourse in over 22% of cases.

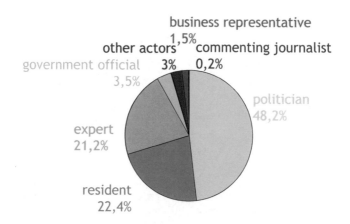

Figure 11. Percentage breakdown of codes in the "individual actors" category

Source: A. Wagner, *Energetyka jądrowa w dyskursie prasowym lat 2007–2012. Analiza zawartości wybranych tytułów prasowych. Raport z badań*, p. 28.

Other categories also occupied marginal positions in the discourse on this occasion: government officials, journalists, and representatives of businesses. The last of these, with just 1.5% of cases of exposure of individual actors, is notable, as in the realities of a capitalist economy, it is they who play the main role in preparations for construction of the nuclear power plant in Poland.

As for collective actors, there is no radical redistribution of places on the map. An important position in terms of the frequency of exposure of collective actors is still held by states – interestingly, the proportion remains identical to that of the 1980s discourse, at around 24%. Despite the sweeping and radical transformations to the political, social and economic circumstances between the two periods, then, the role of this subcategory of collective actors did not change. The countries we find in this segment include Poland, Germany, France, Russia, Lithuania and Japan. Poland is written about as a place of future investment in nuclear energy, and the other countries as either positive or negative points of reference.

Political institutions and international organisations became slightly less significant – whereas previously their total exposure had amounted to a total of 44% of cases of exposure of collective actors, in 2007–2012 the figures were 13% and 10% respectively. Political institutions included the government and ministries, as well as political parties, and among international

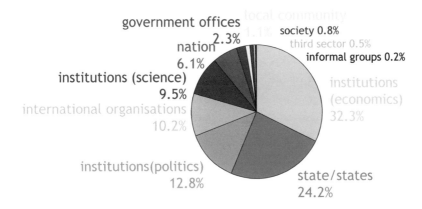

Figure 12. Percentage breakdown of codes in the category "collective actors"
Source: A. Wagner, *Energetyka jądrowa w dyskursie prasowym lat 2007–2012. Analiza zawartości wybranych tytułów prasowych. Raport z badań*, p. 29.

organisations were the EU, the International Atomic Energy Agency, and, less frequently, the UN.

The biggest change, though, is the amount of exposure of the collective actor that appeared most frequently in the discourse in 2007–2012, economic institutions (one third of all instances of collective actors), which were in fact absent in the 1980s as a result of the lack of autonomy of this type of institutions in the planned economy. This category was represented by energy companies such as PGE, PGGiG, Tauron, ENEA and Energa, as well as Gazprom and Areva, and by banks, the stock exchange, supervisory boards and financial markets. The representation of scientific institutions fell, meanwhile, to less than 10%, and that of the media from 9% to almost zero. The position of social communities, informal group and society, on the other hand, was unchanged, with these categories of collective actors remaining marginal at just over 2% of cases of exposure in the discourse, i.e. at a similar proportion to officials. A social category with strongly political and emotional connotations – the nation (6%) – was a new addition to the noticeable collective actors.

The co-occurrence of fragments of the articles defining the contexts with those referring to specific subcategories of actors demonstrates that the most widely exposed context – that of economics – is associated not only with the most obvious actors – economic institutions – but also with international organisations, states and politicians/political institutions, as well as, to a slightly lesser extent, with the nation, experts, scientific institutions and residents. The multilevel network of links indicates a far-ranging connection between the worlds of politics and economics, and thus the economisation of the political discourse and politicisation of economic debate, along with active participation of experts providing scientific validation to the discourse, and notable references to the nation and residents, enjoying a much greater say and agency than in the 1980s discourse. Symbols linked to nuclear disasters – Three Mile Island, Chernobyl and Fukushima – appear in the background of the economic sub-discourse.

The environmental context demonstrates links with actors associated with the third sector and "other actors" (mostly environmentalists), as well as local communities and two methods of expression and confrontation of opposing views assessed in diametrically opposite ways – conflict and social consultations. We can therefore conjecture that the media discourse treats the environmental realm as a natural problem area that permits interdisciplinary discussion and varied debate, which we do not observe with economic discourse as it is more strongly controlled by actors in possession of resources of political power and academic knowledge. The technological context offers the opportunity to cite the experiences of other countries, but also numerical data and visions of the future, as well as a different context – the economic-political one. It therefore generates global references allowing comparison of the situation in Poland with past or current events in other countries. The remaining two contexts, rooted in distinct networks of conceptual links, are that of the lifeworld, meaning the space in which informal groups are active (residents, "certain groups," "opponents"), and also the negative affective background of interpretation of these events, as well as the political-administrative context connected to the society and generating positive connotations. This indirectly points to the negatively delineated image of organised but informal groups as actors in the discourse compared to the dispersed and passive audience of the discourse, in which role the society is usually presented. Society as a category of actors for political and economic actors is a useful quasi discourse partner for political and economic actors, as it does not speak out and is not supposed to represent those entitled to express themselves in the name of this category, and therefore appearing in the role of a passive participation in a discourse placed in contexts chosen by institutional actors.

We did not observe any particular difference with regard to the exposure of the individual subcategories of actors in the various daily and weekly publications. Politicians appear to a comparable degree in all the periodicals, and particularly in *Newsweek*, *Wprost* and *Fakt*, where the exposure was slightly greater). It was a similar case with experts; although they did not appear in *Newsweek* or *Fakt*, this had more to do with the low number of articles than with a conscious and deliberate marginalisation of this group. A similar situation can be observed with a third, relatively strongly exposed category of individual actors – residents – who appeared slightly less frequently in *Rzeczpospolita* and *Wprost*.

The differences in intensity of exposure of the various subcategories can be traced to the diversity in the profiles of the publications – economic institutions are more dominant in *Rzeczpospolita*, but almost invisible in *Fakt*; the presence of states is strongest in the discourse in *Newsweek* and, interestingly, *Fakt*; political institutions feature prominently in *Fakt* and *Gazeta Wyborcza*; scientific institutions do so above all in *Gazeta Wyborcza*. International organisations, meanwhile, receive relatively strong exposure in *Fakt, Wprost* and *Polityka*. However, all these patterns are of limited value owing to the low number of articles in which the various subcategories of actors are present.

Dynamic of discourse

We can draw several conclusions based on observation of the fluctuating exposure of actors in the discourse between 2007 and 2012. Whereas in the case of individual actors politicians maintained a comparatively constant level of exposure in each of the years we analysed – albeit the highest level in 2008 and 2012 – the visibility of experts in the discourse steadily decreased (with the exception of 2009), while that of residents in the role of actors grew (in 2012 we observed a slight drop in their exposure compared to 2011).

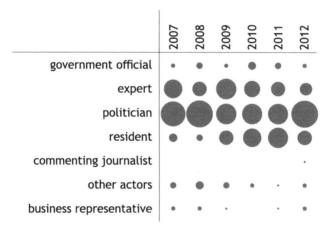

Figure 13. Exposure of individual actors by year

Source: A. Wagner, *Energetyka jądrowa w dyskursie prasowym lat 2007–2012. Analiza zawartości wybranych tytułów prasowych. Raport z badań*, p. 35.

We can interpret this as demonstrating that a category of actors who are ·either consciously and deliberately delegitimised or marginalised on account of their non-expert view of nuclear energy were relatively successful in breaking through to the mainstream of discourse. Yet this delegitimisation and marginalisation cannot and does not take the forms characteristic for the 1980s discourse – social actors are visible, though situated lower in the status hierarchy of participants in the nuclear discourse.

As for collective actors, we observe a discernible downward trend, but not without exceptions, in exposure of state actors (with a minimal reversal of the trend in 2011–2012), as well as a growth trend in the case of economic institutions.

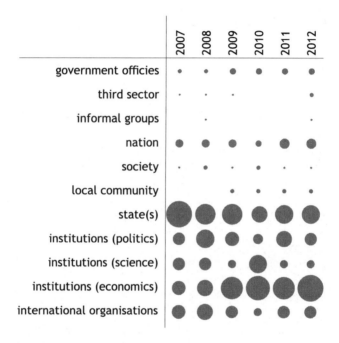

Figure 14. Exposure of collective actors by year

Source: A. Wagner, *Energetyka jądrowa w dyskursie prasowym lat 2007–2012. Analiza zawartości wybranych tytułów prasowych. Raport z badań*, p. 36.

Political institutions received the greatest exposure in 2008 and 2011, and international organisations in 2007 and 2008. Following considerable exposure in 2010, scientific institutions were less prominent in 2011 and 2012. We also observed a minimal growth, year on year, in the significance of collective actors such as the nation and, to a lesser degree, government offices. Based on the trends observed on the map of collective actors, we can conclude that representatives of the business world and community were gradually taking the position of previously more visible actors of academic provenience (who in the 1980s had been the main players in the discourse).

Critical discourse analysis — 2007–2012

An analysis based on the categories of the conceptual triad of power, interests and knowledge leads to the conclusion that there has been a partial, evolutionary change in the positions of the individual actors who control the progression of the discourse. Although it remains an elite discourse in comparison to its 1980s counterpart, there was a distinct breaking of the monopoly in terms of the participation of the actors representing institutions, including politicians and experts, whose opinions served to legitimise the positions and plans presented by politicians. The advance of residents as individual actors co-creating the discourse, from entirely marginal positions to second place in terms of frequency of appearance, is significant. We should treat it as a socially important change in the balance of the powers defining the discourse, although without doubt not a revolutionary change leading to redistribution of the most important positions. Politicians and expert economists, two subcategories of individual actors treated collectively owing to the interests that link them, remain the strongest bloc of individual actors, maintaining the elite character of the mainstream discourse (cf. Wagner et al. 2016).

A change took place in the position of the leading collective actor, which became economic institutions. However, given the radical transformations in the economic-political system after 1990, this does not indicate a revolutionary change. In the 2007–2012 discourse, economic institutions replaced political institutions, as well as, to an extent, the Polish state, as the main power centre. Some of the positions previously introduced to the discourse by entities from the political order, both those concentrating on justifying plans and aspirations and those presenting and announcing concrete actions, in the conditions of the new system were supplanted by entities that were (partly or entirely) organisationally independent from institutions of political power. But institutional independence does not mean independence of interests; the aforementioned entities did not become autonomous in terms of the way of perceiving and hierarchising the priorities for developing Polish energy. The economic and political institutions do not compete with each other, and do not even participate in an interinstitutional discourse taking various positions into account. Instead, they operate as a system of linked vessels, which make them dependent on the changes caused by the evolution in the political balance of power resulting from national – and especially parliamentary – elections, translating into changes in personnel in ministries, but also in State Treasury companies.

The impact of the changes described above (the maps of individual and collective actors) on the progression of the media discourse from 2007–2012 becomes more evident if we take a closer look at the dominant contexts defining the subject framework of the discourse within this time. Since it is the economic context that plays the main role, before the economic-political context in second place in terms of frequency, we can conclude that the centre of gravity of the discourse transferred from the technical to the economic, while simultaneously the centres of power and distributors of elite knowledge seek to maintain the elite, impenetrable character of the discourse. It is therefore clear that there was no change in the essential strategy of the main actors in the discourse to preserve this elite nature, and treat as fundamental those themes and priorities in the discussion for which specialist knowledge is required. In other words, the expert technological discourse with economics in the background was replaced by an expert economic discourse placed in the broader, economic-political context of strategic reflections, without any increase in the egalitarianism of the discourse. Social actors were present as a result of their activity, but were not invited to feature as fully fledged participations in the discourse. The teleological framework affecting the content of the arguments that dominated in the 1980s was also not broken. There continues to be talk of civilisational development and progress, whose manifestation and consequence would be the appearance of the first Polish nuclear energy plant. The topics of sustainable development present in the global media discourse did not make it into the Polish nuclear discourse of 2007–2012.

Without doubt, the increased significance of the environmental context is a factor that we could call a stimulus modifying the balance of power, interests and knowledge. Yet the emergence of this context in the discourse is not a derivative of the activity of actors embedded in orders associated with power and distribution of elite, economic and political knowledge. Rather, it results from grassroots initiatives that are either civic or linked to the work and communications of non-governmental organisations. These are especially the community which the press defines using the rather imprecise and ambiguous, but very much stigmatising and stereotyping label of "ecologists." It is a similar case with the lifeworld context, which also plays a noticeable role in the discourse. It too sprang from the activity of secondary actors, the residents of regions in which investments in development of nuclear energy were to take place, environmentalists or representatives of NGOs, seldom given direct exposure in the discourse in the role of fully fledged actors invested with the legitimacy allowing them to distribute alternative knowledge resources corresponding to alternative social and business interests to the mainstream ones.

The economisation of the discourse, accompanied by marginalisation of the technological context, is directly related to the simplification of the set of key subjects compared to that witnessed in the 1980s. The discourse conducted in the media in 2007–2012 was focused on one core subject – the plans and prospects of development of nuclear energy concerning finding a site for, building, and subsequently exploiting the first nuclear plant, followed by others. Unlike the discourse of the 1980s, with its dual core (the plans to build the nuclear power station and reflections on the Chernobyl disaster), in this case there was no exclusion of non-institutional actors in the discourse, representing – directly or indirectly (through self-definition) – the society or local communities, although the positions that social actors occupy are partly defined by the mainstream actors, who designate the perspective taken on the whole group of actors in the nuclear discourse.

We can therefore observe tactics of media exposure of actors aiming to delegitimise or marginalise the positions they represent (cf. Wagner et al. 2016). It is evident that, despite the presence in the discourse of what we might call social actors, the positions that are a priority for them have not been especially prominent. In other words, the exposure of the actors has not translated into a proportional exposure of the problems and issues that are important to them (as shown by the key word analysis), except for the environmental correlates of investments in nuclear energy, which were marked in the discourse quite distinctly, although not as much as economic correlates. The cluster analysis revealed that the mainstream discussion on topics linked to the economic determinants of the planned investment did admit residents as disparate individual actors and the nation as a collective actor, albeit usually in the role of a source cited by primary actors rather than as independently communicating participants in the discourse. Only the less common environmental context permits environmentalists or local communities to participate in the role of primary actors. Their activity is related either with approval or neutrally when it comes to participation in social consultations, or unequivocally negatively when they are presented as actors stimulating conflict and confrontation tinged with emotional interpretations of the situation.

It is worth stressing that no contexts of the media discourse apart from the environmental one – and certainly not the heavily exposed economic context – are presented in connection with the methods of holding a debate, exchanging opinions, confronting positions, visions or interpretations of a situation. The economic context is placed in categories of dogmas, positions whose source is made unarguable by its validation from the authority of power and specialist knowledge (academic experts, economic institutions, politicians, representatives of the state machinery), whereas environmental issues are placed in context by dialogue. This is an excellent illustration of the unequal approach to various categories of actors, as well as, indirectly, various topics of discourse. It is also important to note that, despite the amount of exposure given to the economic context as well as to actors associated with the political and economic realms, the same cannot be said for strategic questions concerning the country's energy security or threats connected to the energy crisis. Though objectively very important, these subjects, which place the dilemmas presented in the Polish media in a broader, international context, have been entirely marginalised.

As for signs of the delegitimisation that can be observed towards select-ed categories of actors, it especially applies to informal groups, meaning communities playing the role of collective actors that are considered to be organisationally coherent despite their lack of institutional organisa-tion. Their exposure in the discourse is accompanied by negative judge-ments, whereas that of the nation and society are viewed positively (or the exposure is free from evaluation). This means that the abstract, social categories of the nation and society are assigned the role of audience of the discourse and the right to carefully observe events, and possible com-ment on the plans presented by institutions of power, but not to actively influence and shape these decisions. What therefore becomes important is not so much the category of the deliberative potential of the media as that of semiotic visibility, discussed in "The media energy discourse as an object of sociological reflection – the theoretical and methodological context". Informal groups themselves claim the right to play an active role not only in the media discourse, but also in decision-making process of stra-tegic important to the country. This is not accepted by centres of power or by entities responsible for generating economic knowledge, presented dogmatically.

The last of the important changes to the profile of the discourse between 2007 and 2012 compared to its 1980s counterpart is the appearance of politi-cians, representative of state structures and political institutions at the forefront of communicating actors, alongside experts, but this time not behind them. Unlike in the mid-1980s, actors representing the political sphere also, though not exclusively, speak in their own name. As a result, the role of academic actors presenting an expert, and so far mostly technological point of view has been greatly reduced. Given the radical transformation to the socio-political-eco-nomic system, political communication also had to undergo changes. We can therefore observe a new, analytical-economic version of it that legitimises the positions of the people responsible for strategic decisions in the state, whereas some public communication comes directly from the centres of power.

The discourse in 2013 and 2014

The horizontal analysis of the media discourse, examining its progress in the press, radio, television and internet sources, encompassed a 12-month period from 1 April 2013 to 31 March 2014. We started by recording all the state-ments in the selected media types, which provided extensive starting material. The analysis included statements presented in the following sources: the nationwide television channels TVP1, TVP2, TVN, Polsat and local stations TVP Szczecin, TVP Łódź, TVP Katowice, TVP Lublin, TVP Gdańsk, TVP Białystok, TVP Katowice, TVP Poznań; the radio stations RMF, Radio Zet, PR1, PR3, the local Polish Radio offshoots in Lublin, Gdańsk, Szczecin, Białystok, Katowice, Łódź, Poznań; the national press publications and local editions of *Gazeta Wyborcza, Rzeczpospolita, Dziennik Polski*, as well as local press: *Polska – Głos Wielkopolski* (Greater Poland Voivodeship), *Kurier Szczeciński* (Szczecin), *Polska – Dziennik Bałtycki* (Pomerania), *Gazeta Olsztyńska* (Olsztyn), *Gazeta Współczesna* (Podlasie), *Dziennik Wschodni* (Lublin Voivodeship), *Super Nowości* (Subcarpathia), *Dziennik Polski* (Lesser Poland), *Echo Dnia* (Holy Cross/ Świętokrzyskie), *Polska – Dziennik Zachodni* (Silesia), *Nowa Trybuna Opolska* (Opole), *Gazeta Wrocławska* (Wrocław), *Gazeta Lubuska* (Lubus Voivodeship), *Gazeta Pomorska* (Kuyavia-Pomerania), *Polska – Dziennik Łódzki* (Łódź); economics magazines: *Parkiet, Puls Biznesu*; opinion weeklies: *Wprost, Polityka, Newsweek, Gość Niedzielny*; finally, internet sources: 50 selected on the basis of subject matter, popularity, coverage and popularity, and in particular portals such as Gazeta.pl, Onet.pl, Interia.pl and Dziennik.pl and the industry sites Cire.pl (Energy Market Information Centre) and Wnp.pl (Economics Portal).

The year-long monitoring allowed us to compile a database of references to nuclear energy, including 759 on television and radio transmissions, 1287 press articles and 3753 from the internet. We then made a deliberate selection of items from two-week periods in which a trend of increase in the number of press publications was recorded (the frequency of publications on nuclear energy in the press was taken as a reference point for identifying trends of intensity of discourse).

The analysis was conducted using sources (193 press and 444 internet articles, 78 radio and 19 television broadcasts) appearing in the media in the following periods: 25 November to 7 December 2013, 27 January to 8 February 2014 and 24 to 29 March 2014.

Actors

Individual actors

The contemporary discourse on nuclear energy issues is no less impenetrable than those described above – its historical counterpart from the 1980s and its predecessor from 2007–2012. In the press, the main individual actors include, above all, representatives of investors (businesses), as well as (non-academic) experts and scientists, followed by national politicians, who maintain a frequent presence in the discourse.

The actors cited in this final category are Donald Tusk (then Prime Minister), Aleksander Grad (then Treasury Minister), and Janusz Piechociński (then Deputy Prime Minister). Other individual political actors are above all representatives of the ruling parties and of the government (the exception being Andrzej Rozenek, at the time a member of the opposition Palikot Movement). Actors representing such subcategories as activists/local leaders, EU politicians and local politicians are much less visible, and non-organised citizens as well as representatives of NGOs are completely invisible. Interestingly, the map of individual actors involved in the discourse – not expressing themselves directly in nuclear energy, but operating in the discourse through indirect statements and forming a background to it – is somewhat different. These actors are dominated by national politicians, while EU politicians, scientists, activists and local politicians are represented somewhat less often.

The media discourse on nuclear energy taking place on the radio and television in this time period was dominated by politicians as individual actors. These were mostly working at national level, with a smaller role for MEPs and local government politicians. The leading politician actors included Deputy Prime Minister Janusz Piechociński and the government's Commissioner for Nuclear Energy Hanna Trojanowska. Prime Minister Tusk participated in the discourse, but as a background actor. The minister for the environment and officials representing the ministry do not appear in the material, either before or after 20 November 2013, when a new minister, Maciej Grabowski, was appointed to replace Marcin Korolec. The overwhelming majority of the politicians who participated in the discourse representing the coalition government were in favour of the development of nuclear energy in Poland.

The subcategories of actors with a strong presence in the nuclear discourse included representatives of the business sector, i.e. heads of companies and business organisations. They are often supported by experts, who tend to be business analysts rather than researchers representing the academic community, and are usually affiliated to think tanks and consulting firms. Investors perceive advantages of development of nuclear energy, but express doubts as to the prospects of executing the venture as well as the government activity in this respect.

Social leaders appear in the margins of the activity of the dominant individual actors. They are included in the media discourse, occupying positions opposed to the development of nuclear energy in Poland. Those social leaders with relatively high exposure are representatives of Greenpeace Polska such as Maciej Muskat and Iwo Łoś. The collective actors appearing in the background are again Greenpeace, the Green Institute, and the Civic Movement for Nuclear Energy, which supports the development of the technology.

Analysis of the content appearing on the most important websites (portals) confirms the trend observed during the radio and television analysis. It is national politicians that dominate the nuclear discourse, including representatives of legislative (members of parliament, senators) and executive power (ministers, high-ranking officials), to a lesser extent European politicians, and even less, local government politicians dealing with local issues on a daily basis.

Business – major energy firms such as PGE, Tauron, PGNiG, RWE and Areva – constitutes a strongly represented category of individual actors. The individuals who speak on behalf of collective business entities are usually Aleksander Grad, Marek Woszczyk, Jacek Cichosz, Krzysztof Kilian and Piotr Szymanek.

A subcategory of individual actors with a similar level of visibility was the expert community, generally comprising members or associates of think tanks operating in Poland and abroad. These include both those mostly geared towards energy issues (the Energy Studies Institute) and others dealing with wider issues, economics and the labour market (Confederation Lewiatan) as well as various institutes: the Sobieski Institute, Civic Institute, Jagiellonian Club, and Kościuszko Institute. The experts featuring in the discourse are often affiliated to private enterprises that are the largest companies in the Polish energy market (Tauron, Orlen, PGNiG), but also banks (Citigroup, BRE, BZWBK, PKO BP) and consulting firms working on behalf of representatives of the energy sector. Academic experts are relegated to the margins of the discourse, appearing infrequently, and generally as professors of technical sciences within the technical strand of discourse and context.

Representatives of the community promoting sustainable development, i.e. associated with the work of the Green Institute, appear incidentally in the role of expert, as do journalists working for industry publications. They are cited as commentators, or their opinions are used to illustrate a given problem. Journalists not given exposure in an expert position have a similar function.

Collective actors

In the press articles that we analysed, collective actors mostly appeared in the role of implicated actors, building the background for the dominant discourse streams. Two subcategories were dominant among them – states and companies/company divisions. There were individual cases of such institutions and social organisations as Greenpeace, including its Polish branch, Atomic Forum and the Freedom and Peace Movement (whose members are opposed to the development of nuclear energy in Poland).

Radio and television broadcasts told a similar story: here too collective actors formed the background of the discourse, and were dominated by the government, EU institutions and other institutions legitimising the main actors, including the Kościuszko Institute and Energy Institute, as well as those with a position of unequivocal opposition to the development of nuclear energy in Poland – Greenpeace and the Green Institute. The Civic Movement for Nuclear Energy appeared only once in the material.

Residents, viewed as a collective category, are usually associated with civic opposition to the development of nuclear energy in Poland, similarly to the collective category of environmentalists. Yet neither residents nor environmentalists are accorded communicative agency; their statements are quoted either laconically or not at all, when they are said to oppose the discussed direction of energy development in Poland without direct references to their actual words.

Analysis of the content of internet sites confirms the trend described above. The dominant actors are collective ones such as the state, business representatives and the European Union. The Polish state appears in the context of action carried out within the country or the interests attributed to the Polish state. Other countries that feature in the discourse are Russia, Germany, the USA, Japan and South Africa (as reference points for the plans and actions developing nuclear energy in Poland), while the EU subcategory appears in the form of the European Commission, the European Parliament and Brussels.

The subcategory of representatives of businesses in the case of collective actors is represented by energy companies, both Polish – PGE, PGNiG, Orlen, Tauron – and international – Gazprom, Chevron, Shell, BP, San Leon and ENI. Continually noticeable collective actors include ministries, mostly those of the environment and economy, and, importantly, also the Council of Ministers en bloc and the Supreme Audit Office (NIK).

It is important to note the lack of distinct presence of representatives of the social sector, meaning local communities, individuals and institutions representing the third sector, or even those working in local government. This observation concerns both individual actors and collective ones, as well as both leading and background actors.

Resources of knowledge and ignorance

In the spirit of critical discourse analysis, we can treat actors' use of knowledge resources as making use of tools for exercising power, its embodiment in the discourse. In different ways, knowledge and ignorance become important tools that determine the position of individual and collective actors not only on the discourse map, but also in the social structure. First, this involves bringing to the discourse specific knowledge resources, interpreting it in keeping with the interests of the actors in the leading positions in the discourse. Also, though, it means managing the category of ignorance, attributing it to specific groups of actors, and finally according a higher or lower status to actors based on the knowledge resources and ignorance assigned to them. Owing to the complexity of the issue, it was only possible to identify knowledge resources on the basis of the press analysis and internet publications; the instantaneous nature of television and radio transmissions limited the opportunities for drawing conclusions concerning the manner of presentation and the knowledge resources and ignorance that are presented.

In the press discourse on nuclear energy, knowledge is presented relatively frequently as immanent for the discourse, but without specific individual or collective labels. This knowledge is therefore not documented in any way ("it is said," "as we know," "it is widely known", etc.). The high status of the source is sometimes cited when presenting the knowledge resource – it comes from a "study," an "expert report," "research," "from experts," but we are often not told which study, report or research, or which expert is the source of the knowledge resource cited by the texts' authors. Ignorance as a resource very rarely features in the analysed material, and where it does, it is presented in the context of the unknown future that development of nuclear energy entails.

The general knowledge, often without any information on the source, that functions in the social space and sets the tone of the discourse was dominant in the nuclear discourse in numerical terms. Most references to knowledge resources lack information giving an indication as to their origins. Let us emphasise the importance of this, as knowledge resources presented in this way make it difficult to engage in debate or form opposing positions, since, rather than appearing as one of many options, they are presented, and therefore also often interpreted, as resources of unquestioned general knowledge present in the minds of all participants in the discourse.

Apart from the dominant category of distributed knowledge, which we could call knowledge from the social background, the most common type of knowledge in the discourse was empirical, meaning deriving from research or experiments. There was an almost equal number of references in the case of statements based on practical, everyday knowledge regarding specific experiences of state and business entities associated with nuclear energy. The function of practical knowledge in the discourse is therefore to legitimise positions by invoking the development of nuclear energy in other countries, with the active participation of state and economic institutions. References to common knowledge are much rarer, and, just as importantly, there are almost no instances of theoretical knowledge in the discourse.

If we take a closer look at the more detailed categories of knowledge (excluding distributed knowledge from the social background), by far the most cases of exposure of knowledge can be attributed to specific individual sources, meaning experts who present their positions as official multi-source specialist knowledge. A number of instances of knowledge result from research and resources constructed following studies of figures, while some references are based on the specialist industry knowledge of a messenger participating in the discourse. The dominant role of background knowledge becomes even more visible if we consider the list of places in which the knowledge resources are generated, mentioned in the course of the press discourse.

The vast majority of cited knowledge resources are not presented in a way that allows their place of origin to be identified. In the minority of cases, the knowledge is labelled by reference to scientific institutions, less commonly, to the everyday world in the broadest terms (overheard opinions, witness accounts, somebody's personal experiences, information passed from generation to generation), or, even more seldom, to the government or a research department of a commercial company.

Internet resources do not offer any information to fundamentally change the picture painted by the press analysis regarding the proportions of occurrence of various types of knowledge. Here too, penetrating the areas of knowledge that can be identified, the most frequent references are to empirical knowledge, from research and experiments. Practical knowledge, based on the experience of states and/or companies, and theoretical knowledge are presented much less frequently.

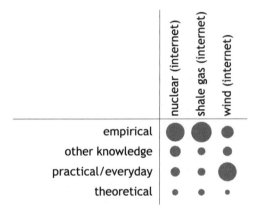

Figure 15. Categories of knowledge functioning in specific areas of the analysed discourse (based on percentage column)

Source: W. Hubert, *Wybrane wątki energetyki w polskim dyskursie internetowym, Raport z badań*, p. 11.

As with the press, a popular source of the knowledge presented was the results of research, either studies of the opinions and attitudes of citizens, or objective studies on secondary, economic, natural or technical data. An important role among the sources of knowledge that appear in the internet discourse is also played by expert reports. These comprise specialist standpoints on nuclear energy presented by experts with a strong emphasis on their personal input, with the experts often being representatives of public administration or business institutions from the energy sector, or, less often, of think tanks. The discourse on nuclear energy more frequently and intensively featured experts as personal sources of a given knowledge resource, rather than portraying expertise as a product that functions relatively independently in the space of the media discourse.

Taking a closer look at the institutions that generate the specific knowledge resources on nuclear energy issues appearing during the discourse, we notice that these mostly result from the work of research teams not based at universities or the research activities of commercial companies. Academic /scientific institutions like universities, as well as consulting firms, play a considerably smaller role as institutional sources of the knowledge resources presented in the discourse.

Areas of ignorance appear in the internet discourse, as with the press one, relatively seldom, which makes it much harder to draw any credible conclusions concerning them. What we can note is that, bearing in mind the analysis as a whole, the low number of cases of exposure of ignorance during the discourse in itself constitutes significant information.

Legislative and axiological points of reference

The discourse taking place in the press contains references to legal systems as tools for legitimising the positions that are presented. This occurs only rarely in the case of the discourse on nuclear energy, with the majority of the few references concerning European Union legislation, and only afterwards laws enacted in Poland.

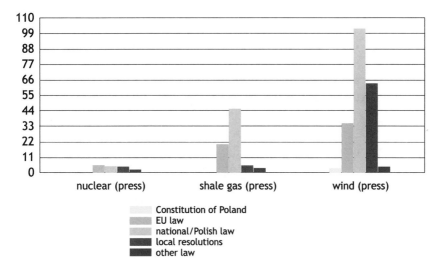

Figure 16. References to legal acts

Source: M. Świątkiewicz-Mośny, *Wybrane wątki energetyki w dyskursie prasowym. Raport z badań*, p. 34.

A similar trend is shown by the discourse that emerges from analysis of internet sources, where the number of references to EU law is again dominant over those to national law. Analysis of the press and website content also demonstrates that local law and the Polish Constitution were not a legitimising point of reference for the positions presented in the discourse.

EU law

Constitution of Poland

national/Polish law

local resolutions   other law

Figure 17. Proportions of codes in the category "legal resources"
Source: W. Hubert, *Wybrane wątki energetyki w polskim dyskursie internetowym. Raport z badań*, p. 26.

Taking into account the fact that there are more axionormative references than legislative ones, which also serve to reinforce the views and opinions actors present on nuclear energy, it is important to underline the signifi-cance and role of references to security as a value constituting the nucle-ar discourse. Security is treated in collective categories as a foundation of a country's energy stability, but also in an international context to the appli-cation of nuclear technology for military purposes. References to symbols that bring to mind the nuclear accidents in Chernobyl and Fukushima also add individual connotations of security to the discourse, in the sense of the safety of the citizen. Incidentally, the development of nuclear energy arouses ambivalent feelings in the actors of the discourse in the context of the safety of residents. While some stress that it is an energy solution that is in principle safe, others highlight the threats, alluding to the examples mentioned above. In this ambivalence we can therefore trace elements of the full-scale delib-eration on nuclear energy, based on various starting positions and aiming at the fullest possible justification of each of them.

The values with significant exposure also include the category of de-velopment – of the community, region or society – which brings with it the possibility of economic advance and creation of new jobs. "The environment" or "ecology," referring to a meta-value, a carrier of values associated with taking care for the natural environment, is much less common, but it allows nuclear energy to be positioned as fulfilling high standards in this respect. The common good is the last discernible value used to build the image of nuclear energy in the press.

Analysis of the content of web portals leads to similar conclusions in terms of the positioning of key axionormative categories. As with the press, security

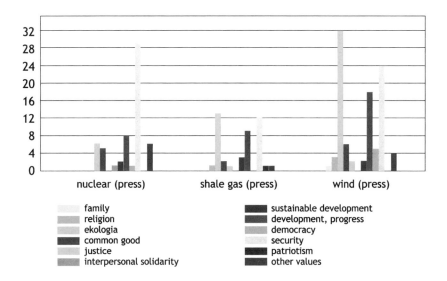

Figure 18. References to key values

Source: M. Świątkiewicz-Mośny, *Wybrane wątki energetyki w dyskursie prasowym. Raport z badań*, p. 34.

Figure 19. Proportions of codes in the category "values"

Source: W. Hubert, *Wybrane wątki energetyki w polskim dyskursie internetowym. Raport z badań*, p. 29

occupies a dominant position, while other values to which the nuclear discourse refers are development and progress (on the scale of the country, its economy, but also the region) and the environment. Exposure of democracy and justice as somewhat more distant meta-connotations of nuclear energy was also noted.

We can therefore regard security as a core value for the question of nuclear energy development in Poland, irrespective of the positions occupied in the discourse by a given actor referring to this value. When speaking of nuclear energy, one must refer to security, whether by showing that it is sacrosanct or by presenting evidence pointing to the numerous threats caused by investment in this area of energy.

Communication strategies

Turning to the linguistic devices used to make the language more figurative, the visions of the future that appear in the discourse are dominated by pessimistic approaches concerning the high costs of nuclear energy, as well as sentimental references to the coal-based economy, presented as a weakening, declining, once powerful as well as more cost-effective mainstay of energy in Poland and other countries.

> To borrow sporting terminology, Polish mining is like a boxer who has taken a series of heavy blows.
> (http://www.wnp.pl/, access: 25 November 2013)

The symbols used are dominated by Chernobyl almost as a synonym of nuclear accidents and the resultant environmental damage and danger to people. A similar role is taken by Fukushima, another city which acts as a symbol of a recent accident. For example:

> No to a Polish Fukushima!
> (*Głos Wielkopolski*, 12 March 2014)

> The fears of a nuclear power station in our country would be smaller if not for Chernobyl.
> (*Gazeta Olsztyńska*, 31 January 2014)

Yet it is not visions of the future or symbols that are the most frequent rhetorical device used to support the presentation of positions concerning nuclear energy in the press. By far the most common is metaphors helping to visualise foundations of Polish energy providing an alternative to nuclear energy (e.g. "coal as the whipping boy") or supporting positive evaluations of renewable sources ("green energy").

The rational arguments that actors use are based on displaying the numerical data to lend support to a given position. Only next, though still frequently, do they cite the examples of other countries. The main country to which Poland is compared in terms of nuclear energy is France, with its cheap and widely available energy. The USA and Japan, on the other hand, are presented as negative examples, as countries where harnessing nuclear energy has generated threats for communities and the environment. The presentations of these prospects of development are often reinforced by emphasising the potential results of investments, and the language of benefits is dominant. However, the arguments employed in the nuclear energy discourse are based on strong emotions, and geared towards arousing them.

The most common argumentative strategies that we can highlight include presentation of numerical data (absolute and percentages) to support positions and reference to economic categories, i.e. the costs of building power stations in Poland. Depending on the position of the actor in the discourse, these are portrayed either as too expensive or as an acceptably costly investment. Arguments employed in the discourse adopt the technological order less frequently, and the environmental one even less.

The language used in the online discourse also features devices making it more figurative. Metaphors are the most common device, appearing more than any kind of visions of the future, symbolic representations or comparisons. An example of a metaphorical view is treatment of progress and accelerated development of nuclear energy in Poland as an activity reminiscent of sporting reality: going from a warm-up to a marathon.

> The warm-up's over, time for the marathon – this was the message of the Ministry of Economy as it announced the decision to build two nuclear power stations. (http://www.wyborcza.biz/, access: 29 January 2014).

The main symbols present in the discourse are nuclear accidents, in the form of the names of the cities where they took place (Chernobyl, Fukushima). The visions of the future are not confined to the prospects of Poland's development through nuclear energy, but present ideas of the future in a broader, European perspective as well as a global one. Comparisons, generally of various national energy policies, are much less frequent in the analysed texts; these are references to German experiences, or European ones in general. Analysis of the thematic profile of the arguments used shows that the most frequent examples refer to the economic order, ahead of the technological or geopolitical ones. Environmental arguments are a constantly discernible, albeit rarer form of argument in the internet-based discourse.

Television and radio broadcasts are dominated by the language of the benefits resulting from the development of infrastructure and the increasing dynamism of the labour market, acting as a boon to Poland's position and the level of its geopolitical security. Politicians, supported by experts, express their readiness to educate society and to explain the government's plans, decisions and actions. These are either in terms of the agency of decision-making bodies or criticised (usually by experts) when the emphasis is on policy makers' sluggishness. Representatives of business, meanwhile, focus on political and economic determinants, financial risk, cost-effectiveness of investments, financial guarantees for investors and EU regulations concerning energy which have a restrictive impact on its prospects for development in Poland. The actors frequently quote figures and examples from other countries, constructing arguments based on rational premises. The positions of residents incidentally participating in the discourse are presented as radical, bound to strong emotions, and geared towards unconditional opposition (cf. Wagner et al. 2016). As for environmentalists featuring in the debate, they use confrontational language which often employs military metaphors ("offensive," "defence"). Like residents, though, they are not allowed to present their views in full, and appear solely in a role materialising a general understanding of civic and organisational opposition. This does not permit the representatives of social communities to participate in the discourse on nuclear energy development in Poland fully, actively and on equal terms with the main actors.

Television and radio broadcasts are dominated by exposure of a more national context (with strong economic and political connotations) than an international one. Nuclear energy development features as the main subject in most cases, and appears as a marginal issue alongside another topic much less often. Actors rarely approach nuclear energy from an environmental and technological perspective in the discourse, generally preferring economic and political angles (the adoption of the Plan for Polish Nuclear Energy and the agreement between PGE EJ1 and the heads of Pomeranian communes). In cases where the discourse is couched in terms of international realities, it is inspired by important events affecting the geopolitical circumstances of energy, for example the earthquake in Iran. Topics involving the funding sources of investments and the high costs incurred occur in the dominant stream of economic arguments. These economic topics also interlock with the category of security, with stress placed on the importance of stable energy supplies and independence on external suppliers, which is in turn connected to emphasis on the importance of competing with foreign entities in the energy sector, on whom we might be more or less dependent.

Dialogue and actions

The media discourse on nuclear energy makes reference to dialogue as a meta-tool supporting the planning and realisation of major investments like finding a site for and building a nuclear power station. The text also refer to actions associated with nuclear energy taken in the past or present, or the subject of plans for the near or more distant future. Our study of the exposure of topics referring to actions showed that in texts published online and in the traditional press there are more descriptive references than in the media discourse, in the form of description of actions that have been taken in the recent or more distant past or are going on at present. The analysed texts contain slightly fewer references to planning, that is prescriptive allusions to actions. Proscriptive messages, comprising references to decisions or recommendations and calls for the best ways to proceed with these decisions, are much less common in electronic and press publications. The situation is somewhat different for radio and television discourse – here the prescriptive dimension is dominant, and visions of the future and planned actions are described more often, but these visions are presented to refer to descriptive topics, decisions already made and adopted legal solutions. The form of these visions is one anticipating the future state of affairs expected by actors active in communications. The future direction of energy in development is presented as certain, rather than only potential.

As for public discussion of nuclear energy, i.e. activities meeting the definition of civic participation or deliberation, the analysed press and internet texts very seldom refer to them. The few mentions that we did find of meetings held in response to participatory and deliberative challenges are dominated by strongly elite-based contexts, which put radical restrictions on access to the discussions that take place by imposing competence- and specialisation-based criteria (conference discussions) or quantitative ones (access for selected circles, e.g. members of parliament, people entitled to participate in a public debate on a given subject). Public meetings and social consultations are hardly ever mentioned, and where they do appear explicitly these tend to be marginal references rather than important topics of the media discourse. With regard to the way in which participatory issues are covered in the material, in almost half the cases references are only judgemental and negative in terms of the current level of social dialogue on nuclear energy.

It is a similar story with the discourse taking place on television and radio, where citizens' dialogue and the associated methods and ideological background are in fact absent. The word "dialogue" appears in the discourse mostly in the context of expressions of its insufficiency or lack, within opinions expressed in emotional terms. With the exception of politicians from the social democratic SLD party, calling for a referendum on nuclear energy development in Poland, the representatives of opposition political groupings, as well as journalists, also fail to mention social dialogue.

Critical discourse analysis — 2013–2014

The discourse from 2013 and 2014 seems to continue the dominant themes and trends from the media discourse from 2007–2012. The triad of key concepts – power, interests and knowledge – was used by a similar configuration of entities and with an analogous structure of interests to those which we observed in the period analysed earlier. We continue to see a media discourse that is strongly monopolised by central power centres (and the business institutions that represent corresponding interests), and to a much lesser extent by local authorities or supranational echelons. What this means is that in terms of both subject matter and style, the discourse is almost a direct reflection of the set of interests of the political communities at the helm, i.e. the coalition government in power at the time, supported by experts – business analysts and think tanks – and only in third place by academic research institutions.

Although the interests represented by society, local communities, informal groups and NGOs are present in the discourse, this is solely through the grassroots representatives of these communities, rather than by any deliberate actions from the media designed to provide balance to the discourse and offer full participation to social actors. This broad category has a smaller presence in the discourse than it did in 2007–2012. Local leaders, citizens not organised as representatives of society and local communities, occupy hard-fought positions in the discourse, which naturally defines their participation in it and relations with the dominant actors. This participation is confrontational, and frequently presented in this way, with the use of metaphors and symbolism alluding to battle or war.

The relations between the key categories of collective and individual actors mentioned above and reflected in detail earlier fits with the similarly continued thematic structure of the discourse, with the economic and political topics as the core themes of its progression, determining the arrangement of the discursive priorities.

The interests of actors occupying dominant positions conflict absolutely with those of the social actors striving for equal positions in the discourse. The representatives of economic institutions and business organisations, politicians and experts legitimising the politicians' positions mostly seek to justify the need for Poland to invest in nuclear energy, even if this conclusion leads to various conclusions, for example demonstrating the potential difficulties involved in funding such an enterprise. The vast majority of social actors, both non-organised – for example residents, society, and sometimes also the nation – and organised – representatives of NGOs (mostly environmental), social leaders and general leaders – are against the idea of Poland engaging in nuclear energy in any of the variants considered in the dominant, strongly economised stream of discourse.

Analysis of the press, electronic publications and television and radio broadcasts showed that the structure of the areas of knowledge dominant in the discourse directly corresponds to the map of actors and the interests which they represent. It is important to underline, however, that knowledge with an economic basis (and therefore deriving from expert statements and reports and research results) is generally presented as being anchored in the space of social discourse, and thus not requiring especially extensive justifications, and certainly not exhaustive disputes with the representatives of positions other than nuclear energy, who make use of other, often competing knowledge resources. The so-called background knowledge on economic subjects that constitutes the basis of arguments supporting investment in nuclear energy is frequently presented as a set of self-evident truths which one can and should not dispute. Such knowledge resources are safeguarded by specialists with the authority of their positions as researchers, analysts and experts, which contributes to making the discourse more elite-based and also impenetrable to outsiders, and thus also naturally contributes to exclusion of the majority of potentially interested parties from the discourse.

Empirical knowledge, deriving from research and experiments, as well as, to a slightly lesser extent, practical knowledge, based on the experiences of other countries that are or have been engaged in nuclear energy, are the two dominant ways in which knowledge is used within this period of media discourse. Subjects who are organisationally involved with the structures of power or business organisations potentially interested in the preparations for selecting a site for and building a nuclear power station, or already involved in these activities, often also engage in the generation and distribution of knowledge resources. This is worth stressing, as it has led to restrictions on the participation of academic institutions in forming an expert knowledge base influencing the progression and priorities of the discourse.

Concerning the normative – whether legislative or axiological – determinants of the discourse, above all we should emphasise the clear dominance of European law over the national one. This would appear to be inconsistent with the stark domination of national political actors over those representing international organisations. Yet this contradiction is only superficial. Although it is domestic actors, representing interests firmly rooted in the national context, who are active, this activity is legitimised with a large proportion of references to the international legal order, as well as experiences, including legislative ones, from other countries. Legitimisation based on supranational regulations therefore stocks up the arsenal of arguments and permits allusions to good practices from other countries, which is especially important considering that the mainstream actors are unable to cite experiences of nuclear energy from Poland.

The value with the greatest exposure is security, with a particular emphasis on security in political-economic terms referring to national interests, and only later to the wider, global context of determinants ensuring security or generating threats. The question of individual safety is present in the discourse, but only as a side issue, viewed with ambivalence – discussion of the development of nuclear energy in Poland both presents threats for citizens and underlines the high safety standards that accompany nuclear technology. Such values as environmental concerns or the common good occupy marginal positions in the discourse, as do the categories of justice and democracy. Security should therefore be treated as an ideé fixe that regulates the axiological background of the nuclear energy discourse, without being directly related to any positive or negative appraisal of it.

When examining the communication strategies, something that stands out is the major role of metaphors supporting the energy discourse. These are often used to depict the trends in energy development or the relations between the various directions of this development in ways that are attractive and easy to understand for passive participants, i.e. the consumers of the media. Owing to the largely impenetrable nature of the nuclear discourse, both in its technology-heavy 1980s incarnation and after 2007, with a concentration on the economic aspects of nuclear investment, use of metaphors is no doubt popular as they offer an excellent way to give simplified summaries of complicated, multifaceted processes and phenomena. The discourse also often features visions of the future as persuasive tools describing potential future states of affairs. These are often characterised by uncertainty and ignorance regarding the direction of any investment being taken (or not) in Poland, ignorance of what course this might take, and finally ignorance concerning the costs of realising such a venture, and consequently its economic justification. We can also speak of ignorance to refer to the cases, present in the discourse, of negation of segments of the knowledge presented by mainstream actors. It surfaces too when organised social actors enter the discourse and present competing knowledge resources. An implicitly present element in the disputes is discrediting of the source of an opponent's opinion, or of the opinion itself, resulting in its treatment as an area of ignorance or false knowledge, which has been intentionally or unintentionally introduced (according to the opponents as false) to the mainstream. Popular linguistic means of expression also include symbols. These include places as symbols, i.e. the names of two cities, Chernobyl and Fukushima, strongly connoting with the circumstances of nuclear power station emergencies. Also popular are example images from other countries used as means of expression to support the position of the protagonists or antagonists of nuclear energy in Poland. Its proponents frequently invoke the example of France as a stable country as regards energy matters, providing its citizens with access to cheap energy. The USA and Japan are used as negative examples, as places where nuclear energy has got out of control, which is treated as a bad omen for the development of this branch of industry in Poland.

The dominant, thematic argumentative streams present in the discourse show an evident division into rational-economic and emotional arguments, accompanied by the rhetoric of protest, and sometimes even battle and war. Environmental issues are therefore present, but since they are introduced by social actors, positioned (and presented as such in the media by mainstream actors) as actors of opposition and destruction, as opposed to the actors defending the ideas of development and creation, such topics have no chance of being discussed at a level of rational deliberation. As a result, the economic discourse takes place within a small circle of actors equipped with the necessary qualifications required for competent participation, whereas the environmental discourse, which in any case only achieves second or third billing, is carried out by a larger group of actors, but not in depth, and concentrating on simplified, stereotypes labels of actors presenting the "green" community. This then results in delegitimisation of the positions that they present.

The relations between the discourse and past, present and future actions are arranged in a way that exposes references to past or present facts; the descriptive stream is therefore dominant. We can also find many references to the future, expected, and often anticipated state of affairs concerning nuclear energy development in Poland. Prescriptive topics, on the other hand, are secondary to the dominant position of the descriptive dimension of reference to actions undertaken by actors or remaining as plans.

Questions of social dialogue, social participation or deliberation occupy unchangingly marginal positions during the progression of the discourse on nuclear energy, almost undiscernible alongside the most visible subject dimensions of the media discourse. Actors in dominant positions do not give these issues prominence at all, whereas actors struggling for equal participation in the discourse (which, incidentally, would demonstrate a good understanding of participation and balanced dialogue) introduce this subject to the discourse, emphasising the deficiencies and neglects in this regard.

To sum up, the discourse on nuclear energy is conducted mostly by politicians pursuing interests concerned with power and representatives of the business world following short-term business objectives whose achievability depends directly and overwhelmingly on political solutions, themselves dependent on international political-economic factors. Of the remaining actors, the function of non-organised ones – society and the nation – is that of a passive background, an audience for the media discourse, while the organised ones – NGOs, academic experts, environmentalists – participate in the role of secondary and tertiary actors in the discourse, present solely of their own accord and due to their own activity. The media and key actors in the discourse define their role as one of protest and struggle, which effectively (considering the mosaic of media representations) delegitimises them and hinders their participation in the mainstream of the discourse.

An examination of the contemporary discourse on nuclear energy issues leads to surprising conclusions. The slow, yet marked development of civil society in Poland is not reflected on the map of the energy discourse in the media from April 2013 to April 2014. As in the 1980s and 2007–2012, the discourse retains a high level of elitism, while its level of alienation towards society and local communities does not differ from the level noted during the 1980s press discourse.

Conclusion

We can draw several main conclusions from our review of the discourse concerning nuclear energy in the 1980s, 2007–2012 and 2013–2014.

First, in each period, discourse remained exclusive. Those with full access to it were the few actors in possession of elite knowledge: in the 1980s, this meant specialist technological knowledge, and then in the latter two periods, it was economic knowledge. Any attempts to break down the barrier of access to the discourse were interpreted in the media as emotional and destructive manifestations of the activity of certain parts of society.

Second, participants in the discourse representing society and the nation as a whole or the community whose members live close to the planned investments, as well as informal groups and NGOs, including those focused on environment protection, having earned the chance to participate in the discourse, remained marginal actors. This meant at least in a qualitative sense, if not in quantitative terms (in 2007–2012 there was a relatively large number of instances of actors in this meta-category, and only slightly fewer in 2013 and 2014). The key was that they never participated as fully fledged actors constituting an axiological counterweight to the mainstream actors (experts, politicians, representatives of economic institutions).

Third, the dialogical, participatory or deliberative dimension of the discourse was marginalised not only in quantitative terms, but also in terms of value judgements. These questions did not acquire the rank of an important area of discourse on nuclear discourse, but were treated more as a weapon to battle with the mainstream actors and their positions than as a way of conducting a democratic debate giving its participants the freedom to present the multifaceted nature of their positions. The discourse was dominated by black-and-white images of nuclear energy, which, transferred to the positions of actors occupying opposing positions, did not meet anywhere and at any point. Nuclear energy was usually presented either as flawless or as lacking in any merits, and this made any deliberation on its development in Poland rather impossible.

Fourth, in most cases the nuclear discourse took place in isolation from its geopolitical context. Though references to this did appear in the media discourse, their arguments were never decisive. In the 1980s, advanced technology and its correlation with civilisational progress represented the most effective area of teleological authority of the presented positions, whereas in the later periods it was fundamental, detailed economic analyses that served to legitimise the positions of the proponents of nuclear energy in Poland. The country's international situation and political and economic connections did not leave a mark on the profile of the media discourse, except for unambiguous but rare normative references to European law in the 21st-century sources. It was for these reasons that no kind of community of interests of actors of differing views on nuclear energy development in Poland was evident in the discourse. The subjectively perceived interests of the main actors proved to openly and radically conflict with the interests of other categories of actors. The media did not debate the objective – independent of the views of any particular individual or collective actor – convergence of interests, and the actors themselves did not notice it.

Fifth, the media discourse analysed in each of the three separate time periods, including two after the radical socio-political-economic transformations of 1989, reflected a structuralistic model of power assigned to few positions – decision makers. In the cases we analysed, the rule of the few translates into discourse of the few, with extremely limited access to it for non-institutional and non-political actors except for those linked in terms of interests to political actors (representatives of business and expert institutions). The picture of power that emerges from the media discourse on nuclear energy also conforms to the vision of Foucault, an immanent element of various dimensions of social life, including media discourse, whose progression reflects the relations between various communities and interest groups. Power in the analysed cases is manifested in the regulation of positions and roles in the discourse, resulting in the overrepresentation of political-economic positions, and previously political ones, supported by technological analyses, with a simultaneous insufficient representation of positions reflecting the distribution of public opinion.

Bibliography

Bulcaen, C. (2000), "Critical Discourse Analysis," *Annual Review of Anthropology*, 29.

Fairclough, N., Duszak, A. (2008), "Wstęp. Krytyczna analiza dyskursu – nowy obszar badawczy dla lingwistyki i nauk społecznych" [in:] A. Duszak, N. Fairclough (eds.), *Krytyczna Analiza Dyskursu. Interdyscyplinarne podejście do komunikacji społecznej*, Kraków.

Foucault, M. (1995), *Discipline and Punish: The Birth of the Prison*, trans. A. Sheridan, New York.

Howarth, D. (2000), *Discourse*, Buckingham-Philadelphia.

Wagner, A. (2014), "Shale Gas. Energy Innovation in a (non-)Knowledge Society. A Press Discourse Analysis," *Science and Public Policy*, 7 August.

Wagner, A., Grobelski, T., Harembski, M. (2016), "Is Energy Policy a Public Issue? Nuclear Power in Poland and Implications for Energy Transitions in Central and East Europe," *Energy Research and Social Science*, vol. 13, March.

Warzecha, A. (2014), "Krytyczna analiza dyskursu (KAD) w ujęciu Normana Fairclougha. Zarys problematyki," *Konteksty Kultury. Pismo Kolegium Nauczycielskiego w Bielsku-Białej*, vol. 11, no. 2.

Unpublished reports:

Hubert W., *Wybrane wątki energetyki w polskim dyskursie internetowym, Raport z badań.*

Świątkiewicz-Mośny M., *Wybrane wątki energetyki w dyskursie prasowym. Raport z badań.*

Wagner A., *Energetyka jądrowa w dyskursie prasowym lat 2007–2012. Analiza zawartości wybranych tytułów prasowych. Raport z badań.*

Wagner A., *Energetyka jądrowa w dyskursie prasowym lat 2007–2012. Analiza zawartości wybranych tytułów prasowych. Raport z badań.*

Maria Świątkiewicz-Mośny

THE MEDIA DISCOURSE
ON WIND ENERGY

The harnessing of wind as an energy source has a long history. One merely has to look at the sailing boats that used its power to traverse seas. Wind has also been used to mill grains and to pump water. The Netherlands were the homeland of windmills in Europe – and even now the variations on post mills, with four sails placed on wooden or walled buildings, are one of the country's main symbols and tourist attractions. Today, in Europe it is Denmark that leads the way in wind energy, along with Germany and Spain.[1]

The importance of windmills decreased with the arrival of steam machines, followed by electric engines, and the advent of the steam and electricity era. Only in the late 19th century was the first wind turbine producing electric energy constructed. Charles Brush erected the first such construction to produce electricity in his own garden, using it to illuminate his mansion. Although wind is a free energy source, the electricity generated was too expensive owing to the high costs of building a turbine. The wind-generated electricity could not compete with the power from a fossil-fuel power station, whose availability did not depend on the weather.

Modern wind energy began to develop in the 1970s, when the oil crisis made it necessary to search for alternative energy sources. The beating heart of the sector was in California, home not only to strong winds, but above all to inviting tax breaks as well as the Public Utility Regulatory Policy Act (PURPA), which meant that energy had to be bought from small producers. The Californian wind craze acted as an incentive for innovative solutions in Europe. Wind farms were built in California, but the technology was Danish.

---

[1]   *BP Statistical World Energy Review*, 20 June 2015, BP, http://www.bp.com/en/global/corporate/energy-economics/statistical-review-of-world-energy.html (access: 25 June 2015).

Denmark had a wealth of "wind" traditions, out of which technological ideas grew. By 1987, 90% of the new wind turbines installed in California were Danish-produced (Yergin 2011: 1146).

In the early 1990s, energy prices began to drop, tax breaks were scrapped, and the wind industry collapsed. Its renaissance began in the second half of the decade, following protests from environmentalists, and its growth is helped by demands for reduction of CO_2 emissions.

The first wind turbines producing electricity in Poland were installed in 1991 at the Żarnowiec Hydroelectric Power Plant[2] (where the Lisewo wind farm can now be found) in the Pomeranian Voivodeship. The first industrial farm was opened 10 years later in Barzowice (West Pomeranian Voivodeship[3]). In 2015 Poland was among the top ten countries in terms of installing new capacity.[4] Data shows that wind turbines generate 3% of energy produced in Poland (Lacal-Arantegui, Serrano-Gonzalez 2015). This is a modest result in comparison to Denmark, which in 2014 covered 40% of its energy needs with wind energy (Lacal-Arantegui, Serrano-Gonzalez 2015). This difference is explained by the fact that Polish energy is largely based on coal,[5] a local resource, and entered the renewable energy sources (RES) market considerably later than Denmark or Germany, as well as by the moderately favourable conditions for building wind farms. Wind energy is the most dynamically growing renewable energy source, and yet it does not get a great deal of exposure in the general news media. Materials on the subject appear relatively rarely – only a few programmes broadcast on radio and television[6] in the analysed period (2013–2014) covered the subject. Wind appears either in opposition to other energy sources, or marginally as an element of RES, which themselves tend to be discussed in relation to other energy topics. It is a similar story in the press.[7] Although there are more articles in terms of numbers, wind energy appears only sporadically, and wind turbines are presented as local energy sources. Issues related to energy feature in the local press much more often than nationally, remaining

---

2   The Żarnowiec Pumped Storage Power Station is the biggest hydroelectric power plant in Poland. It has worked since 1983 and was prepared as an additional storage of energy for a nuclear power plant which was planned to be built in Żarnowiec.

3   The West Pomeranian Voivodeship is still the region that dominates with regard to generating capacity. This is because seaside belt conductive a good condition for wind energy plants. (Wind Energy in Poland 2010, http://www.paiz.gov.pl/files/?id_plik=14293) (access 20 May 2016).

4   Global Wind Energy Council, 2015, http://www.gwec.net/wp-content/uploads/vip/GWEC-Global-Wind-2015-Report_April-2016_22_04.pdf (access: 20 May 2016).

5   The Polish energy system is in the process of restructuration, but coal remains the most important source of energy.

6   The methodology of the research project was outlined in detail in A. Wagner, "Organising the research."

7   The major Polish daily newspapers and opinion weeklies were analysed between 2007 and 2014. More information in A. Wagner, "Organising the research."

a subject of interest to the local communities that have or will have wind farms nearby. The press does not present wind energy in a global context. Examples from other countries do occur occasionally, but only as positive reference points. The media discourse appears to be atomised, localised to specific places, and concentrated around individual wind farms.

In periodicals, information about wind as an energy source is usually given by brief snippets of news, with little room for in-depth analyses and explanations. Radio and television broadcasts are seldom devoted to wind energy – it is more frequently discussed as a certain type of RES. There is a lack of extensive information and thematic or educational programmes on wind energy, or on RES as a whole.

Actors engaged in the wind discourse

The discourse on wind energy is dominated by men. The actors who are most active in the press are politicians, mostly local – city and mayors and heads of communes and villages – while it is investors who are dominant in internet sources (we analysed texts from the following information services: Gazeta.pl, Onet.pl, Interia.pl, Dziennik.pl, Cire.pl, Wnp.pl). Experts also include individuals associated with the Environmental Protection Fund, the Agricultural Market Agency, the Institute for Renewable Energy, unnamed representatives of the RES sector, and current and former ministers. Representatives of other areas of renewable energy also appear: hydroelectric power stations (Society for Development of Small Hydroelectric Power Stations), solar energy (Polish Photovoltaics Society) and agricultural energy (Polish Chamber of Biomass). Giving organisations of this kind a voice indicates a civil society involved in energy issues.

The investors presented in the press are usually company presidents (Geo-Wind Polska, Eco Wind-Contruction S.A., Tauron Polska Energia S.A., RWE, SUneks[8]). Their full names are given, as well as the company names. Only in the case of PGE[9] is there a more lengthy description ("vice-president for development of the country's largest energy company"). Readers are given no, or only rudimentary, information on investors or any affiliations they might have. Such presentations make social worlds distant. This distance is not shortened. Knowledge on partners potentially interested in the processes of deliberation and participation proves to be minimal, which makes the process inefficient.

---

8   Companies form the energy sector in Poland.
9   The PGE is the largest energy sector company in Poland.

The processes of deliberation and participation generally take place with the participation of third-sector organisations. It is important to note that the NGOs appearing in the analysed material include both the Polish Wind Energy Association (e.g. *Puls Biznesu*, 21 October 2013; *Gazeta Olsztyńska*, 24 January 2013), and the Stop the Planned Wind Power Station in the District of Gołcza Association (*Dziennik Polski*, 19 April 2013, 18 April 2013), i.e. both proponents and adversaries of the development of wind energy in Poland. These are often local organisations (Eco-Rymanów Association, I Love Warmia Association), but also include those operating on a wider scale (Institute for Renewable Energy, Polish Power Transmission and Distribution Association, European Wind Energy Association).

It is characteristic of the wind discourse that actors are given the floor more frequently than in the nuclear energy or shale gas discourse. In these two cases, actors seldom have the opportunity to express themselves directly, as instead their words are used and woven into the discourse, serving as argumentative strategies. The main primary actors in the wind energy discourse, permitted to make independent statements, are politicians – mostly local and national – and investors. "Citizens" (meaning people not representing either a political party or a non-governmental organisation) rarely have a voice. They more often feature in the press as a local community or informal group. Local leaders or activists are usually linked to NGOs. No teachers or priests figure in the discourse. School, according to Michel Foucault, is "a political way of maintaining or modifying the appropriation of discourses" (Foucault 1981), and could therefore be used as a means to lobby and exert influence. Schools and churches continue to be important opinion-forming centres, and could perhaps also become a deliberation space. Yet they do not exist in the media discourse; the press does not cover their engagement. Actors involved in science – scientists as well as institutions – play a similarly small role in the dialogue, and the marginal role they play impoverishes the discourse. Those experts who do feature tend to be associated with economics and financial markets, as well as, less often, technology. The absence of representatives of the social sciences and humanities is an example of "sepisation," i.e. the procedure of ignoring things that are "someone else's problem" – SEP), exclusion of actors from the discourse, and in this case also their knowledge resources and interpretive perspective.

Figure 1 presents the frequency of occurrence of the various primary actors. The larger the font, the more frequently a given actor appears in the collected material.

Alongside the primary actors, we also identified implicated actors, i.e. those with no opportunity to make a direct statement – they are cited, and their statements are interpreted, and sometimes taken out of context. In the press, it is companies/company departments, local government and the state

Journalist **expert** scientist domestic politician

local politician citizen activist, local leader

NGO representative other investor

local community research institute NGO, association EU

parliament

company, company department, enterprise

government office **local government** state informal group medium

governmental and intergovernmental agencies

Figure 1. Primary actors appearing in the press
Source: own elaboration.

other expert EU politician domestic politician

local politician investor citizen

activist other governmental and intergovernmental agencies medium

informal group state

local government government office

company/company department political party

parliament EU NGO/association

local community research institute

Figure 2. Implicated actors appearing in the press wind discourse
Source: own elaboration.

that are dominant. As with primary actors, the representation of citizens is marginal and marginalised, meaning that it is not only ignored, but also not given the opportunity and possibility to participate effectively in social life. This discourse seems to reflect the possibilities of participating in the distribution of goods.

The wind discourse map is Polish-centric, as this form of energy is discussed in the context of Poland. Other countries appear only sporadically, generally used solely as examples of good practices and attractive solutions in this sector. The countries cited in this way are dominated by Germany, which is the European leader in exploitation and production of wind energy as well as construction of power stations (cf. Lacal-Arantegui, Serrano-Gonzalez 2015). Denmark, in second place in Europe on the list of countries harnessing wind power most effectively, appears only occasionally in the analysed discourse, as do other countries – Spain, France and the USA.

As in the case of primary actors, investors (companies and company departments) are involved in the discourse. Local government is also represented. The investor-local government duet models the discourse in the economic perspective. Business representatives, i.e. actors of the economic market, use arguments based on profits and losses. It is a similar story with local government, for which the key word is "development," usually meaning investment in infrastructure or new jobs.

The wind discourse is dominated by local politicians and investors, who construct an independent economic subdiscourse, consisting of rational arguments based on profits and losses. There is no room here for other, non-economic arguments, such as environmental ones. The residents of the actual or proposed sites for wind farms also refer to measurable profits and losses, but also attempt to discuss issues concerning the environment, health, and the quality of the landscape.

Power — interests — knowledge

In the Foucauldian vision of discourse, knowledge and power are inextricably linked. Knowledge is a product, as well as a tool, of power. Yet Foucault does not explain either concept precisely, and one can trace their evolution (Czyżewski 2009: 85). In the poststructuralist phase of his work, he understood power no longer as just the external effect of a structure on individuals, but also as "an immanent process tied to knowledge and discourse which operates as a technique on all levels of society" (Lemert, Gillan 1999: 82). It is hard to imagine any social reality without the relation of this kind of power. It "cannot but evolve, organise, and put into circulation a knowledge [...] (Foucault 1980: 102).

In the online discourse concerning wind energy, the role of creators of knowledge has been taken by experts, and specifically (non-university) research groups, commercial companies and NGOs. We can observe expert knowledge presented by the specialists cited in the articles, for example investor representatives, government officials, and employees of consulting companies.

> According to the investor's expectations, turbines are capable of producing over 100 GWh of electric energy per year. (http://www.tygodnik.onet.pl/, access: 1 June 2014)

The power of the farm would then reach a level of over 45 MW. These investments will increase the total installed power of RWE Renewables in wind energy in Poland to 197 MW (http://www.www.cire.pl/, access: 22 April 2013)

Similarly to the case of press discourse, we can mention the Polish Wind Energy Association, the leading consulting company Ernst & Young, the Energy Regulation Office and the International Energy Agency (once each), i.e. the third-sector organisations and consulting firms that would in this case produce the knowledge resource. The knowledge "produced and introduced into circulation" by the mentioned actors mostly concerns issues related to economics.

Data from the Polish Wind Energy Association shows that the average value of property tax in 2011 was 65,800 PLN for each wind turbine installed. The local communes earned a total of 66 million PLN. In 2020 this could pour 212 million PLN into commune coffers. (*Dziennik Polski*, 14 May 2014)

One wind installation brings the community 653,000 PLN annually, according to the consulting company EY, which *Rzeczpospolita* quotes. (*Gazeta Pomorska*, 24 October 2013)

In the wind energy discourse, the most frequent references are to practical knowledge concerning everyday matters.

Let's try to produce even small amounts of energy on our own, where possible. [...] In Germany this type of solution is very popular. (*Gazeta Lubuska*, 23 April 2014)

The dominance of common, everyday knowledge probably results from wind's cognitive accessibility. The empirical studies quoted in the discourse are used as an argument to support a specific position (in this case showing the positive aspects of wind energy). Paradoxically, ignorance can also be an argument.

I haven't heard of them bothering anyone. (*Echo Dnia*, 25 March 2014)

[...] these estimates will remain very uncertain. (http://www.www.wnp.pl/, access: 7 January 2014)

Also unknown is the future scale of micro-production, which will enter the market with a result that is perhaps surprising, because – to quote a comment heard recently – how can one understand the fact that a tiny turbine is 20 times as expensive as a washing machine? (http://www.wnp.pl/, access: 18 April 2014)

"Production" of knowledge is not everything; access to channels of distribution of information and knowledge constitutes the source of domination, and is thus equally important (Bourdieu, Wacquant 1992). Power is generated in the institutional field thanks to specific resources, and remains accumulated in the hands of the symbolic elites – or in other words, the privileged classes.

Interest groups concerning energy issues in Poland are most clearly visible in the context of coal. The economy is based on this raw material, and in need of transformation. In the case of wind energy the stakeholder groups are not defined especially sharply. The first such interest group comprises residents, yet their place in the discourse does not receive much exposure. With the exception of a radio programme in which residents of the commune of Miastko protest as the mayor did not consult with them on the construction of a wind power station, the presence of residents in the press is scarcely visible. They are mentioned in the context of social consultations, and sometimes also protests against the construction of a power plant. Usually, however, they are portrayed as being satisfied with the new investment and proud of the turbines, perceived as symbols of the commune's development. The residents' interest seems to be purely economic. Financial gain dominates timid mentions of issues relating to quality of life ("Participants in an excursion asked the locals whether they weren't bothered by the turbines," *Echo Dnia*, 25 March 2014).

The rhetoric of examples that characterises discourse immediately gives a reassuring response. The quality of life with turbines in the background differs from that without them only in terms of the health of one's purse. The financial benefits are presented as being the most important and obvious factor. The actors – residents of the sites where wind farms have been built – speak of the money that these farms have brought them. The financial gains are described as significant and large, but are not specified with concrete sums. Both residents and the representatives of local government also point to the additional income to the commune, but no details are given.

The next group of stakeholders, who are also present only to a limited extent, is trade unions (in this case the West Pomeranian branch of Solidarity) representing the employees (and potential employees, as in this case) of the wind industry. According to television reports, the lack of legal regulations delays the process of appointing a new board, which is supposed to produce the foundations for offshore wind power stations. Trade unions are interested in work and appropriate pay. The unions operating in the wind industry are also concerned with assuring suitable legal regulations to support the opening of wind farms.

Politicians have a large representation in the wind discourse, especially local ones – heads of communes and villages and mayors, and much less often those operating at a national level. The power of local politicians is based on their knowledge of an investment. In accordance with Foucault's conception, knowledge generates inequalities. Local authorities are generally presented as being in favour of investment, with the leading motif being financial gain. For small settlements the taxes paid by investors are a serious injection into their budget, which is why the representatives of the authorities can talk of the development of the commune, mentioning investments in the infrastructure and potential jobs.

The knowledge and power of local structures can lead to the release of mechanisms of corruption, and there are traces of such situations in the analysed discourse. The source of this corruption is exclusive knowledge of the planned energy investments. The owners of the plots in which the turbines are erected receive compensation. An example shown on television is the case of the commune of Kleczew, where turbines are located on a plot belonging to the mayor. Local authorities do not always actually support investments. The media note that officials demonstrate sluggishness in making decisions, and sometimes also a lack of good will.

The next group is investors. Their interests are not articulated, as they are players of the economic system and their actions are subordinated to the logic of profit, yet it seems obvious that their objective is financial gain. For example, a television programme presents a company with a very strong position on the market, as it produces parts for power stations used by half of Polish wind farms.

The dominance of investors in the media demonstrates that their power over channels of communication is of some significance. It is they too who have access to sources of empirical knowledge. The links between investors and third-sector organisations, especially those supporting development of wind energy, are not clear. The media often cite data generated by NGOs, their expert reports and estimates, which are used as an argument in favour of the development of wind energy. Environmentalists, meanwhile, remain the great absentee of the wind discourse. The only representatives of the community promoting sustainable development in the internet wind discourse are people associated with the Green Institute, cited in the role of experts. Environmentalists also appear sporadically in the press, as representatives of NGOs, including the Safe Energy coalition, or as an informal group. Paradoxically, they are opponents of wind energy.

> One of the Polish paradoxes is the fact that among the strongest opponents protesting against wind power stations are environmentalists, who should surely by definition be in favour of clean renewable energy. (*Nowa Trybuna Opolska*, "Nie używajmy demagogii do walki z wiatrakami" [Let's not use demagoguery to tilt at windmills], 20 June 2013)

Diagnosis of communication strategies

The wind discourse is dominated by positive value judgements. Positive discussions of wind energy highlight wind farms' contribution to development, which is treated as an important positive value and desirable characteristic. Development is better and faster (when the commune has a wind farm on its land), the energy is ecological, and the investment prestigious ("we have gained prestige," *Gazeta Wyborcza Kielce*, 20 March 2014) and modern. The residents of the communes that are home to these investments are presented as being satisfied ("we have good lives here," *Echo Dnia*, 25 March 2014], also in material terms ("they received a decent sum of money," *Echo Dnia*, 25 March 2014).

> The construction of wind turbines contributes to better and faster development of the commune and to satisfying the needs of residents by realising a larger number of investments. (*Dziennik Polski*, 19 April 2013)

The enthusiasm seems incredible: "according to 70% of respondents, wind turbines have a positive impact on the landscape" (*Dziennik Wschodni*, 25 April 2013). While windmills are a picturesque addition to the Dutch landscape, it is another matter to appreciate the charm of modern wind farms composed of several enormous posts with revolving sails.

Development is a value that often occurs in texts on wind energy, usually understood from the perspective of economic calculations. Sustainable development, environmental issues or quality of life do not feature. There is a clear orientation towards the future, connected with the foreseen future benefits that individuals and the entire local community are likely to experience. Constructing a vision of the future is the next communication strategy used in texts on energy. In the press discourse, the future tends to be painted in darker hues. It is hard to speak of a bright future when an energy-guzzling world needs more and more energy, which is becoming increasingly expensive. Furthermore, the media adopt a catastrophic tone to proclaim the end of the world as we know it, meaning the end of coal as the most important source of energy in Poland: "The era of coal using the current technology is ending, and we need new ideas for using it" (*Dziennik Wschodni*, 14 March 2014).

The world needs clean, green energy from renewable sources. Wind energy is a solution. The visions of the future in this context are positive and concern a rather distant or not precisely defined time. An example is these online comments on a Bloomberg New Energy Finance report:

> As much as 70 percent of new generation capacity in global energy by 2030 might be provided by renewable energy, according to the Bloomberg New Energy Finance (BNEF) report. (http://www.cire.pl/, access: 24 April 2013).

> Marcin Wójcik of the Foundation for Sustainable Energy believes that the Pomeranian and West Pomeranian voivodeships could gain tremendous benefits from offshore wind energy. "Not just from taxes and fees for location permits," he explained, "but also from creating new jobs." He said that in 2030 the development of 6 GW of installed power could bring 35,000 jobs, and that developing this branch of energy will contribute to the development of the port infrastructure. (http://www.cire.pl/, access: 24 April 2013)

According to the conducted research, the future of wind farms seemed to be optimistic.[10] The media discourse is lacking, however, precise explanations, or even attempts to show the relations between various energy sources.

Alongside very positive descriptions of wind farms we also find those that paint a somewhat different picture. Above all, these concern the emotions that make it difficult or impossible to decide to open a farm.

> Wind farms have become a new source of unhealthy emotions among the region's inhabitants. (*Dziennik Polski*, 17 April 2013)

Contrasting emotions – negative ones – with rational knowledge – which is judged positively – leads to marginalisation of the position of groups following their emotions. Residents, whose actions are most often described from this point of view, are not included in the rational debate on the opportunities for wind energy.

Yet most of the texts containing adverse value judgements are those giving a negative verdict on wind energy development in Poland ("Unfortunately Poland does not have suitable legal regulations," *Gazeta Lubuska*, 23 April 2013). This means in particular a law and tax relief system favourable to investments. Development of wind energy is now so advanced in the world that the perception of wind as an alternative source of energy is slowly coming to an end. It is a fully fledged part of the energy system.

The lines of argument are constructed around a strategy of "the example of others." The press often cites other communes with already active wind power stations. It also reports on visits made by the residents of communes mooted as sites for turbines to places where they are already in place.

> Participants in an excursion asked the locals whether they weren't bothered by the turbines.
>
> "There's no problem. I live about 500 metres from a turbine. It doesn't bother me at all," said a man from near Margonin in Wielkopolska Voivodeship. [...]"
>
> "I haven't heard of them bothering anyone. Sometimes you can hear them – it depends on what the weather's like, how strong the wind is and from which direction. But it's not a noise that causes any amount of annoyance. [...]"
>
> "I've lived right in the middle of the farm for four years. Our property is surrounded by turbines on all sides. None of us has got ill from that. I had a healthy granddaughter born three months ago. Don't believe any strange stories," says a resident of Kowalowo in Margonin commune who attended the meeting. "Yes, I do profit from it in various ways, as I get money for leasing the land." (*Echo Dnia*, 25 March 2014)

---

10 In 2016 in Poland a new act was passed that regulates the conditions for the construction of new wind power plants. Many RES organisations protested against the new law. They claim that it will slow down or even stop the progress in the wind energy industry.

The residents' opinions on wind farms reported by the press are very positive. The interviewees barely notice any difficulties at all with the proximity of wind turbines to their homes. They also possess knowledge that is empirically tested, and therefore presumably more credible, on the negative consequences of wind power stations. The residents deny beliefs that wind turbines cause illnesses, basing their positions on their own experience.

"Study visits" are a consequence of the frequent protests of local communities against wind farms. The protests themselves are neither described nor analysed in any great detail in the press, but rather mentioned with reference to information on the consultations that have taken place.

> Investments in wind farms often encounter opposition from the local communities. These fears are associated, for example, with noise. [...] The majority of the residents of the villages where wind farms are planned are generally against the investment. (*Gazeta Lubuska*, 22 March 2014)

The aforementioned "study visits" are part of social consultations. The residents have the opportunity to learn about places where wind investments already operate and acquire knowledge about them.

The "example of others" argumentative strategy discussed above also has an international application, as journalists frequently cite examples from abroad. In Poland there are considerably fewer wind turbines than elsewhere. "The saturation of wind power stations in Poland is among the lowest in Europe" (*Dziennik Wschodni*, 25 April 2013).

Poland's engagement in RES is also lower than in other countries in the continent. Denmark, Germany and the Netherlands are presented as models worthy of imitation, as modern and progressive states:

> The new paradigm of the 21st century is flexibility in the supply of energy and managing the demand for it: modern (private) network operators in Denmark, Germany, the Netherlands, France, Switzerland and the USA base their planning on the lowest possible marginal costs. The network in these countries is supplied by sources of all kinds [...] renewable sources not using fuel, such as wind and solar power. (*Gazeta Wyborcza Tricity*, 24 March 2014)

Renewable energy, mainly wind and solar, is treated as a synonym of progress and development. For many experts this is the only possible path in contemporary energy matters.

The next argumentative strategy is to use numerical data, both absolute and percentages. These are often large numbers – thousands, millions ("The EU does not take into account the fact that 90% of energy in Poland comes from coal," *Polska – Dziennik Zachodni*, "Pakiet antywęglowy" [Anti-coal package], 28 November 2013). The numbers provide order to the discourse, making it seem more credible. Quantified economic arguments are more persuasive.

According to an analysis by DnB NORD and Deloitte, thanks to extraction [of shale gas] Poland's GDP will grow in 2013–2022 even by 3%, and 1000 people will find work. (http://www.tygodnik.onet.pl/, access: 1 June 2014).

As Poland Wind Energy Association (PWEA) president Wojciech Cetnarski said during the 8th PWEA Wind Energy Conference, this sector has already invested 18 billion PLN in building 2.5 GW of power in Poland, and according to the national action plan it could spend another 86 billion PLN by 2020, including one third directly in the country on services and equipment (reo.pl) (http://www.www.cire.pl/, access: 24 April 2014).

Arguments are strongly economic, subject to the logic of profits and losses.

We want to have our own energy at the lowest cost. (*Gazeta Lubuska*, 30 January 2014)

The investment can be profitable not just for the commune, but for residents too. (*Dziennik Wschodni*, 25 April 2013)

The wind discourse is not only an economic discourse, but a legal one too. Many situations are explained by the lack of appropriate laws. The imperfections of the law, but also officials' incompetent application of it, cause delays to the investments, and even to negligence. The law works too slowly, which makes institutions ineffective both economically and politically. It is generally national/Polish law that is discussed, as well as local resolutions; legal matters are seldom covered, commented upon and discussed in broader terms. References occur in the context of reports from sessions of commune /district councils.

"I think that the Commune Council will take the result into consideration," he said. "What that means is that in the spatial development plan it won't be able to designate areas for constructing wind turbines." (*Dziennik Polski*, "Koniec walki. Wiatraków nie będzie" [Tilting over. There won't be any windmills], 23 April 2013)

The referendum on turbines is the first in Małopolska. The decision to hold it was made by the Commune Council. (*Dziennik Polski*, 18 April 2013)

The media do not become a field of deliberation on the law. There is a lack of proposals and discussion on legislation. They only inform, report and provide reference points. The problem that remains is the lack of legal regulations, usually understood as an obstacle to development. The law is the mechanism that hinders investments or results in their discontinuation. In this context EU law features mostly in a negative context as a source of repression. The CO_2 limits introduced result in high fines being imposed on everyone who does not keep to the new rules ("According to the EU directive, by 2020 Poland is to attain a 15% share in renewable sources in energy use," *Dziennik Polski*, 17 April 2013).

The analysed materials contain scant references to climate policy. Emissions reductions are presented as a technical objective that must be conformed to.

Between quality of life and development

Quality of life and development are two paradigms of the modern world. Though understood in different ways, they are viewed in positive terms. Development is a guided process of positive social changes (Sztompka 2002). In the analysed discourse, development is construed from an economic point of view. Wind farms assure financial gain at the level of both individual households and the commune. The benefits are measurable, and perceived as attractive.

> Lesław Blacha, head of the commune of Gołcza, who argued that wind turbines will allow the commune to develop faster. (*Dziennik Polski*, 23 April 2013)

> Waldemar Pawlak said, among other things, that it is a myth that renewable energy is more expensive than traditional sources. Referring to the situation in the Świętokrzyskie region, he said that when looking for ways of development and a better life for the residents of less economically developed areas, one should see their chances for a civilisational advance in production of green energy. (*Echo Dnia*, 25 March 2014)

In the analysed discourse, there are two dominant values: the environment and the safety (health) of individuals (as opposed to the country's energy security). Wind turbines are not always presented as safe and not detrimental to the health of the people living close by.

> "We protested, because wind farms are dangerous to people's health. I am not completely opposed to them, but they should be built far away from homes. In our village this distance was definitely too small. There are lots of health risks, and you can easily find them online," explained Kazimiera Wąż of the protest committee. (*Dziennik Polski*, 17 April 2013)

> The situation is further aggravated by individuals who wage an information campaign showing the impact that turbines allegedly have on health and quality of life. (*Echo Dnia*, 25 March 2014)

> Resident of Żary commune: "Wind farms lead to decrease property value, and owing to the risk of failing health, noise, and a ruined landscape it will be harder for us to find a buyer for the house." (*Gazeta Lubuska*, 22 March 2014)

As these examples show, there may be a worsening in the quality of life of the residents of communes proposed as sites for wind farms. Quality of life is determined on the basis of a set of criteria identical for everybody. According to Angus Campbell (1976), it depends on the level of satisfaction in such areas of life as marriage, family life, health, neighbours, friends, household tasks, employment, living in a given country, place of residence, free time, living conditions, education and standard of life. With the discourse we analysed, questions of health security remain problematic. Yet this is not an argument that appears frequently. Mostly, wind turbines are treated as a symbol of progress.

> Information appeared on the commune website, saying, "Construction of wind turbines contributes to a better and faster development of the commune and to satisfying the needs of residents by realising a larger number of investments." (*Dziennik Polski,* 19 April 2013)

> THE COMMUNE HAS CASH. Deputy mayor of Margonin Łukasz Malczewski claims that the wind power station has had a large impact on the functioning of the commune. "We're much better off," he says. "This adds around 5 million PLN to our budget, that is one fifth of the entire budget. As a result we can develop. (*Echo Dnia,* 25 March 2014)

Progress means development, usually measured by the economic situation and residents' prosperity. A wind farm is an additional source of income for the commune and its residents. Development is promised both by local politicians (heads of communes and villages) and by their national counterparts. The benefits that a wind farm brings hide the potential discomfort.

An important value is the environment. Wind farms are presented as a clean, environmentally friendly source of energy. In this respect too they are definitely appraised positively.

> Wind turbines are an exceptionally clean source of energy. (*Nowa Trybuna Opolska,* 26 March 2013)

> Communes are now increasingly often being approached by investors wishing to invest in an environmentally friendly energy source. (*Dziennik Polski,* 17 April 2013)

Examples of topics not covered in the material are the question of birds or the environmental friendliness of the production of the turbines themselves. The emphasis and frequent underlining of financial gains and the cleanness of the energy leads to the sepisation of topics that do not fit into the idealised image of wind energy. Also almost absent in the wind discourse are such values as justice, interpersonal solidarity and democracy. This points to a dehumanised way of thinking about energy issues. The economic-technocratic perspective does not leave any room for tackling social problems.

Renewable Energy Sources are idealised, and treated even as a kind of religion of postmodernity, to which one must surrender if one wishes to be regarded as progressive.

> Renewable energy sources. In the secularising European Union, this notion has taken on almost a religious character. Anyone against RES is backward and an ignorant bumpkin. Anyone who sees the ideal absolute in RES is a progressive and a proper European. Yet renewable energy sources are by no means the gift from the gods portrayed by their advocates... (*Polska – Dziennik Zachodni,* 18 April 2013)

The discourse on wind energy stretches between development and quality of life. The idealisation of green energy means that critical opinions on wind energy are marginalised. The development and progress made thanks to turbines have an impact on the lives of local communities. The analysed discourse emphasises arguments that support a positive relationship between development and quality of life. Money is a tangible factor that improves residents' quality of life, on both an individual and a social level. At the other extreme to this enthusiastic perspective are claims regarding worsening quality of life owing to health issues. Yet these are not tangible, but rather a scenario that could, but does not necessarily have to materialise. The media construct a positive image of green wind energy, but do not show the possible connections between this and other energy sources. The perspective of strategic management at state level is absent. As a result, wind energy is treated as a local energy source that is of low significance compared to coal or gas.

Democracy and participation

Democracy, and especially participatory democracy, is treated as an important element of civil society. Deliberation is defined as joint, rational reflection on issues of importance for the community (Fishkin 2009). Debate is becoming central for the processes of democracy (Dryzek 2000).

Democracy is not a dominant value in the discourse that we analysed. Only on a few occasions is it noted that questions of energy investments should be the subject of a vote.

> One of the main points of discussion in conference rooms and corridors turned out to be the presidential so-called landscape bill, whose regulations, according to the representatives of the wind energy sector, could hamper the development of wind energy and break the constitutional principle of self-government of communes.

> "Warmia and Masuria is one of Poland's poorest regions, and needs new investments. We must therefore ask whether the communes should not themselves decide on the future and profitability of using wind energy?" wondered President Krawcewicz. (*Gazeta Olsztyńska*, 30 October 2013)

> The councillors from Miastko are giving power back to the residents. In Miastko the democratic responsibility for the most important decisions for the commune goes down a rung. To the village councils. The authorities want to include in the commune statute the obligation to carry out social consultations on the most sensitive issues. Importantly, the council will be supposed to make decisions in accordance with the will of the local community. (*Polska – Dziennik Bałtycki*, 20 April 2013)

> "The council is not obliged to make a decision identical to the result of the social consultations, but I think that the voice of society should be respected," admits Chairman Borowski. (*Polska – Dziennik Bałtycki*, 20 April 2013).

The success of deliberation depends on a minimal level of trust and re-spect. When they begin the debate, the authorities of the communes create a space for shaping the decisions that affect them.

In the discourse, democracy is understood as voting or participation in social consultations. Newspapers inform of the possibility of participation sporadically (six articles were coded). They either write that a referendum will take place (when, where, whom and what it will concern – so an an-nouncement of sorts), or give information about the conditions that must be fulfilled for the referendum to be deemed valid. On the internet too we mostly find references to public discussions.

The analysed press material contains several brief pieces of informa-tion about a referendum having taken place, or a consultation meeting or excursion to a place where wind farms operate. Generally provided in this information are numbers (how many people participated in the meeting), references to who took part (councillors, mayor, representative of association, representative of investor, residents), and what the result was. The consul-tations are usually on planned investments.

> Meanwhile the residents of the commune of Lipno do not even want to hear about turbines. In the referendum the majority of them (approx. 90 percent of voters) opposed the building of farms, which Zbigniew Boniek's[11] company Bonwind planned to locate there. The councillors respected the people's position and removed places where the wind power stations could have stood from the spatial development study. (*Polska – Głos Wielkopolski*, 21 October 2013)

Social consultations are a tool of participatory democracy. In many cas-es, failure to employ it means breaking the law. This is discussed by a radio report from Miastko commune, in which the residents protest that nobody talks to them about the new investment. The commune head did not hold social consultations, and thus break the law.

The social consultations reported in the media usually concern invest-ments in a wind power station, and sometimes also broader problems, such as the question of the division of EU money:

> The Employers' Union of the Renewable Energy Forum (EUREF) made a number of comments on the proposals for allocation of the next tranche of EU money. Above all they are demanding larger sums for RES and preference to producers of machinery. A total of 24 billion euro is supposed to be available. The EUREF took part in social consultations of the Operating Programme Infrastructure and Environment for the years 2014–2020. (*Kurier Szczeciński*, 29 October 2013)

Democracy and participation do not have a strong presence in the an-alysed discourse and are not treated in categories of obligation as an ideal

---

11 The famous former footballer Zbigniew Boniek now owns Bonwind – a company which builds wind power plants.

state. The media therefore do not create the conditions of deliberation. They do not promote participation, for example by encouraging people to take part in social consultations. The *post factum* report fulfils important information functions, but does not open the possibilities of participation.

In the press articles we analysed, there is a lack of space for building a compromise or consensus, or even for building significant differences in the positions taken by the actors. One position is presented, or sometimes two opposing ones, focused on strong emotions, and this tends to favour polarisation rather than building a consensus.

Conclusion

Polish energy is in a process of transformation. The changing political situation (the case of Russia) and EU policy on CO_2 emissions means that the strategy realised to date cannot be sustained. A distributed model in which prosumers – users consuming and producing electricity – participate, seems an attractive proposition. Wind energy is supposed to be one of the solutions to fill Poland's energy portfolio. Yet the discourse observed in the media does not support this option. Above all, it does not provide sufficient knowledge resources regarding RES. There is a lack of suitable educational programmes on radio and television. It is also hard to find such materials in the press or online.

The discourse is dominated by the economic context. Arguments concern the "profitable – not profitable" relation. This is the perspective taken by both investors and local politicians, residents and representatives of NGOs. An important value that often appears in the analysed material is development, which means financial success. Prestige is also understood in economic categories.

The economic context of the discourse is imposed by the groups of investors and local politicians. The perspective of financial gains also proves to be attractive for local communities. The domination of politicians and the economic context can be treated as a kind of counter-sepisation (Czyżewski et al. 1991) involving publicising and making into a subject of interest something that others view as unimportant. Questions of quality of life, meanwhile, which depend not only on the material conditions, but also, for example, on health or the nature of bonds, are overlooked. Residents' fears, expressed during seldom reported-on protests concerning the noise caused by turbines and their effect on health, are depreciated. A similar mechanism can be observed in the environmental field. Wind turbines are presented as a clean, environmentally friendly source of energy, while the subject of how environmentally friendly production of turbines is and their impact on animals and plants is overlooked.

Wind energy is presented as an important project influencing the development of communes. It is treated in very local terms, however, and not explored from a national point of view. This makes it hard, for example, to discuss the competitiveness of wind power compared to coal or nuclear energy. The language in which the dialogue takes place does not make it open. As a result, we can hardly speak of any field of deliberation or of joint reflection on the problems of the local community or participation. The examples of social consultations reported in the press demonstrate that the media are emphatically not a place of deliberation. The appropriation of the media space by politicians and investors marginalises other groups with a potential interest in the issue.

Bibliography

Bourdieu, P., Wacquant, L. J. D. (1992), *An Invitation to Reflexive Sociology*, Chicago.

Campbell, A. (1976), "Subjective Measures of Well-being," *American Psychology*, 31, pp. 117–24.

Czyżewski, M. (2009), "Między panoptyzmem i 'rządomyślnością' – uwagi o kulturze naszych czasów," *Kultura Współczesna*, 2 (60), pp. 83–95.

Czyżewski, M., Dunin, K., Piotrowski, A. (1991), "Cudze problemy czyli wstęp do sepologii" [in:] M. Czyżewski, K. Dunin, A. Piotrowski (eds.), *Cudze problemy. O ważności tego, co nieważne. Analiza dyskursu publicznego w Polsce*, Warszawa.

Fishkin, J. (2009), *When the People Speak. Deliberative Democracy and Public Consultation*, Oxford.

Foucault, M. (1972), *The Archaeology of Knowledge: And the Discourse on Language*, trans. A. M. Sheridan-Smith, New York.

Foucault, M. (1980), *Power/Knowledge: Selected Interviews & Other Writings 1972–1977*, ed. C. Gordon, New York.

Foucault, M. (1981), "The Order of Discourse," trans. I. McLeod [in:] R. Young (ed.), *Untying the Text: a Poststructuralist Reader*, Boston, pp. 48–78.

Jabłońska, B. (2012), "Władza i wiedza w krytycznych studiach nad dyskursem – szkic teoretyczny," *Studia Socjologiczne*, 1 (204), pp. 75–92.

Lacal-Arantegui, R., Serrano-Gonzalez, J. (2015), *2014 JRC Wind Status Report. Joint Research Centre of the European Commission*.

Lemert, C., Gillan, G. (1999), *Michel Foucault. Teoria społeczna i transgresja*, trans. D. Leszczyński, Warszawa–Wrocław.

Sztompka, P. (2002), *Socjologia. Analiza społeczeństwa*, Kraków.

Yergin, D. (2011), *The Quest. Energy, Security, and the Remaking of the Modern World*, New York.

Aleksandra Wagner

SHALE GAS
IN THE POLISH MEDIA DISCOURSE

Introduction

The discourse on shale gas in the Polish media actually began in early 2010 (the first two mentions were recorded in late 2009), and held a large amount of the media's attention until the end of 2014.[1] The context of the subject's emergence and development in the media discourse is multifaceted, shaped especially by economic, political and geopolitical factors, but also by historical ones, including those associated with Poland's economic history, and cultural determinants – the sense of national identity, relations with Russia and the United States, but also with the earth and nature, with the traditions shaping the relationship with fossil fuels, ways of thinking about the environment, etc.

Debates on shale gas continued apace at a similar time outside of Poland too. In Germany and the United Kingdom, their scope is national, accompanied by numerous references to the countries' energy policies. A generalised picture of the global discourse based on the media representations of the debates in these countries, as well as the USA and France, therefore seems relevant. Although they are outside the field of interest of many consumers, they serve as a point of reference for the framers of the discourses in the Polish media: politicians, journalists, business leaders and experts. These foreign discourses construct and reproduce both the success story of sorts observed in the USA, and the controversies on hydraulic fracturing (fracking) technologies there and in Europe. Interesting analyses have been conducted

---

1   At the time of writing, in 2015, shale gas is a practically forgotten subject in the public consciousness. References to the topic appear only occasionally in the media, and the policy statement given by Prime Minister Beata Szydło on 18 November 2015 also ignored it.

on the public discourses in narrative topics related to energy policy in the United Kingdom (Cotton et al. 2014), the dynamic of the media discourse on this subject (Jaspal, Nerlich 2013), and attempts to reconstruct the controversies caused by shale gas in the USA and in the international discourse (Mazur 2014).

Economic conditions

Gas does not occupy a prominent place in the energy use of Poles compared to other energy sources (particularly coal), at around 15% of final energy consumption (GUS 2015). The main consumer of gas in Poland is the industrial sector. Approx. 28% of the gas consumed comes from domestic production, and the remainder is imported, largely from Russia. Poland's dependence on Russian gas stretches back to the 1970s and is connected to the export strategy employed by the Soviet Union at the time. Owing to the current pricing policy of the Russian company Gazprom, the cost of gas for Poland is higher than that for North-Western European countries, such as Germany.

Despite its influence on Poland's relatively low energy dependence level, the domination of coal in the country's energy sector proves to be an economic risk factor owing to the higher costs of energy obtained in this way (as a result of the stipulations of the EU Emission Trading System, in force since 2013). The low degree of diversification of suppliers of coal, gas and oil also creates an additional area of risk: Poland is among the countries with the lowest diversity of energy mix in the EU, although its energy policy undertakes to increase this diversity (EE 2013345).

Poland also continues to have high CO_2 emissions, albeit decreasing steadily since 1998. A concentration on domestic natural gas, regarded as a source of low emissions, is therefore a potential strategy for minimising risks. As mentioned above, Polish energy policy undertakes to diversify the sources of energy acquisition by introducing nuclear energy and increasing the proportion of RES by 2030.

A significant aspect of the discourse on shale gas is the rival economic interests of entities representing various sectors of the energy industry: coal, producers and operators of nuclear reactors and RES infrastructure. The transformations of energy systems can result in threats to some interests and an opportunity for others, consequently enforcing a reconfiguration of the dominant players and verification of their action strategies.

Economic conditions are also affected by the appearance on the Polish market of foreign companies themselves owning concessions, or acting as partners of companies with concessions, to search for shale gas in Poland. A large proportion of these companies withdrew between 2013 and 2015.

Geopolitical conditions

The security of gas supplies to European countries gains significance in the light of the conflict in Ukraine (a transit country for supplies of Russian gas to Poland) as well as Polish-Russian relations. Despite Poland's aforementioned low energy dependence compared to other EU countries – around 30% – this dependence is mainly on Russia. It will be reduced if, as forecast, the proportion of gas in the Polish energy mix increases, making use of domestic gas resources. The prospect of acquisition of unconventional gas is therefore perceived as an opportunity for reduced dependence on Russian raw materials.

The potential exploitation of shale gas would mean closer cooperation with the USA, exchange of experiences, and perhaps also import of technologies and knowhow. This would result in a weakening of Russia's geopolitical position in the region by undermining Gazprom's economic power. The hoped-for strengthening of Poland's geopolitical position as a potential exporter of shale gas is reflected in the future-oriented and wishful tone the country's politicians use in their statements. The factors of economic risk mentioned above can therefore be interpreted in terms of Poland's energy security and independence, opening a path to giving them a status of raison d'état.

The political debate on exploring for and exploitation of shale gas taking place in European Union institutions is also related to the strategic interests of individual countries – Germany, France, the United Kingdom – and the political balance of power in both the countries themselves and the European Parliament. This context influences the media discourses of the individual member states. The main dimensions of the overlapping geopolitical and economic references in the Polish media discourses are illustrated in Figure 1.

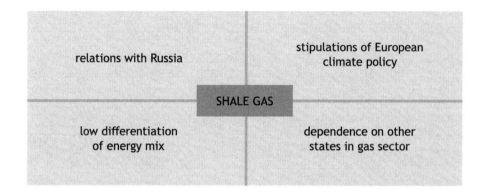

Figure 1. Outline of geopolitical and economic references
Source: own elaboration.

Political conditions

The political balance of power provides a significant reference point for the analysed media discourse on shale gas mostly because of the model of the public sphere in Poland, which we assume to be close to the model of a representative liberal democracy (Ferree et al. 2002). As an ideal type, this model is based on the principles of representativeness, transparency and proportionality. It is based on rational discourse with a privileged position for symbolic elites. We can therefore assume that it is the representatives of these elites – politicians, experts and journalists – who will be most visible and permitted to speak most often in the public sphere. In accordance with the principle of proportionality in the media discourse, the largest political parties and NGOs will also be represented in the media discourse. We can therefore expect the media discourse sphere to become one set aside for presenting positions on shale gas, making and justifying proposals, and explaining decisions to consumers in a rational manner based on respect for opposing points of view.

In the period of analysis, the political scene was generally divided between the two largest parties – Civic Platform (PO), centrist, defining itself as liberal, in power between 2007 and autumn 2015, and the conservative Law and Justice (PiS) party, in opposition throughout this time. In the initial phase, i.e. 2010, both parties expressed enthusiastic support for the shale gas project, viewing it as offering economic and geopolitical opportunities for Poland. The opposition became increasingly vocal in its criticism, but this concerned the government's sluggishness in executing the project rather than disapproval of its premises. The other parties – the Polish People's Party, representing above all farmers, and the Democratic Left Alliance – did not take up a position opposing utilisation of shale gas in Poland. They neither introduced the concerns voiced by environmental organisations to the media discourse nor supported the protests of the population living in the areas where exploration was taking place, although individual politicians did speak out against the heavy-handed policies of corporations towards local communities and the failure to abide by the principles of social dialogue.

The parliamentary elections of 2011 led to frequent references of politicians to shale gas concerning energy security and economic development. Visions of the future emphasising the potential benefits figure among political parties' propaganda statements, with the optimistic visions of a prosperous future that go with them helping to secure political capital. After the 2011 elections, Prime Minister Donald Tusk included the subject of shale gas in his policy statement, while the Supreme Audit Office (NIK) report naming the errors and oversights in the legislative processes and administration of the shale gas project and the withdrawal of the largest companies from explorations for gas in Poland meant that the issue lost its political attractiveness.

The next dimension of the political context is questions of legislation. Both the exploration and extraction of shale gas in Poland take place on the basis of concessions awarded by the Ministry of the Environment. On 1 September 2015 there were 40 active concessions, issued to ten Polish and foreign licence-holders (Ministry of the Environment data), on 70 appraisal wells.

The explorations and potential exploitation were initially regulated by the Geology and Mining Law of 4 February 1994, amended by the Geology and Mining Law of 9 June 2011 (GML2011), and then adjusted by the Act of 11 July 2014 on a change to the Geology and Mining Law and several other laws. The form of the legal solutions foreseen in GML2011 is affected by EU legislation in areas associated with awarding concessions for exploring for hydrocarbons as well as environmental protection. Fiscal issues are also governed by the Act of 25 July 2014 on a special hydrocarbon tax.

The previous lack of detailed regulations, as well as the work required to prepare and then announce them, are an important aspect of the context of the public sphere, related to the media discourse forming around shale gas.

Media discourses in the USA and European countries

The media discourses that have developed in other countries are not self-contained, but, like the Polish one, entrenched in the social, political and cultural conditions of their own systems of reference. Their peculiar materialisations in the form of a set of media statements, mutual references, repetitions, omissions and interpretations constitute an intertextual external context, a space in which the symbols, iconic representations, metaphors and labels that affect communication in the Polish media are formed – even though it is sometimes hard to recognise direct allusions to them. In the age of globalisation, the internet and social media, these contents are widely accessible, and can both be a point of reference to the discourses of specific groups and find their reflection, often somewhat transformed, in the public sphere.

For obvious reasons, it would be difficult to describe the extent and complexity of this discursive sphere at length. From the point of view of analysis of the Polish shale gas discourse, however, two of its dimensions stand out: first, the discourse creating an optimistic vision of the spectacular economic success of shale gas extraction in the USA, and second, the area constructing and reproducing controversies on fracking technologies present in the USA and other European countries. These controversies are expressed in the form of various narrative strategies by diverse groups of actors and actants which form something like dispersed epistemic communities that can be studied through the discourses revealing the resources of knowledge and power rooted in the language, as well as contexts and organisational structures (Cotton et al. 2014).

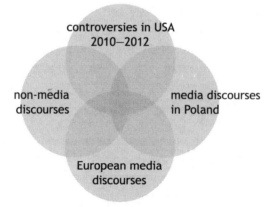

Figure 2. Media discourses in the setting of the Polish media discourse
Source: own elaboration.

It is important to note that the areas divided in this way are not internally uniform, and are constructed by diverse sources using various logic and semantics and with different objectives. These vary from expert, technological, environmental and economic discourses to political ones, and even the products of popular culture. Among the latter are John Fox's renowned film *Gasland*, which is critical of shale gas extraction, illustrating the social consequences of extracting unconventional hydrocarbons in the USA, and a production that is something of a response to it, *FrackNation*, directed by Magdalena Segieda, Phelim McAleer and Ann McElhinney. In the discourses on public policies these slot into argumentative coalitions and oppositions, which can be positioned on discursive maps of the public sphere.

The main axis of division in international discourses runs between the proponents of shale gas, who underline its beneficial impact on the economy and/or climate policy (low emissions), and its opponents, who highlight pollution of groundwater, methane emission, increased risk of seismic activity, and contamination of land. A major part in the controversies is played by areas of uncertainty and ignorance concerning fracking, as well as disagreement on its role in energy transformation. The depictions of shale gas in the narratives vary from the view of it as an ideal technology, via those that regard it as a transition on the road to "clean" energy, to the conviction that shale gas technologies block the development of alternative energy forms, profoundly contradicting the idea of energy transformation and sustaining the order based on fossil fuels.

Allan Mazur analyses the role of the media in creating these controversies in his article "How Did the Fracking Controversy Emerge in the Period 2010–2012," noting the major role played by the media in forming perceptions of a given technology and its consequences for political decisions (Mazur 2014). The sensitivity of policy makers to questions of social approval therefore additionally increases the economic risk involved in investments, which is often the key (and even only) reason for investors to engage in social dialogue. Research on the media discourse regarding shale gas demonstrates the important role played by these investors in shaping the social representatives of this source of energy and the associated technology (cf. Jaspal, Nerlich 2013; Jaspal et al. 2014) and the roles and significance of media discourse for the prospects of social dialogue and transformation of energy policy (Upham et al. 2015; Wagner 2014; Wagner et al. 2016).

The dynamic of the Polish shale gas discourse

Shale gas appeared as a topic in the Polish media discourse in late 2009, as a result of the public announcement of estimates of Poland's shale gas resources made by Advance Resources International and Wood Mackenzie in 2009. The subject remained firmly in the media attention in subsequent years, featuring prominently in the public discourse on energy issues. Apart from nuclear energy questions, it has been the most frequently tackled energy topic in recent years. The largest increase in contents published on shale gas issues can be observed in 2011.

The dynamic of this discourse is connected to the political and economic activity of its leading actors. The initially optimistic approach that accompanied the exploration phase slowly gave way to slightly more critical appraisal, largely as a result of the succession of companies withdrawing from Poland. The media discourse in 2010–2011 was characterised by optimism regarding shale gas, and politicians' pre-election activity was conducive to building optimistic visions of the future. Shale gas was mostly described in terms of opportunities and possibilities, which corresponded with political decision makers' outlook on the shale gas project (Johnson, Boersma 2013). These observations on the media discourse from this period are also corroborated by the interim research of press discourse conducted independently by various researchers (e.g. Jaspal et al. 2014; Wagner 2014). The initial enthusiasm was followed by a period of confrontation with the realities of operational explorations. Criticism mounted regarding the government's actions, and especially the incompetence of officials and the slow legislative process. A significant event in this phase of development of the discourse came in January 2014, with the publication of the NIK report criticising the actions of businesses and the administration concerning exploration for shale gas in Poland. The tone and character of the media discourse was also affected by further reports of withdrawal of significant market players from the project of shale gas extraction in Poland. In March 2014 the media also showed interest, when the government enacted the law regulating extraction of shale gas.

This period can be defined as a wave of moderate criticism compared to the previously aroused hopes, then disappointment, and finally a decline in interest in shale gas in the Polish media, temporarily revived by the political event of the passing of the law. Essentially, however, in this period the popularity of shale gas gave way to the topic of the construction of a nuclear power station. The most significant events in the shale gas media discourse can be illustrated in the form of a timeline (see Figure 3).

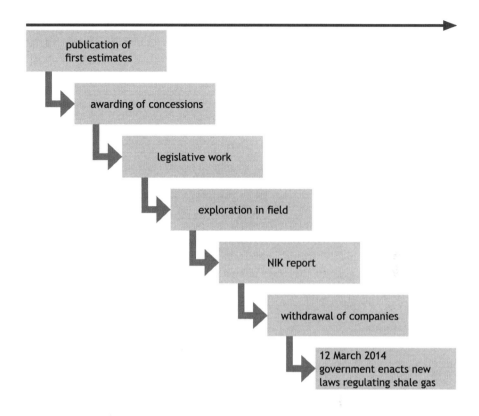

Figure 3. Communicative events in the media determining the dynamic of the shale gas discourse until 2014

Source: own elaboration.

In the next phases of development of the discourse we can observe dynamic changes to particular aspects of the situation – communications of the actors in the discourse, mobilised resources, argumentative strategies and the resultant discursive constructions.

Shale gas as a discursive construct

The issue of shale gas has been accompanied by a degree of ambivalence from the outset: on the one hand, it is mostly described as a resource, and as such as anchored in social knowledge by the following concepts: deposit, asset, resource, land, nature, and even treasure. In this context, even when it is exploitation that is being discussed, it does not command attention itself, but rather is treated instrumentally, from the perspective of optimisation of the extraction process. This optimisation is understood economically, in terms of profitability, gain, and economic risk. However, this way of speaking about shale gas places a strong emphasis on links to national identity, and patriotism in the context of energy independence from Russia. Rusi Jaspal, Brigitte Nerlich and Szczepan Lemańczyk (2014) explain this way of constructing the social representation of shale gas by referring to the construction of identity vis-à-vis the Other (here Russia), perceived as a threat. The crisis in Ukraine only focuses this perception of Russia even more sharply. Extraction of shale gas becomes a chance for independence, something which gains the status of raison d'état in light of Poland's strained relations with Moscow. This opens the field of construction of social representation of shale gas with reference to the level of macropolitics and macroeconomics. Questions of social support and residents'/citizens' perception of the issues are only reflected in an aggregate form, as the results of surveys probing the level of declared support for realisation of shale gas projects in Poland. Reports of social protests (e.g. the case of Żurawlów[2]) are presented solely as local issues concerning a small number of residents, although with this comes a narrative constructed around the figures of a strong, evil corporation and the heroic civic resistance from those who are far weaker, but acting for a good cause.

The second type of discussion on shale gas emphasises not so much the resources as the technologies used for extracting them. This discourse covers hydraulic fracking, and is characterised by greater controversy: from arguments that it is harmless, and even beneficial to the objectives of climate policy, to harsh criticism of fracking as an untested technology with potential harmful effects for the environment and human health. The latter topic, developed by environmental organisations, is considerably less visible in the media, however.

The three areas indicated by the keywords with the highest frequency in the analysed discourse – nature, economy, politics – therefore result in various semantic constructions: shale gas as a resource, an asset, a treasure (here there is a clear predominance of positive connotations: opportunity, asset, hope), as well as perceived through the lens of fracking. The latter representation is not unequivocally positive, but rather more clearly linked to areas of uncertainty and risk, often described as controversial, although the controversies themselves are seldom articulated in the media discourse.

Although for years the main subject connected to shale gas has been its extraction – the prospects for profitable exploitation and distribution, the

---

2   Żurawlów is a village in Lublin Voivodeship which became the site of a protest of residents lasting more than a year against Chevron and its plans to search for and utilise shale gas in the area.

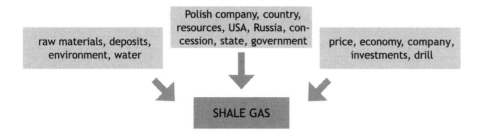

Figure 4. Nonhuman factors shaping the discursive representations of shale gas
Source: own elaboration.

associated barriers, regulations etc. – it is the first way of discussing the topic that has been the dominant one. The media frequently describe shale gas as being a controversial issue, but these controversies are not reflected in the mainstream media: either in the opinion polls they cite, in which Poles declare almost unanimous support for the shale gas project, or in their own standpoints. The "controversial" label is in fact perhaps more of a reflection of the discourses taking place abroad, which raise the issue of the harmfulness of hydraulic fracturing and the new, untested technology, and are characterised by a much more diverse spectrum of viewpoints.

To sum up, shale gas in Poland is for the most part discussed in terms rather of valuable resources than of the extraction technology (fracking). The main participants in the discourse are politicians and economic experts, referring to the macro level – geopolitics and the state economy. The construction of the law that they employ treats it as a resource making it possible to realise the (economic, political) actions of the system. The intensifying criticism of the state administration in the second phase of the discourse concerns the slow pace of legislative actions from the point of view of economic entities, and the complex procedures that hinder enterprises in realisation of their investments. As a result, the law figures in the discourse less often as a guarantee of justice (including fair use of natural resources) and protection of people in relatively weaker social positions, instead being treated instrumentally as a tool for realising specific interests – in this case as a barrier to commencing exploration and extraction processes. Politicians respond to this criticism by announcing acceleration of the legislative process and simplification of procedures, to act as an incentive for investors. In this context, discussions of potential protection of the environment or of the interests of the local population are much rarer. The concept of justice as objectivity that lies at the foundation of deliberation, and in particular the principle of protection of the positions of the weakest groups in a social order, is acutely marginalised here.

Language

The actors featuring in the discourse generally have a positive view of the question of exploitation of gas. In the first phase, this is the dominant tone of the media representations, which position these topics as a big issue, a matter of prime importance. The language used in the press also expresses this – Poland is often called a "gas Eldorado," and the exploration for shale gas a "valuable, one-off opportunity," "which might not happen again," "the greatest hope for Polish energy." Shale gas is also "excellent business," the "most important subject," something that "will become the driving force of our economy." The experiences of other countries are often cited by way of comparison, especially the USA and Norway, which made large economic gains after the discovery of energy raw materials. Description of the recent past therefore becomes the foundation for building a vision of the future:

> Although the Ernst&Young report concerns the past, it also draws conclusions on the future. The main one is that, following the American example, more countries with shale gas deposits will seek to increase extraction, becoming independent from external supplies. Countries equipped with the most unconventional deposits could be especially active in this respect. (*Rzeczpospolita*, 17 December 2012)

The positive image of shale gas is also affected by the idea that it is profitable ("it will be possible to earn good money from shale gas"), but in particular by the perception of it in the context of energy independence from Russia. Sceptical voices tend to express caution, pointing not so much to the dangers as to the areas of risk resulting from failure of the enterprise (insufficient resources, impossibility of exploitation). No direct proponent–opponent conflict line concerning shale gas exploitation in Poland is evident. In symbolic terms, then, shale gas is associated with the chance for independence from Russia and freedom ("freedom smells of gas," *Rzeczpospolita*, 25 July 2012). As time goes on, the statements become more direct, especially in the context of the Ukraine crisis: "The conflict between Ukraine and Russia has demonstrated irrefutably that Poland must become energy-independent from gas supplies from the East. Shale gas deposits are what give the chance to do so" (*Dziennik Bałtycki*, 12 March 2014).

In the process of construction of the media representation of shale gas, allusions to the myth of the gold rush (or "gold fever," as it is called in Polish) also play a significant role. The symbolism that follows this not only places hopes and enthusiasm in the semantic field of shale gas, but also reinforces the positive perception of the resource as something valuable and unique ("shale gas fever," *Gazeta Wyborcza*, 24 March 2012; "Poland the second Norway," *Polityka*, 18 January 2012).

In the following years, despite the decline in general enthusiasm and criticism of the government's actions, the positive perception of shale gas persisted:

> "I think that our natural resources can be an even stronger stimulus for development of the country, and I believe that acceleration, which is most important for me, of extraction of unconventional gas from shale is what is, and will be, the priority for me," Grabowski declared. (Polish Radio 1, 20 November 2013)

The increasing criticism concerning actions involving the shale gas extraction project, as opposed to be extraction itself, treated the circumstances as a reason for concern.

> Since the beginning of the year, further blows have rained down on the Polish shale gas exploration programme. The NIK report presented last week is scathing, pointing to officials' incompetence, the danger of corruption and the lack of legal basis. The latest foreign investor, ENI, has begun to withdraw from Poland, having lost two (of its three) concessions for shale gas exploration. On top of this worrying news comes the alarmingly low number of shale gas exploration wells. (*Dziennik Polski*, 16 January 2014)

The shale gas discourse is future-oriented – the future presented usually takes the forms of:

- Planned actions
- Estimates concerning resources, prices, potential inflow of extracted gas onto the energy markets
- Far-reaching visions of development of Poland and the geopolitical situation.

The statements take the form of forecasts running to the near (from a year to one or two decades) or, less often, more distant future (several decades or centuries). The former are dominant, with precise times given, e.g.:

> The breakthrough will take place in 2016, when the USA and Canada will commence exporting LNG on a large scale, according to Sbierbank. (*Gazeta Wyborcza*, 22 May 2012)

> "The investments in energy begun now will in 2020 lead to a situation in which Poland could have an excess of its own energy," said Treasury Minister Mikołaj Budzanowski recently. (*Rzeczpospolita*, 31 October 2012)

The visions of the future presented above also vary in their modality (indicating the speaker's degree of certainty that the forecast would come true). Some sentences appear that affirm the assumed state of affairs:

> Gas will come from shale in 2014. (*Rzeczpospolita*, 27 March 2012)

> The first wells for exploring for shale gas in Poland have been made. Prime Minister Tusk predicts a real abundance. (*Polityka*, 1 June 2011)

Or in a somewhat less categorical form:

> [...] there is much to suggest that 2013 will be a breakthrough year – in every mea-
> sure: global, European, Polish, financial, social and geopolitical. (*Rzeczpospolita*,
> 29 December 2012)

> There will also probably be a breakthrough in the energy market. In 2013 development
> of shale gas will be accelerated on a global scale, and this new trend might change
> the global balance of power within a decade. (*Rzeczpospolita*, 29 December 2012)

Some sentences refer to the future actions planned at present:

> By the end of the year, exploratory work is due to be completed or to start at 29 sites.
> (*Rzeczpospolita*, 6 August 2012)

Others can be classified as wishful thinking. The visions of the future they
present, based on estimated data, encompass a time frame even of several
centuries, for example:

> 300 years – this is how long shale gas resources in Poland are estimated to last.
> (*Rzeczpospolita*, 10 October 2011)

The scenarios that are presented are conditional, dependent above all
on discovery of shale gas in Poland and confirmation of the profitability of
its extraction. These two fundamental conditions delineate the main areas
of risk conceptualised in the press discourse. Yet both can essentially only
be verified by practical action. There is therefore a need to act, and permit
exploration and exploitation attempts, in order to assess their effectiveness.
The potential negative effects of these actions are not discussed.

Social worlds and arenas

Krzysztof Konecki (2010), following the ideas of Paul G. Cressey, describes
"social worlds" from the point of view of the actions around which these
worlds are formed. They arrange a physical and symbolic space for themselves, and within them norms develop, subjected to action, as well as
a particular division of work. The main action is accompanied by auxiliary
ones. In public communication, social worlds will therefore be a reflection and measure of socially existing worlds, while the media discourse
space will become an additional measure of their creation and reproduction.
We will henceforth understand arenas as scenes constructed in media statements, in which events are presented and actors operate. They are a space
of the conflict going on within the social world, and can be the nucleus of
creation of a new sub-discourse (Konecki 2010). They become part of the
perspective of a specific area of social life (e.g. politics, economics, science,

and, in the case of lifeworld, work, family, recreation, habits and individual likes) that is dominant in a given extract.

In keeping with the trends anticipated by the presence of collective and individual actors, the world of economics and politics are dominant. Also present, but with less exposure, is the world based on the perspective of environmental protection, as well as the marginal lifeworld, incorporating the perspective of "everyday life," of so-called ordinary people.

The dominant meanings of the world of economics are subordinated to the perspective of profit, expressed in terms of making money, costs, prices, the market etc. The world of the market and economics is complemented by a variously characterised economic-political perspective. In the latter case, the perspective of profit is linked with an orientation towards reproduction of power. Costs, supply and demand therefore become tools or effects of political actions. The two first perspectives encompass the entire spectrum of systemic presentation of shale gas – on the one hand in the light of the potential gains, investments and necessary expenditure, and on the other in the context of independence from other states (mostly Russia), possible alliances and cooperation (mostly with the USA) and strengthened position in the political balance of power in the domestic (parliamentary elections) and international arena (within the EU). This world also has a political-administrative dimension, being subject to the principle of efficient organisation of systemic actions, and thus legal regulations, administrative control and ensuring security. This is the world of the state. The separate world of environmentalists, whose horizon is marked by an orientation towards environmentally friendly activities, including preserving natural resources where possible in an untouched state for future generations, is weakly represented in the media discourse. Yet it is not an invisible or unnamed world. It is named, not by its own representatives, but by politicians, business representatives and journalists in external roles, who speak of the efforts, actions and logic of "ecologists." We therefore find slivers of this world in the media discourse, but they seldom set the dominant atmosphere of the text or programme, instead appearing as additional arguments accompanying other perspectives.

The main arena in which various ways of interpreting shale gas can meet is the battlefield of economic and political interests. The latter involve reproduction of power through controlling the situation, including strategic goods. Elements of the environmental discourse, focused on protection of nature, intergenerational solidarity and the perspective of sustainable development, occupy marginal places here, and are non-existent in the main, central part. This has consequences for the nature of the conflicts that are played out, which do not include the dispute over the safety of fracking technologies for the environment. Something that we can observe is the efforts made by actors of the environmental world to enter the economic and political arena – in both cases without significant results. For example, the representatives of environmental organisations emphasised the financial expenditure associated with the realisation of the shale gas project as a factor hindering the development of RES (lack of funds to subsidise this sector), and Greenpeace launched an offensive timed to coincide with the UN climate summit in Warsaw. This is an important narrative, however, as it directly concerns questions of energy policy and of setting its priorities, as well as – although this is not articulated directly – certain moral assumptions of which sources of energy are good. This strategy is based on the metaphorical opposition of "dirty" and "clean" energy sources noted in external discourses (Cotton et al. 2014). Yet the media do not give much attention to the issues highlighted within this, such as the pollution of water and methane emissions, and the media discourse fails to develop them. The actors of worlds marginalised in the discourse therefore endeavour to increase their visibility in the public sphere, not always successfully. The main problem is doing battle in the economic arena, in which a unique weaponry applies: vocabulary associated with profit, money, growth and economic development. In the material we analysed, we found no attempts to introduce a new semantics based on alternative lexica.

The world of extraction technologies, engineers and geologists is also only lightly sketched, and not clearly articulated in the mainstream media. The key actions for this world appear as key words, as the problems or possibilities of extraction. Its actors, symbolic determinants and resources are seldom cited in the discourse, and do not form their own symbolic space. The lifeworlds of the residents of potential sites for exploration, or the world of the everyday lives of inhabitants of Poland in general, in which individuals' beliefs, approaches and emotions would find their place, is an unknown space. The residents or local communities cited in the discourse tend to be treated as passive addressees of actions rather than active agents. The few statements that refer to social protests provide us with a partial, one-dimensional picture of this world. These are essentially solitary islands in a sea of opinion polls expressing aggregative support for shale gas investments. The perspective of the everyday, norms and values with a bearing on the perception of energy issues is in fact non-existent in the press we analysed. Topics problematising the industrialisation of rural areas (as a consequence of shale gas extraction) also do not appear, and the narrative observed in the United Kingdom, of the uneven distribution of risk and the expected benefits, appears marginally in the form of a story about a gargantuan, avaricious corporation and desperate, weaker farmers, in the few materials that describe the conflict between the residents of Żurawlów and Chevron.

Both the lifeworld and the world of technology are characterised by certain processes that serve to develop the technologies or perspectives of residents through hegemonic worlds – that of economics and politics. This phenomenon can be described using the concept of colonialisation of the lifeworld, in a sense also the world of technology, as a world of practical possibilities, by power and money, i.e. the aforementioned hegemonic worlds of the state and economy.

Actors

Our analysis methodology distinguished socially individual actors (people) and collective ones (organisations, groups), as well as primary and background actors. Primary actors are those who play active roles in the discourse, are quoted (press, internet) or directly presented (radio, TV), have the chance to state their views independently, take a standpoint, and make independent use of symbolic resources. Background actors, on the other hand, are those cited by others, appearing in absentia, so to speak. Positions and resources are attributed to them, as they become a point of reference for other contributors. Background actors sometimes speak independently – their statements are presented – but these appearances serve to illustrate information (e.g. shots showing protesting members of local communities).

In a quantitative sense, collective actors dominate individual actors. Though there are more of them, however, they are usually background figures. Economic organisations predominate here: companies and enterprises, including Polish – PGNIG, Tauron, Energa – and foreign ones – Gazprom, Areva, Chevron. Alongside them we observe such institutions as the stock exchange, banks, and financial and energy markets. As for the major individual actors, these are domestic politicians – initially, Prime Minister Donald Tusk was very active, joined increasingly by the ministers of the economy and – after the change in this position in 2013 – the minister of the environment.

The main background actors to join these domestic politicians are other countries, whose leaders are mentioned as synonymous terms for state organisms (Poland, but also Merkel, Putin, Obama, Germany, Russia, USA). The media visibility of scientific and research institutes is insignificant. They neither publish their own views on the shale gas project, nor give their verdict on expert opinions or reports that appear, with the exception of the first estimates concerning resources of Polish deposits. The Polish Geological Institute (PGI) and the Energy Information Agency (EIA) both figure in the discourse, but much less frequently than the aforementioned economic institutions. Experts are an important category of actors, as they prove to be active. Expert status is defined either explicitly, where a journalist presents the individual's role as such, or by reference to the specialist knowledge. Experts in the shale gas discourse are mostly actors of the world of economics, and usually employees of consulting companies, businesses and think tanks or business analysts, rather than engineers or geologists working in R&D departments. There are a few appearances in the discourse of environmentalists or representatives of the social sciences. Universities do not operate as a notable place of generation of important knowledge or as an institution legitimising the actions taken in the world of economics or politics. In comparison with the discourse concerning nuclear energy, we can observe a migration of knowledge from the traditional centres of its generation (academic research and theoretical institutions) towards the economic system (businesses' analysis departments, company laboratories, consulting agencies). Hybrid institutions symbolically located somewhere between the system of science and those of economics and politics – think tanks, science-business consortia, etc. – are also being formed. This observation is consistent with Nico Stehr's (2012) definition of knowledge as the foundation of taking actions (as opposed to information, which constitutes a resource not necessarily connected to an actor's actions). However, economics does not seek knowledge beyond its own world, but rather generates and obtains it in its own scope and for its own use. We should note that the discursive map of energy issues has certain blank spaces. Above all, there is no local community, residents, and citizens in a broader sense. The representatives of the local community generally function in the roles of passive actors, addressees of actions, and constructs used as points of reference in the statements of politicians and experts. There is also a weak showing from representatives of the third sector, limited to selected environmental organisation and two civic institutes (Sobieski Institute, Kościuszko Institute).

From the first phase of development of the discourse, a certain order of dominant actors began to form, which did not change substantially in the subsequent period. Using the similarity map (Figure 5), we can clearly reveal the links between codes within one cluster. Evident here are mutual links between economic and political institutions taking an economic perspective, i.e. employing the criterion of profitability and the language of profits and costs. We see a strong connection between experts and the institutions forming the economic system, as well as with the state and politicians. The field of influence also includes the media with weak links to the first sector, as well as slightly more distant political institutions and informal groups (and then residents and the local community).

The press analyses we conducted demonstrate minimal differences between the various publications when it comes to the exposure of the individual categories of actors. Three categories are dominant: politicians, experts and representatives of business.

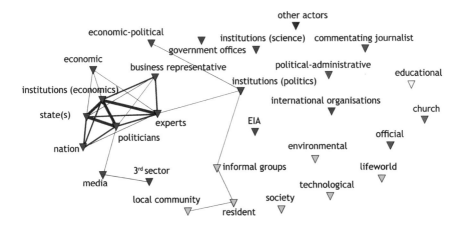

Figure 5. Links between codes in the discourse 2009–2012
Source: own elaboration.

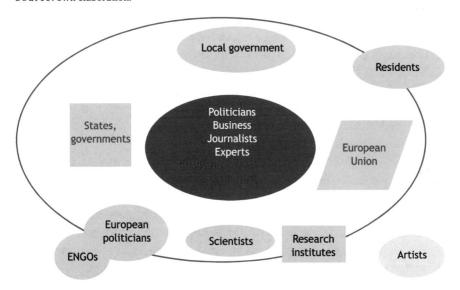

Figure 6. Actors and actants of the shale gas discourse 2013–2014
Source: own elaboration.

In the collective actors category, there is also a lack of fundamental differences from a synchronic (publications) and diachronic (years) point of view. The main categories are still states and economic institutions. Subtle differences can be found between the national and local media. In the latter, local government politicians appear somewhat more frequently.

As noted above, there are blank spaces in the reconstructed discursive map. Above all, there is no local community, residents, or also citizens in a broader sense. Where the representatives of the local community do appear, they generally function as passive actors, addressees of actions, constructs used as a point of reference in the statements of politicians and experts.

The exposure of representatives of the third sector is also relatively weak, confined to selected environmental organisations (Greenpeace, Green Institute) and two civic institutes (Sobieski Institute, Kościuszko Institute). They are therefore unable to share their perspectives and positions in the arena, which means that this dimension of conflict is not articulated in the public space.

Conflicts played out in arenas

In the discursive arenas, we therefore observe a crossing of the interests of actors, especially political and economic ones. Experts are placed in the role of adherents of the conflicting sides. The conflict of interest concerning the economic actors representing the industry interested in exploitation of shale gas is mostly about distribution of the expected profits between the enterprise and the state – which is expressed in the discussion of tax issues.

The subject of shale gas in the media discourse shows a clear tendency towards representations using binary oppositions. The shale gas–coal opposition, along with the associated energy models, proves to be fundamental here. Oppositions are also invoked in the media discourse, however, in the form of negation.

The second of the strong oppositions is the representation of the EU's climate policy as incompatible with Poland's economic interests. The axis of tension between various orientations concerning energy policy – the position considering protection of the environment and climate, and that which prioritises industrial development – runs between the European Union and the Polish government and the investors and experts in coalition with it. Owing to the weak visibility of other actors (ENGOs, scientists, social activists), it is EU climate policy that occupies the indicated counter-position. It is worth noting, however, that the EU position that is cited appears in terms of technicised legal instruments – questions of emissions, requirements for obtaining environmental decisions etc. There is no discussion on its axionormative foundations or strategic objectives.

The third opposition is that of Poland, as well as the EU and the West, with the Russian company Gazprom, which is identified with Russia's expansive policy. This dimension mainly corresponds to the politicisation of the issue of shale gas extraction. Gazprom is perceived as the chief antagonist of shale gas, and the relatively rarely recorded protests of environmentalists meet with commentary on the implicit connections with Gazprom and its stimulation of adverse presentation of shale gas.

An opposing voice observed in the discourse is *Gasland*. The occasional comments of the local community refer to the film, and experts and business representatives also assume a position towards it, disavowing the image it presents of the negative environmental effects of shale gas.

The conflicts outlined are played out within the arenas of the economic, political and social worlds. Each defines the roles separately, as well as equipping their actors with slightly different symbolic resources.

Among the main conflicts is that between Gazprom and the allied forces of Polish and American companies. At stake is Russian domination on the European market, with the conflict going beyond a strictly economic dimension to touch upon geopolitical spheres of influence. Gazprom assumes the form of a negative protagonist endangering other participants of the energy markets. This demonic image of Gazprom is also referred to by those who question it:

> This is the most fantastical part of the myth, but it is so attractive that it has already inspired sensational novels. The cover of Zbigniew Machowski's *Greed is Good*, the first shale-gas novel, features the question, "Will Russia seize Polish gas deposits?". (*Polityka*, 18 January 2012)

The conflict between Gazprom, represented by Russia, and the Western world, is also played out in a strictly political dimension:

> The final victory of the Russian authorities will take place if we do not reach agreement on shale gas in Poland. (*Rzeczpospolita*, 26 November 2012)

It is often accompanied by military metaphors:

> The agreement on shale gas does not mean that we will win the battle for exploitation of this raw material (the opposition, meaning the Russians and the Western renewable energy lobby, are still strong and will not give up). (*Rzeczpospolita*, 27 September 2011)

> The Russians' irritation was triggered by the assault of American concerns seeking shale gas in Poland, which Gazprom treats as its own sphere of influence. (*Gazeta Wyborcza*, 14 June 2010)

> This year's Wrocław Global Forum, which took place on 9–11 June, was largely devoted to questions of freedom and democracy, as well as energy and raw materials. Although this seems like a backbreaking combination, it is unsurprising given the consistency with which the Kremlin uses gas and oil to manipulate its upstart neighbours and the huge scale on which China is exploring Africa and South America to search for strategic raw material deposits. (*Wprost*, 20 June 2011)

The political conflict is also played out on the EU scene, between the proponents and opponents of shale gas exploitation.

> France does not agree to shale gas exploitation and is in favour of its prohibition in the whole European Union. This is contradictory to Polish interests. (*Rzeczpospolita*, 16 November 2012)

A simultaneous juxtaposition is "coal versus shale gas" or "nuclear versus shale gas." Here, the various energy technologies are treated as alternative, and therefore rivals.

> Will nuclear energy not tolerate shale gas in Poland? (*Gazeta Wyborcza*, 16 October 2012)

> The problem is that we do not have enough money to build a nuclear power station and search for shale gas using technology we do not yet possess and in which the Minister of the Treasury told state companies to invest. (*Rzeczpospolita*, 31 October 2012)

Less confrontational voices also appear in the discourse, calling for diversification of the technologies employed. These, however, are often articulated as wishful thinking, alongside the discussed presentation, which is clearly present and contained implicitly in the press articles.

> I believe that the wealth of Pomerania will be based on energy and raw materials. It is not just shale gas and nuclear energy. (*Gazeta Wyborcza*, 5 November 2011)

The social discourse is only hinted at in the discourse, without extensive discussion of the causes and determinants. The conflict is only noted in this arena, while at the same time it is played out beyond the main media representations.

> The Kashubians versus shale gas. Protests in Pomerania against shale gas exploration. (*Rzeczpospolita*, 12 October 2012)

To an extent simultaneously with the political and economic discourse – dominant in the press and on radio and television – in the field of social media, popular culture, and also individual commentaries, conflicts are played out between local communities and their representatives – activists, environmental organisations and farmers – and big corporate business. The positions of participants in the dispute are presented as asymmetrical in terms of power and influences, which are shown as sources of oppression. The role of corporations portrayed here is decidedly negative, and their economic interest is contrasted not so much with individual interests as with autotelic values: justice, human decency, and respect for nature.

In short: I prefer for a thousand Polish peasants to live in a clean environment than for five shareholders of an enormous corporation to change their wood on board their yachts to a more refined one (because these are the objectives for which enormous corporations usually exist). And I also don't like it when the big guy kicks the little guy, because how else can you describe Chevron's lawsuit against 13 rather randomly selected farmers out of 150 protestors?

Although this kind of conflict seldom appears in the arenas constructed in the media discourse, to an extent it develops independently from the mainstream, mostly reaching the consumers associated with this world.

The presentation of arguments, portrayal and reference to values brings it closer to the perspective of residents' everyday lives than the political and economic discourse, which refer to macro-problems. Moreover, it makes use of evocative and communicatively strong means of expression – for example, on YouTube one can watch numerous films illustrating burning water coming out of a tap (https://www.youtube.com/watch?v=4LBjSXWQRV8, access 29 September 2014, views: 1,635,516).

Arena or agora?

In the background of the conflict axes illustrated here, so to speak, we can find numerous (albeit disparate) topics on cooperation. Most are proposals referring to economic collaboration, but taking the political consequences into account. Poland's main partner identified in the analysed articles is the United States, followed by Canada.

> "American companies have a large financial potential, and we know that explorations come with a certain risk. This is why such collaboration is important for PGNiG," he adds. (*Rzeczpospolita*, 27 August 2010)

> For now Orlen is funding its shale gas exploration itself. However, it is speaking to the companies with the experience and technology required to extract gas from shale deposits and who might be interested in joint projects. This is hardly surprising – a well costs several million dollars, so it makes sense to share costs with companies that have hundreds of such wells behind them. The natural partners for such collaboration are companies whose concession territory borders with Orlen's, so ExxonMobil, Chevron and Encana, for example. (*Wprost*, 6 September 2010)

> Geofizyka has decided to take the opportunity, and boasts the position of leader of the domestic search for unconventional deposits of natural gas. It is working with the concerns PGNiG, ExxonMobil, Chevron, ConocoPhilips and Aurelian. (*Gazeta Wyborcza*, 8 December 2012)

This cooperation space, however, concerns business and administrative partners; there are no efforts to construct a plane of common actions for a larger number of stakeholders, such as local governments, state power, business, NGOs, research centres and the local population. There is no attempted empowerment of citizens, by making actors from outside politics and economics additional stakeholders discussing the problem of shale gas, allowing them to add to the discourse the perspective of sustained development, and thus quality of life, health issues and protection of the environment, understood as a common good. The emotions incorporated in the discourse are managed ideologically, and these include extreme emotions: from enthusiasm and national pride, supporting visions of successful exploitation, to fear, frustration and anger, from which perspective positions opposing the exploration and exploitation of shale deposits in Poland are perceived. We should also note here that it is not cognitively legitimate to attribute these negative emotions to lack of knowledge, as ignorance is also connected in the discourse with positions in support of shale gas, and actors even use it strategically (cf. Wagner 2014).

Actors in the discourse make use of various types of symbolic resources which they cite or attribute to other actors, constructing their positions and argumentative strategies. Among the main ones are resources of knowledge and ignorance, from which the understanding and definition of risk often result, but they also include the law, norms and values, and power and economic capital possessed.

Although shale gas can be, and is, viewed in terms of technological innovations (Stankiewicz 2013), and as a result one might expect the discourse to include attempts to construct a corpus of shared knowledge on the subject and a process of distribution of this knowledge featuring experts and decision makers, in fact the media discourse in Poland is constructed on a peculiar ignorance, and moreover one that in certain areas is strategic (Wagner 2014). Rather than extreme oppositions, knowledge and ignorance function in the discourse rather as ends of the same continuum. Knowledge here is defined as a process at the basis of the actions taken by social actors (Gross 2012). One might expect knowledge to give the opportunity to take these actions, and ignorance not (Stehr 2012). Yet this issue is complicated in the shale gas discourse. The knowledge continuum does not so much convey a quantitative increase – somebody knows more, somebody less (or its qualitative differentiation in various social actors) – as the degree of certainty of these statements. For example:

> There is no certainty that extraction of gas from shale deposits will be profitable. The boss of PGNiG also warns that it is premature to give any estimates or forecasts concerning extraction. (*Rzeczpospolita*, 27 July 2010)

> But thanks to unconventional gas deposits, especially those in shale, that could change. Because according to a report of the US Energy Information Agency (EIA) published in April this year, the *forecast resources of extraction of shale gas* in Poland are 5 billion cubic metres, and their market value exceeds tens of billions of dollars. *Except that these are estimates* not of geologists, but only of a consulting firm. (*Gazeta Wyborcza*, 18 July 2011)

> According to the US Energy Information Agency, resources of shale gas are also present in Poland, and *may total 5.3 billion cubic metres*, the most in Europe. *For now these are theoretical estimates*, because the explorations for shale gas are only now taking place, the government stresses. But PiS wants to guarantee profits from shale exploitation now. (*Gazeta Wyborcza*, 24 May 2011)

> It is *in fact already certain* that Poland, and in particular Pomerania, is "sleeping" on vast resources of shale gas. Suffice it to say that if it was only Poland using the gas, the resources would be enough for approx. 300 years. (*Gazeta Wyborcza*, 10 October 2011)

The states close to the end of the continuum described as ignorance – and thus supposition, estimates, lack of facts – by no means constitute obstacles to taking actions. Uncertainty is treated as an intrinsic aspect of human activity, and actors referring to the unknown at the same time describe what is not yet known. This is a type of ignorance which Matthias Gross (2012), following Georg Simmel, calls specified ignorance. In communicative actions, actors refer to knowledge, constructing areas of ignorance, and also attributing specific resources of knowledge and ignorance to other actors. This is an element of negotiation concerning which actions must or should be taken. Presumptions suffice to initiate them and, regardless of the later effects, taking actions itself triggers a change. This type of action usually becomes the basis of making political capital.

> Even if it turns out that the scale of extraction of gas is not large, it will improve Poland's situation. The investments begun now must be continued by the next governments. (*Fakt*, 11 June 2010)

> For now these are only estimates. How much gas there really is in Polish shale will become clear in a few years after the explorations conducted by the biggest fuel companies in the USA and Western Europe. Since 2007 the Ministry of the Environment has already issued 85 concessions for searching for shale gas. (*Gazeta Wyborcza*, 18 May 2011)

> It is not known how much gas there is in Polish shale and whether exploitation of deposits will pay. But PiS wants to inscribe in the law now a provision that the state budget will receive 40 percent of income from sales of gas. (*Gazeta Wyborcza*, 24 May 2011)

The discourse even includes the position that these changes should be preceded by actions taken on the basis of incomplete/dubious knowledge, in order to make competition possible.

> Today models are needed. The law should precede investments, and not straggle behind them. It is time to think about who we want to base our business model on. Do we want in future to earn as much on gas as the Canadians, as much as the Norwegians, or perhaps as much as the Americans? The comfortable moment when we have hard data allowing precise calculations to be made will come only when the Ministry of the Environment receives the results of gas explorations conducted by private investors. If we were to wait till then, that would mean that only in 4–5 years' time would financiers and lawyers set about writing the strategies for managing this good. This will potentially be a huge financial conflict. Yet it looks as if our strategists will be joining a game that is already underway. They will no longer be able to play the gambit deciding on its subsequent course. (*Polityka*, 1 June 2011)

In the economic discourse, the financial and political risk and the constructed area of uncertainty, juxtaposed with enthusiastic visions of future gains, opportunities and possibilities, means that the shale gas extraction technologies can be defined as innovations, which therefore provides a basis for favourable financial regulations (Wagner 2014). This is an example of strategic use of ignorance, in which the actor makes deliberate use of its resources in order to attain specific objectives (McGoey 2012). Understanding knowledge and ignorance as lying at the foundations of human actions directs attention towards the concepts of risk and uncertainty (Wagner 2014). Gross defines the differences between them as follows: risk is an undesirable possibility that we can foresee; uncertainty, meanwhile, is an undesirable possibility that cannot be foreseen at a given point (Gross 2010). Estimations of risk often involve its quantification – they not only require knowledge and awareness of its gaps, but when actions are taken they entail readiness to expose oneself to specific threats, whereas in the case of uncertainty potential threats cannot be foreseen until they occur (Tannert et al. 2007). It is impossible to prepare for them or accept them. There are two types of ignorance here: closed – when in uncertainty we reject and deny existing knowledge, choosing ignorance, or open – when we perceive the need to know more (Tannert et al. 2007). Both types of ignorance are articulated in the discourse, but with differing aims. Closed ignorance is connected to arguments for abandoning the explorations and exploitation of shale. Owing to the marginalisation of this position in the discourse, this type of ignorance also appears relatively seldom. Open ignorance is also cited by proponents of shale gas – experts in science making tentative attempts to cool the excessive and premature enthusiasm, economic experts stressing the significance and essence of the risk associated with investment in shale gas, and finally business representatives themselves, emphasising the high degree of uncertainty of the field and seeking additional support for their actions from the political community.

Conceptualisations of risk

The most common connotations of the concept of risk in the discourse are those referring to the economy. Above all, the media articulate the financial risk borne by investors owing to the uncertain profitability of exploitation of deposits, as well as the political risk associated with the unpredictability of political decisions made on the basis of criteria other than rational analysis of costs/gains. Part of this perception of risk is instability of the legal setting and the insufficient pace of adaptation of regulations to the new challenges that shale gas exploitation brings. The next dimension of economic-political risk is the controversies over shale gas played out in the international arena, and particularly in EU regulations. This is rather an area of uncertainty than one of risk – in the initial phase of development of the discourse it is hard to predict the position of European institutions and the restrictions that they will impose on member states.

Therefore, although the area of the unknown concerning the profitability of exploitation of deposits seems to be expressed in the language of risk (i.e. a language of numbers giving estimates, likelihood and financial calculations), political factors affect the interpretations of issues of extraction in terms of uncertainty – of the unpredictable political and geopolitical circumstances.

The next threat in terms of exposure is the energy dependence on another country, especially Russia.[3] The uncertainty associated with Moscow's unpredictable international policy and the recognised risk incurred by a potential block on gas supplies or unfavourable purchase conditions act in the media space as something of a counterbalance to the marginalised actions of the shale gas opposition.

The question of dangers to the environment is seldom discussed, and the risk to human health caused by fracking more rarely still. The problem of in-dustrialisation of rural areas does not exist in the media discourse, and where topics of social risk do arise, they are relatively weak, and reduced to potential conflicts between the investor and residents. The issue of distribution of possible risks and benefits between social actors is also not covered in the media.

References to seismic activity, water pollution or uncontrolled gas emissions are lacking. Risk is perceived as directly linked to human activity. To a great extent this is the risk of incorrect assumptions in relation to the actual state (size of deposits, conditions of exploitation), as well as connected with the unpredictable actions of other actors (social, political risk). Strategic decisions are made with awareness of incomplete or unconfirmed (hypothetical) knowledge and under time pressure. Speed of action here is a condition for obtaining the market advantage, while scientific knowledge gained through research provides only estimates which must be confirmed in companies' operational activity. Therefore, it is only the practice that is the consequence of decisions that can verify their pertinence.

As mentioned above, the knowledge leading to decisions on exploration and exploitation of shale gas requires verification. The resources of the-oretical knowledge are insufficient to eliminate the investment risk (also environmental, although this is discussed much less frequently). This prac-tice has now become the domain of economic entities, rather than scientific research institutions:

> Until the companies complete the exploration, we will not know what the actual reserves of shale gas in Poland might be and how many of them can be exploited profitably. (*Gazeta Wyborcza*, 17 March 2011)

---

3 The presence of Russia appears in various contexts, and it is therefore coded in terms of both conceptualisation of risk and economic or political conflict.

And let's not forget that the technology for extracting gas from shale is experimental. Nobody has done it yet over a longer period, so what will really happen underground is to a great extent still theory. (*Gazeta Wyborcza*, 23 March 2011)

What did the miners' representatives say? That everything is super-safe. Except that they don't have any proof. (*Gazeta Wyborcza*, 23 March 2011)

We can observe a significant difference concerning the perceived field of uncertainty between the position represented by professionals and decision makers and that attributed to the protesting members of the local community. The igloo of uncertainty model developed by Tannert et al. (2007) can act as a basis for mapping the differences in the positions that actors in the discourse occupy regarding knowledge and ignorance.

The position most frequently represented by politicians – especially the government and above all the prime minister – corresponds most to the position of "closed knowledge" – "we know enough to make decisions on the future." This enthusiastic position, geared towards gathering social support capital, does not fully match the positions held by the institutions from which this knowledge comes. Experts occupying positions of knowledge mostly concentrate on "what we do not yet know," and less often on "what needs to be learnt." They make a kind of estimate of the potential risks, which, as we have seen, are political and economic risks. In the technological field we observe what Piotr Stankiewicz (2009) has called a "strategy of declared safety" as a strategy for lessening conflict by reducing it to its market dimension.

The dominant actors in the discourse usually couch the positions assigned to members of the local community in terms of ignorance. On the sporadic occasions when local community voices are quoted (often under the influence of *Gasland*, and its criticism of shale gas extraction), the state of awareness present corresponds to "open ignorance," whereby the ignorance comes with the strong belief that in order to make a rational decision it is necessary to "know more." Only then can the perceived danger be transformed into acceptable or inevitable risk.

Law

A large proportion of social actors' statements concern issues of legal regulations. The dynamic of the legislative process is linked to that of the discourse in the sense that media interest is piqued by any new bill, agreement or entry into force of regulations and the surrounding circumstances. From the beginning, the law is treated as a framework shaping the possibilities and extent of investors' activities. This perspective of the relationship between the law and the economy is certainly at the forefront of the discourse. It is treated as one of the factors with an impact on the bill's economic effectiveness. This is also the perspective from which the actions of ruling politicians are judged: on the one hand they make declarations concerning the preparation of regulations which will above all facilitate the actions of representatives of business, while on the other they are criticised for sluggishness and incompetence. It is worth noting that economic topics are usually connected to issues of domestic law, whereas environmental matters tend to refer to EU regulations.

It is hard to find another group of actors whose perception of extraction law has comparable media exposure. In comparison to the German media, for example, which frequently raise the question of cautious regulations safeguarding the interests of the community and environmental safety, in the Polish discourse there is in fact no reference to a law protecting the interests of shale gas opposition groups. On the whole, the law as a guarantor of citizens' safety functions only in the form of generalised references.

It appears more frequently as a tool of domination, for example in the few descriptions of the Żurawlów protest, where the corporation's argument that it is acting in accordance with binding civil law is confronted with natural law, the right to land and to the legacy of future generations. The law is also often presented as a tool of pressure from the European Union. It is referred to by the marginalised actors of environmental civic movements, which invoke it as a safeguard from the individual interests of global corporations and local politicians.

The dominant actors usually treat the law incorporated in the shale gas discourse as a tool to enable them to act in a way favourable to their interests, and essentially protecting above all those of the elites. From this point of view, it is viewed as "friendly" to investors or a "barrier" to realisation of economic interests, often identified with those of the state.

The media as a space of deliberation: exclusion and inclusion mechanisms

The characteristics of the shale gas discourse we have observed seem to fit the concept of "post-normal science" proposed by Silvio Funtowicz and Jerome Ravetz in 1991. This envisages situations in which facts are uncertain, values debatable, the stakes high and decisions urgent (Funtowicz,

Ravetz 1991; 1992). Despite the gaps in the available knowledge and the high level of uncertainty, it is necessary to make a quick decision on what to do. The way in which the discourse on shale gas in Poland has progressed seems to go beyond the field that the authors' model refers to as professional consultation. The areas of risk surpass the competences of experts, the risk itself is unquantifiable, and the existing methods for solving problems prove to be inadequate (Funtowicz, Ravetz 1991: 5). The authors therefore propose widespread deliberation and participation of stakeholders in the decision-making process. We cannot find any traces of such an approach in the media discourse. The members of the community are treated as passive recipients of actions and decisions and are not properly represented in the discourse. Efforts to incorporate into the discussion forms that the authors point to as possible alternative knowledge resources – collective wisdom, "real-life" examples, neighbourhood stories, secret documents or the result of journalistic investigations – are extremely rare. Where do they occur, as with *Gasland*, they are denied validity, and their objectivity, rationality or instrumental intentions and ideological obstinacy are questioned. The media as broadcasters do not undertake to promote active civic deliberation, stimulate dialogue, or organise a space for exchange of arguments.

The question of whether the media constitute a space of deliberation concerning shale gas is a question of the vision of the public space that they pursue, to whom they provide visibility and who is lacking in this space. Further questions are how the mutual relations of actors present in the discursive worlds are arranged, which actions are presented and how they gain legitimation. Finally, how are actors' positions built and what strategies do they employ to be present in the communicative space and to make the meanings of their world common meanings.

The first and most obvious exclusion mechanism is omission and absence. Some social actors do not appear at all in the shale gas discourse, while others do very seldom. Although in the former case it is difficult to say whether the reasons for the lack of certain communities active in the media discourse of other countries (artists, religious organisations, industry associations, e.g. farmers) is a lack of interest or rather intentional omission, we can certainly observe large disproportions between the actors present in the discourse. The quantitatively lower presence of actors associated with the third sector, including especially representatives of environmental NGOs, social movements, local associations and groups involved in strategic regional development (e.g. local action groups), along with the marginal presence of local government politicians, scientists representing research institutions, and finally residents, is an evident exclusion mechanism. The communicative public sphere, subject to and in fact limited to the perspectives of the worlds of economics and politics, not only excludes widespread deliberation, but even restricts debate within symbolic elites. The consequence of this is inter-systemic communication (politics–economics) aiming to form a favourable environment or political decisions geared towards reproduction of power and profit-centred economic actions. This communication is closed within the sphere of macropolitics and macroeconomics, and far removed from the lifeworld of residents. The buzzwords of public consultations and public dialogue are usually no more than a political game either targeted at legitimising decisions or used as a political weapon (when political opponents are accused of a lack of dialogue or conducting consultations improperly).

We found no information or reports in the media on organised dialogue meetings. Common, on the other hand, were references to scientific or industry/business conferences on shale gas. There is a lack of materials supporting civic participation, and showing how to be included in dialogue and what residents have the right to expect. The media make no effort to increase the number of actors involved in the discourse or to identify excluded voices and standpoints.

Actors representing environmental organisations are presented differently from business actors or politicians. The main difference is that they are less likely to be directly supported by people to whom the media convey expert status. They sometimes cite experts' views, but in this situation they play the role of background actors, with positions, views and knowledge being attributed to them. NGOs appear more frequently as collective actors or together as "environmentalists." On the radio and television they are presented in the field, often in everyday situations and informal dress. Their statements are emotional and close to colloquial language. The media often contrast them with a clinical, rational expert discourse with politicians and business representatives sitting in studios and the experts who support them. The latter group are given importance by the formal situation, their dress, and academic and professional titles (director, president, expert), and the virtue of objectivity is suggested by their theoretical or practical, specialist knowledge. Such titles tend not to be used for environmentalists and activists (with some exceptions), who are instead described with reference to the organisations to which they belong. They are perceived from the perspective of their personal engagement, which on the one hand makes them more persuasive, but on the other removes their objectivity. Although activists are much closer to the everyday world, in the media space the imbalance of positions is underlined. The reason for this is probably the model of the public sphere attached to the current media discourse – prioritising of elites, hard economic data, legitimation of positions through expert knowledge. The partners for journalists organising the discourse are said besuited guests sitting in a studio, holding a discussion close to the analytical style. Actors who are usually quoted in snapshot reports do not have the opportunity for active participation in the discussion, while what they say is commented upon by other, privileged actors. The activists shown in the field inspire sympathy, but do not convince us of their arguments at the level of state policy.

A similar mechanism is at play with residents representing local communities. Here the workings of exclusion mechanisms are demonstrated more starkly as they are assigned specific interests, motivations and ignorance. These actors function as illustrations of the point of view of the "ordinary person," a construct which is objective in nature – on the one hand legitimising the media themselves as representatives of citizens and a public opinion forum, and on the other managing the discourse by assigning specific positions to actors who are actually excluded from it.

A further exclusion mechanism concerns specific arguments. The most visible one is attributing the arguments increasing the possible environmental harmfulness to unspecified "opponents," which sometimes means local oppositions and other times the European environmental lobby. Their positions are contrasted with the raison d'état of the Polish state, i.e. energy independence and economic security. A further argument is placing the position of Russia, and specifically Gazprom and its interests threatened by shale gas, on the same side of the line.

The next exclusion mechanism is the strategy of overlooking specific arguments and a kind of semantic shift entailing treatment of certain issues as primary and others as insignificant or marginal. An example might be a scene in an interview given by Deputy Prime Minister Janusz Piechociński, who, asked about the role of green energy, responded, "As regards Polish energy, our main intention is to develop coal..."

Although the Polish media note the opposition of environmentalists to the exploitation of shale gas, this is not linked to an extensive discussion on the reasons for this protest. They also accentuate the protests over other environmental investments, which might lead to the belief that environmentalists protest always and about everything.

The media lack any awareness of social dialogue – which tools it uses, what its expectations are linked to and what are or should be its consequences. The very idea of dialogue appears in the context of the failed investment in Żurawłow, which has become an example of incapacity to reach an agreement between an investor and the community.

Although the media play an important role as distributors of information about what is currently happening with the shale gas project in the public sphere, it is hard to observe any intentional actions in favour of broader deliberation. Journalists are more likely to adopt the role of observers rather than activators of social engagement.

Bibliography

Cotton, M., Rattle, I., Alstine, J. V. (2014), "Shale Gas Policy in the United Kingdom. An Argumentative Discourse Analysis," *Energy Policy*, 73, pp. 427–38.

Ferree, M. M., Gamson, W. A., Gerhards, J., Rucht, D., (2002), "Four Models of the Public Sphere in Modern Democracies," *Theory and Society*, Vol. 31, No. 3, June, pp. 289–324.

Funtowicz, S., Ravetz, J. R. (1991), "A New Scientific Methodology for Global Environmental Issues" [in:] R. Constanza (ed.), *Ecological Economics. The Science and Management of Sustainability*, New York, pp. 137–52.

Funtowicz, S., Ravetz, J. R. (1992), "Three Types of Risk Assessment and the Emergence of Post-normal Science" [in:] S. Krimsky, D. Golding (eds.), *Social Theories of Risk*, Westport, CT, pp. 251–74.

Gross, M. (2010), *Ignorance and Surprise. Science, Society and Ecological Design*, Cambridge, MA.

Gross, M. (2012), "'Objective Culture' and the Development of Non-knowledge. Georg Simmel and the Reverse Side of Knowing," *Cultural Sociology*, 6, pp. 422–37.

GUS (2015), Główny Urząd Statystyczny: *efektywność wykorzystania energii w latach 2003–2013*, Warszawa.

Jaspal, R., Nerlich, B. (2013), "Fracking in the UK Press. Threat Dynamics in an Unfolding Debate," *Public Understanding of Science*, 13 August.

Jaspal, R., Nerlich, B., Lemańczyk, S. (2014), "Fracking in the Polish Press. Geopolitics and National Identity," *Energy Policy*, vol. 74, November, pp. 253–61.

Johnson, C., Boersma, T. (2013), "Energy (In)security in Poland? The Case of Shale Gas," *Energy Policy*, 53, pp. 389–399.

Konecki, K. T. (2010), "W stronę socjologii jakościowej. Badanie kultur, subkultur i światów społecznych" [in:] J. Leoński, M. Fiternicka-Gorzko (eds.), *Kultury, subkultury i światy społeczne w badaniach jakościowych*, Szczecin, pp. 17–37.

Mazur, A. (2014), "How did the Fracking Controversy Emerge in the Period 2010–2012?," *Public Understanding of Science*, 8 August.

McGoey, L. (2012), "The Logic of Strategic Ignorance," *British Journal of Sociology*, 63, pp. 533–76.

Stankiewicz, P. (2009), "The Role of Risks and Uncertainties in Technological Conflicts. Three Strategies of Constructing Ignorance," *Innovation – The European Journal of Social Science Research*, 22, pp. 105–24.

Stankiewicz, P. (2013), "Razem o Łupkach": czyli jak prowadzić dialog publiczny przy poszukiwaniu i wydobyciu gazu z łupków," *Przegląd Geologiczny*, 61 (6), pp. 374–80.

Stehr, N. (2012), "Knowledge and Non-knowledge," *Science, Technology and Innovation Studies*, 8, pp. 3–13.

Tannert, C., Elvers, H.-D., Jandrig, B. (2007), *The Ethics of Uncertainty*, EMBO Reports, 8, pp. 893–96.

Upham, P., Lis, A., Riesch, H., Stankiewicz, P. (2015), "Addressing social representations in socio-technical transitions with the case of shale gas," *Environmental Innovation and Societal Transitions*.

Wagner, A. (2014), "Shale Gas. Energy Innovation in a (non-)Knowledge society. A Press Discourse Analysis," *Science and Public Policy*, 7 August.

Wagner, A., Grobelski, T., Harembski, M. (2016), "Is Energy Policy a Public Issue? Nuclear Power in Poland and Implications for Energy Transitions in Central and East Europe," *Energy Research and Social Science*, vol. 13, March.

Wit Hubert

REPRESENTATION OF SELECTED ENERGY TOPICS ON THE POLISH INTERNET

Introduction

According to Niklas Luhmann, contemporary media should be treated as "the evolutionary achievements that enter at those possible breaks in communication and that serve in a functionally adequate way to transform what is improbable into what is probable" (Luhmann 1995: 160). The role of the media is therefore to provide order to the information world by linking broadcasters with users (van Dijk 2006: 26). This continual transmission of the information contained in symbols by self-reproducing media networks accompanies individuals in all decision-making processes. The media – both traditional (press, radio, television) – and new (internet) are an intrinsic element of the organisation of social life, including the processes taking place in the public sphere. It is thanks to the information transmitted through the media that social actors are able to make political decisions, and thanks to the media that the social order is reproduced and power is legitimised (or delegitimised), or, more broadly, the social structure is reproduced (van Dijk 2006). The discourse itself is a "tool" of the deliberative processes leading to political and economic decisions, as well as of semiotic visibility, which was discussed in the introduction to this book.

In order to more precisely define the roles and places of new media (especially the internet) in the socio-political system, we need to briefly recall the features that characterise these forms of communication. Important here are the constitutive characteristics of new communication technologies, such as interactiveness, integration (multimedia) and hypertextuality (see Introduction). These characteristics are responsible for the transition from mass communication towards distributed communication. The "few to many" communication model is replaced by a "many to many" model, which in theory favours a large differentiation of broadcasters and a demassification of media (Goban-Klas 2004). As noted by van Dijk, "the new media cause a shift from allocution towards consultation, registration and conversation" (van Dijk 2006: 12). This means that the internet helped to leave behind a model in which the subject matter, time and speed of contents were up to broadcast centres (allocution model). The turn towards other models of communication (consultation, registration and conversation) leads to empowerment of peripheral (local) individuals.

In order to understand how the popularisation of new media can change the structure of communication in systems of holding power, let us recall the features of new media identified by Marc Smith. The "five As" characterising communities built via the internet, Smith writes, is that they are aspatial, asynchronous, acorporal, astigmatic and anonymous (Smith 1992). If we assume that these are also characteristics of internet discourse, then online public communication partly corresponds to Jürgen Habermas's conditions of an ideal communicative system. Some forms of internet communication seem to fulfil the conditions of inclusiveness of the public sphere. These are the associated equality of the participants in the communication, voluntary expression of opinions or lack of self-excluding fallacies and illusions (Habermas 2008).

As Barry Wellman (2001) points out, it is mostly the low transmission costs and asynchronicity of internet communication that increase citizens' engagement in it. This, he argues, helps to break individual and group particularisms. Solidarity based on an internet model can be more effective, owing to the spatial dispersal and heterogeneity of the actors communicating with each other (Wellman 2001). Robert Putnam, meanwhile, believes that internet communication has the chance to be less burdened by the hierarchical nature of the communicative structure, meaning that more pluralistic dialogue can precede the adoption of solutions (Putnam 2000). According to Anthony Giddens, "where television and newspapers [...] are dominated by commercial interests, they do not provide a focus for democratic discussion. Yet public television and radio, together with the Internet, offer many possibilities for developing open dialogue and discussion" (Giddens 2006: 119).

Unfortunately, the above conclusions are considerably limited in their explanatory potential. Firstly, they do not derive from thorough empirical studies. Secondly, they refer to the state of the internet from over a decade ago, and moreover were made on the basis of observation of the American part of it. Thirdly, the internet is treated as a relatively homogeneous medium. This is a gross category error of sorts, meaning that we assume the similarity of all phenomena triggered by the popularisation of this technology (Geiger 2009). Yet the internet is in fact many different digital technologies integrating diverse communication models. To evaluate the influence of such different tools as forums, blogs, vlogs and social networking sites on civic participation it is necessary to abandon thinking about the internet as a "uniform and finite" medium.

Matters are complicated by the fact that the internet has also become an extension of traditional media: press, radio and television. One of the main dimensions describing individual internet technologies is who sends the messages. What proves to be most important is whether it is a professional media worker or an amateur. The former case concerns publications by journalists posted on web portals. The latter type of broadcasters are individuals publishing on forums, social networks or sometimes also the blogosphere. The following analysis of the energy discourse will be described from a perspective that highlights this division of the internet space. First, though, let us examine what internet discourse itself is.

Analysis of the models of social discourse proposed below shows that the key categorisation can be based on the type of medium mediating in a given dialogue. For this analysis I distinguish four levels of discourse: social (transmitted by speech, text not made public), media (transmitted by the media, e.g. press, radio, TV), internet (via internet 1.0 technologies) and social internet (via internet 2.0 technologies, e.g. social networking sites). We can differentiate this division on the basis of the types of mediating technologies (see Figure 1) or in terms of the source of the published contents (see Figure 2).

At this point we should note that the social discourse is presented in not linguistic or philosophical terms, but rather sociological ones, whereby it is almost identical to the concept of the public sphere. I understand this to mean "a discursive space in which strangers discuss issues they perceive to be of consequence for them and their group. Its rhetorical exchanges are the bases for shared awareness of common issues, shared interests, tendencies of extent and strength of difference and agreement, and self-constitution as a public whose opinions bear on the organization of society" (Hauser 1999: 64). What is important here, though, is the concept of media discourse that I propose understanding, following Małgorzata Lisowska-Magdziarz, as "a set of ways of deliberate, non-accidental use of language to communicate information, opinions, values, concepts, and the views of media on various subjects" (Lisowska-Magdziarz 2001). When these communicative practices are transmitted through computer networks, this becomes internet discourse. In such cases where those sending messages on the internet are not professional broadcasters and the content appears on forums, blogs and online communities, I see this as "internet community discourse."

The most important information that can be interpreted from this simplified outline is that any content can, but does not have to, function in all designated areas (Figure 1). A discussion on a blog will always constitute an element of social discourse (speech situation). Yet it does not necessarily concern the issues present in mainstream media, both those conceived as traditional (e.g. newspaper, radio station) and internet ones (web portals). From the technological point of view (Figure 2), each newer technology must contain older technologies. Social networking sites, for example, use text present in all other "discourse technologies."

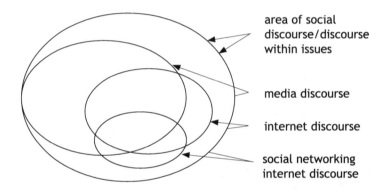

Figure 1. Discourse outline – content model
Source: own elaboration.

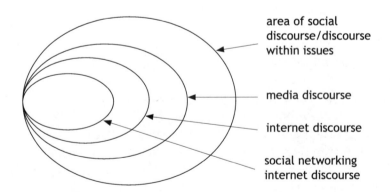

Figure 2. Discourse outline – technological model
Source: own elaboration.

Methods used in analyses

The below analysis is based on data gathered during research carried out within the grant "The media as a deliberative plane – an analysis of models of public discourse based on the example of key energy issues in Poland: building of a nuclear power station, shale gas exploitation and wind energy." At the research planning stage a comparative analysis of the construction of media discourses around selected energy issues was planned. Alongside television, radio and the press, the internet as a whole was one of the areas considered a potential space for deliberation among social actors. The scope and character of the material collected was thus not originally designed for studying the relations between the expert internet and the community internet. Rather, it was supposed to serve to reconstruct the areas of online communicative actions as well as the narratives generated there. However, these relations were observed during collection of the material and analysed as far as possible.

This chapter therefore aims to provide a qualitative description of the internet discourses functioning within selected energy issues. The analysis that follows describes the representations of issues discussed in the media (expert discourse) as well as the accompanying dynamic of increase in statements made by web users (social media discourse). This analysis is not, then, comparative in a quantitative sense. It provides a reconstruction of the maps of mutual links between actors, topics and issues.

The results presented below are based on:

1) qualitative analysis of selected news and industry websites
2) quantitative analysis of social media trends.

The first area of analysis encompasses a survey of the texts written by professional journalists and opinion formers published on Poland's top information and industry websites. Some texts are reprints – copies or slightly amended versions of press articles. We shall call this research area "expert internet discourse." The second area comprises contents appearing on social media, forums and blogs. These contents are usually published by internet users, who may be professional or not, but are not regular editorial contributors. I will use the category "social media internet discourse" for this kind of content.

For the first survey, the database was collected with the aid of the company Press-Service Monitoring Mediów and supplied in the form of a library of .xml and .pdf files. The necessary data for analysing social media content was provided by the company SentiOne, and the analysis was conducted in a data provider online service.

All three categories of energy areas constituted a foundation for classifying texts on account of the occurrence of accordingly selected key words. In both cases, the sample selection was inspired by "trends analysis" (nesting of information). This means that we selected periods characterised in the written press (reference medium) by the greatest number of publications (see Table 1).

Table 1. Periods of transmission of analysed publications

Nuclear	25 Nov–7 Dec 2013	27 Jan–8 Feb 2014	24–29 Mar 2014
Shale gas	17–30 Nov 2013	6–20 Jan 2014	10–16 Mar 2014
Wind	15–29 Apr 2013	20 Oct–2 Nov 2013	20–26 Mar 2014

Source: own elaboration.

Study of expert internet discourse – method

The unit of analysis for the "expert internet" comprised journalistic texts appearing on Polish internet sites. The material selected for the key words analysis consisted of 580 articles posted on the eight largest Polish news and industry websites (December 2014, Megapanel PBI/Gemius data). The news sites are dominated by Gazeta.pl, Onet.pl, Interia.pl and Dziennik.pl. Energy issues were also presented on industry websites – we made use of press materials appearing on the following sites: Cire.pl (Energy Market Information Centre) and Wnp.pl (Virtual New Industry – Economics Portal).

An important characteristic of the internet as an information source is the fact that content is often repeated and reproduced on many websites. The hypertextuality of the web means that one text can often function on a few sites in an identical or similar form. As a result, we had to conduct a three-stage sample selection.

1. The objective of the first step was to make the sample selection. The method is described in more detail in A. Wagner, "Organising the Research".
2. We then, using the Python language libraries, made an automatic selection of repeated texts. At this stage we eliminated repeated texts on the basis of similarity of titles. We also converted files to HTML format, in accordance with the demands of the QDA Miner analysis software.
3. The third stage of the sample selection concerned 508 texts published on the Polish internet in the selected periods. Here, at the coding stage, the researchers rejected repeated texts that had not been eliminated automatically in the second stage.

The final study sample consisted of 404 texts published in the periods presented in Table 1. The materials categorised as referring to issues of shale gas and oil therefore numbered 210 (52% of the sample). Texts on nuclear energy comprised 30.2% of the sample (122 cases), and wind energy issues were represented in 72 articles (almost 18% of the sample). Although there were some texts that examined issues from the three energy areas, all three sets of texts were separate. The coders therefore had to decide which of the topics was dominant in a given texts, in this way assigning them one of the three values of the variable "research area/unit of analysis."

Since we also observed repetition of texts on industry sites (Cire.pl, Wnp.pl) and general online portals, the texts from the first publication were used for the analysis. In many cases, source texts offered a more comprehensive description of a problem than their "reprints." To some extent, the phenomenon of reproduction of contents on the internet explains the overrepresentation of texts appearing on Cire.pl.

Table 2. Structure of study sample by energy areas

Research area/unit of analysis	Number of cases	Percentage of cases
shale gas_internet	210	52.0%
nuclear_internet	122	30.2%
wind_internet	72	17.8%
	404	100%

Source: own elaboration.

Table 3. Structure of study sample by information sources

Websites analysed	Number of cases	Percentage of cases
cire.pl	195	48.3%
wyborcza.biz.pl	84	20.8%
wiadomosci.onet.pl	45	11.1%
wnp.pl	36	8.9%
fakty.interia.pl	30	7.4%
wiadomosci.dziennik.pl	7	1.7%
wideo.onet.pl	4	1.0%
tygodnik.onet.pl	3	0.7%
	404	100%

Source: own elaboration.

Study of social media internet discourse — method

Research on the trends in social media is an important complement to analysis of the expert discourse. The data provided by SentiOne comprises statements selected by the keywords method from a database encompassing social media sites, microblogs, internet forums, blogs and comments on web portals, video sites and opinion comparison services. The results were obtained on the basis of monitoring of over 2.9 million statements originating on the Polish internet, published between April 2013 and April 2014. Users' posts were collected automatically using web crawlers (indexing robots). This tool permits collection only of statements of a public nature, i.e. those available to people who are not in the writers' private social networks. Discussions taking place, for example, in social groups were therefore omitted. Researchers also do not have access to contents posted in various expert niches and closed online groups, i.e. areas of the "deep web."

It is important to note that this type of sample selection differs in several ways from that used for description of the "expert discourse." First, it is conducted on data aggregated with the service provider. All lists are limited by the interface of the provider's analytical panel. Second, the analysis is limited only to a quantitative analysis of the intensity of statements of users of the websites in the study. No qualitative content analysis was conducted on the collected materials. The text selection was carried out using an automated keywords method, without corrections from an analyst or coder. This resulted in a lack of control over the sample quality and made it hard to assess the reliability of the survey. The data collected in this part were therefore supplementary, and could not be used for a comparison with the data from the "expert discourse." Yet they are of significant value for checking the frequency with which topics are referred to by people making their statements publicly visible. This is useful as we will be particularly interested in whether the intensity of the expert internet discourse goes hand in hand with an increase frequency of statements of social media users. Does the media visibility of subjects in the public sphere then generate a growth in their visibility in discussions on the cusp of the public and private spheres, and can social media discourse therefore influence the agenda of issues?

Expert internet energy discourse

Summing up the results, we can state that this area was dominated by politicians (mostly domestic, parliamentary), who were the actors – both primary and implicated – who appeared most frequently (see Figure 3). In the diagrams provided below, the size of the circles shows the frequency of a value of a given variable (actors category). The thickness of the line indicates the number of mutual links between the categories shown in the course of the cluster analysis. The colours of the circles reflect the number and type of cluster (number of clusters limited to 5).

The issues discussed generally occurred together with the representatives of companies as experts on the energy market. Furthermore, this discourse is clearly dominated by men. In the category of collective actors, meanwhile, the debate was based on the state–company axis, with a relatively significant representation of European institutions (see Figure 4). Of course, the list of coded categories of the actors who build the discourse is considerably longer, but the above categories are the dominant ones. This order applies to all the energy areas we studied.

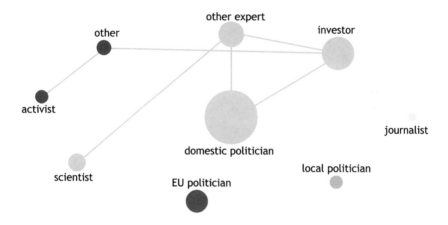

Figure 3. Co-occurrence of codes of combined categories: individual primary and implicated actor (number of groups 5, Jaccard index)
Source: own elaboration.

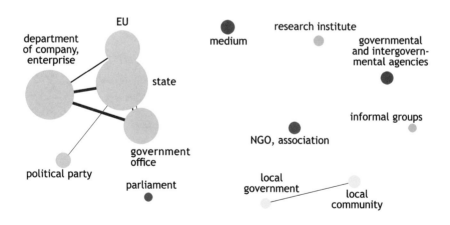

Figure 4. Co-occurrence of codes of combined categories: collective primary and implicated actor (number of groups 5, Jaccard index)
Source: own elaboration.

The actors who appear in the texts are the main source of the knowledge that functions within them. This is usually empirical knowledge, i.e. it derives from research or experiments (Figure 5). The below bubble charts illustrate the frequency of occurrence of the values of a given variable (type of knowledge or place of its generation) in relation to all occurrences of a given variable (cases of use of knowledge), divided into the researched fields (areas of energy issues). Column percentages were used.

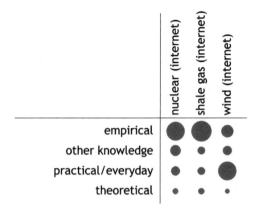

Figure 5. Categories of knowledge functioning in the individual areas of the analysed discourse

Source: own elaboration.

The practical knowledge resulting from individuals' experience can also be distinguished. This type is present to a greater extent in texts on wind energy. The knowledge that appears has not only broadcasters, but also sources and places of generation. The cited knowledge usually comes mainly from public opinion research centres and expert reports of ministerial institutions (Figure 6). These are not the only areas of knowledge generation present in the energy discourse, of course, but they are clearly dominant. Notable here is the relatively limited role played by Polish science (research institutions as the place of knowledge generation) and Polish scientists.

Knowledge is generally accompanied by arguments, which appear in such forms of rationalisation as describing possible gains or losses, presenting numerical data, quoting authorities or demonstrating benefits. Alongside knowledge, ignorance is another rhetorical element. This occurred not only much less often than knowledge, but also relatively independently from it, which we can view as showing a lack of direct connections.

Analysis of the legal acts cited by actors shows that domestic (Polish) legislation is dominant as a source of law. European Union laws are quoted much less frequently in the texts. Direct references to the constitution appeared only in the case of wind energy. This no doubt shows a connection to references to axionormative systems.

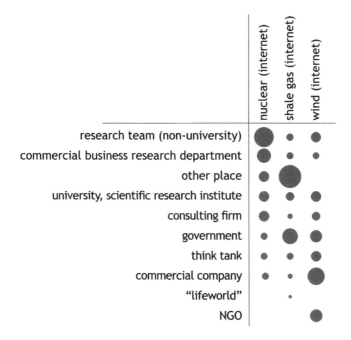

Figure 6. Place of generation of knowledge functioning in the individual areas of the analysed discourse (based on column percentage)

Source: own elaboration.

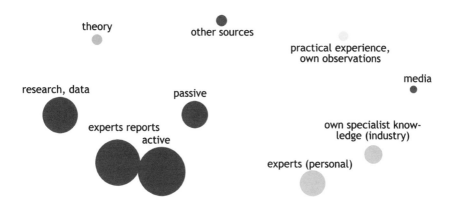

Figure 7. Co-occurrence of codes of the categories: type of knowledge use; source of knowledge (number of groups 6, Jaccard index)

Source: own elaboration.

The texts we examined contained many references to such values as security, as well as, less often, development (progress) and the environment. The first of these values appeared mostly in the context of nuclear energy and shale gas. Wind energy is not often connected to values-based discourse. Shale gas, on the other hand, was tied to statements coded as references to the common good.

The actors in the discourse used appropriate arguments and figurative speech to support all of these elements. The most common device was allusion to a vision of the future, while metaphors and symbols appeared less often, and generally within the nuclear energy discourse.

All these devices were accompanied by arguments dominated by the economic dimension. Economic discourse applied to all three areas of energy issues. Of course, other argumentative fields were also present – the technological, geopolitical and environmental ones, for instance, with environmental arguments usually functioning in the context of shale gas. Figure 8 illustrates the connections between the code categories that were distinguished. The presence and thickness of a line shows the number of mutual links occurring between the categories of variable values (codes) shown in the course of the cluster analysis.

As illustrated by Figure 8, the social media discourse most frequently refers to a set of values linked to security, the common good, development and progress. Security/safety is placed centrally, operating as a kind of anchor for arguments from various angles: geopolitical, environmental, economic or technological. This concept therefore acquires various contexts, and to an extent conceals other contents. It is interesting that values such as democracy or justice (which could occur, for instance, in the form of fair distribution of risk and benefits) remain outside of the network of main connections and function on the margins of discourses in the social media.

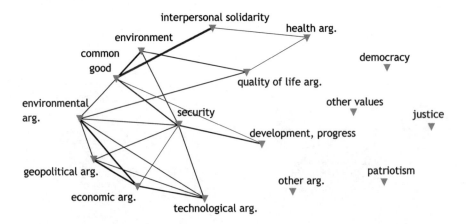

Figure 8. Co-occurrence of categories of codes: arguments, values (number of groups 1, Jaccard index)

Source: own elaboration.

Analysis of the collected material points to a high degree of exclusivity of the discourse. The texts not only overlooked or marginalised some groups of actors, but they also rarely employed mechanisms of inclusion for many interest groups. References or other elements supporting civic participation were relatively rare. There were in fact no descriptions of holding a dialogue of interest groups with citizens. More often, though, came criticism of this state of affairs.

The online/social media energy discourse

In the period in question, most statements of Polish internet users in the selected areas concerned wind energy or shale gas. There were considerably fewer comments on nuclear energy (see Table 5).

Table 5. Number of statements on selected energy issues

	Number of statements in research periods		
	Nuclear	Wind	Shale gas
For the period 1 April 2013—1 April 2014	53525	75994	75275

Source: own elaboration.

One of the main characteristics to describe the online social media discourse is where it functions (publication source). Analysis of the SentiOne data showed that nuclear energy was the area with the largest number of statements on Facebook. This subject was the topic of discussion in comments below articles on news sites slightly less frequently. Internet forums accounted for considerably fewer – slightly over one fifth – posts on nuclear energy on the Polish internet (see Figure 9). Shale gas demonstrates a similar structure of proportions of various types of social media services. In this area, however, forums, comments on news sites and Facebook posts each account for around a third of all published statements (Figure 11). The situation is different with wind energy (see Figure 10), in which almost half (46%) of statements come from internet forums. The popularity of this form of online debate can be explained by the prosumer approach to RES issues. The wind energy discourse also includes questions of the level of investments of individual households. The majority of statements are found on forums of enthusiasts and constructors of wind power stations. This is confirmed by an analysis of the most popular domains for this subject area. The top ten sites ("forums and portals" category) include such titles as Elektroda.pl, Forum. pcland.pl and the forum Wiatraki.memu.pl (*wiatraki* = turbines).

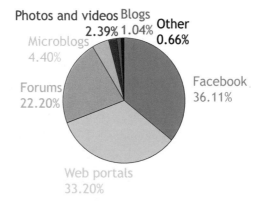

Figure 9. Representation of the subject "nuclear energy" in social media
Source: own elaboration based on Sentione data.

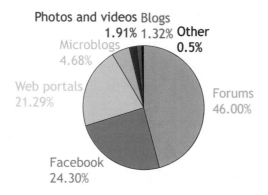

Figure 10. Representation of the subject "wind energy" in social media
Source: own elaboration based on Sentione data.

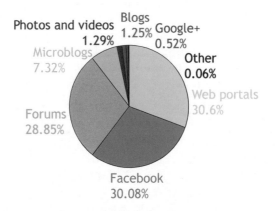

Figure 11. Representation of the subject "shale gas energy" in social media
Source: own elaboration based on Sentione data.

If we analyse the titles of the domains of the most active communities, we can notice certain significant difference between the various energy areas. In the case of nuclear energy, we can observe a large proportion of comments published on forums on industry websites (e.g. forum.wnp.pl), as well as those on news sites: finanse.wp.pl, forum.gazeta.pl, niezalezna.pl and wiadomosci.onet.pl. Notably, the list of the most popular domains among people commenting on shale gas is dominated by the forums of information/opinion websites with a right-wing profile: prawica.net, wpolityce.pl and niezalezna.pl.

As for wind energy, apart from the aforementioned popularity of technology forums, we can also note that these issues have a greater "locality." The list of the most popular domains with comments on wind turbines include addresses such as forum.dawnygdansk.pl ("old Gdańsk") and forum.echodnia.eu (a Świętokrzyskie Voivodeship local service). Perhaps unsurprisingly, given the reach in all three subject areas, most statements were recorded on facebook.com and twitter.com as well as the content aggregator wykop.pl.

Looking at the data on the social media discourse, let us note that this area of the media too is very much dominated by males. In all three subject areas they are in the clear majority, with an average of 82% of statements categorised as being made by men (see Figures 12, 13, 14).

The graphs in Figures 12–14 also contain information on the changes in frequency of appearance of posts in social media on energy issues. In the analysed period (April 2013–April 2014), we can observe that the graphs for both nuclear energy and shale gas contain very high growths in internet user activity. In the former case this increase took place in February 2014. We can assume that it was linked to the appearance of many texts concerning the government's adoption of the Polish Nuclear Energy Programme. Online activity regarding shale gas, on the other hand, made a jump following the publications of the results of experimental wells in Pomerania, in late December 2013 and early January 2014.

There are no clear dominants on the graph of internet activity on wind energy. We can perhaps attribute this to the lack of significant and "media-friendly" events in the course of the research, as the period in question does not cover the work on the adoption of the so-called prosumer law (February–March 2015).

These observations suggests that the social media discourse is very susceptible to the debate initiated by the mainstream media. Unfortunately, the research material does not prove whether this pattern also exists at the level of local debate.

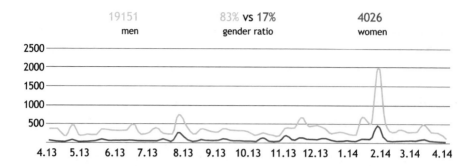

Figure 12. Gender in social media discourse – nuclear energy
Source: own elaboration based on Sentione data.

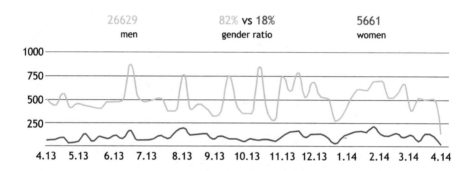

Figure 13. Gender in social media discourse – wind energy
Source: own elaboration based on Sentione data.

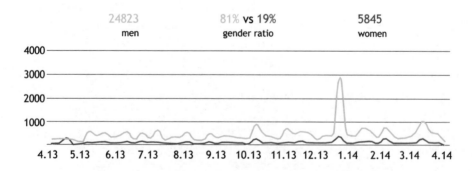

Figure 14. Gender in social media discourse – shale gas
Source: own elaboration based on Sentione data.

Conclusion

The description presented provides an approximate illustration of the energy discourse operating on the Polish internet. The most important characteristic is its exclusivity, which also applies to the press discourse (see M. Świąt-kiewicz-Mośny, "The Media Discourse on Wind Energy"). The exclusion of many actors (e.g. local communities, consumer representations) combined with the domination of certain categories of them (politics, business) means that it is impossible to speak of the representation or visibility of all social groups engaged in energy matters. Rather than constituting an alternative, including unrepresented interest groups in society, the social media discourse functions solely as an extension of the existing discursive order. As a medium serving the demassification of broadcasting, the internet does not break the model described by Michel Foucault of a reflexive relationship between power and knowledge (Foucault 1972). The above analysis is therefore not an illustration of a model in which the "long tail" of the internet is decisive in the extension and democratisation of discourse. As one science blogger notes, "contemporary society executes its power not only through access to information (knowledge) but also through processing it and reflexive sending of the 'social interpretation' of information" (Networked Digital 2012).

Taking this perspective would suggest that energy does not function in the network of dialogue and searching for agreement, but only in the game of particularisms. As a result, the loss of the sense of what the common good is, diagnosed among others by Zygmunt Bauman (2007), might risk become heightened still further. Yet it does seem that the "internet has produced a change in the structure of access to information – power centres continue to control key information that is inaccessible to others, but the knowledge contained in billions of pieces of data scattered around the internet (and unattractive to power) is today being interpreted and formed into a whole by the collective intelligence of millions of internet users" (Networked Digital, 2015). This is a subject that requires more extensive analysis.

In conclusion, we can make use of the conception of Christian Fuchs (2014), who points out that in order to understand the essence of the internet one should reduce it to the phenomenon of capitalism. Both function thanks to the opposing forces of cooperation and competition. According to Fuchs (2014), this antagonism is the reason not for the weakness, but for the potential of the web. However, when there is a lack of balance between the two the internet discourse will be a tool not of an electronic form of participation, but of an electronic form of domination.

Bibliography

Bauman, Z. (2007), *Consuming Life*, Cambridge.
Dijk, J. van (2006), *The Network Society: Social Aspects of New Media*, London.
Foucault, M. (1972), *The Archaeology of Knowledge: And the Discourse on Language*, trans. A. M. Sheridan-Smith, New York.
Fuchs, C. (2014), *Social Media. A Critical Introduction*, London.
Geiger, S. (2009), "Does Habermas Understand the Internet? The Algorithmic Construction of the Blogo/Public Sphere," *Journal of Communication, Culture, and Technology*, issue 10, vol. 1.
Giddens, A. (2006), *Sociology*, Cambridge.
Goban-Klas, T. (2004), *Media i komunikowanie masowe. Teorie i analizy prasy, radia, telewizji i Internetu*, Warszawa.
Habermas, J. (2008), "Communicative Action and the Detranscendentalized 'Use of Reason'" [in:] J. Habermas, *Between Naturalism and Religion, Philosophical Essays*, trans. C. Cronin, pp. 24–76.
Hauser, G. (1999), *Vernacular Voices. The Rhetoric of Publics and Public Spheres*, Columbia.
Lisowska-Magdziarz, M. (2001), *Analiza tekstu w dyskursie medialnym*, Kraków.
Luhmann, N. (1995), *Social Systems*, trans. J. Bednarz, Jr. with D. Baecker, Stanford, CA.
Morozov, E., "How Democracy Slipped through the Net," http://www.theguardian.com/technology/20911/jan/13/evgeny-morozov-the-net-delusion (access: 03.11.2005).
Networked Digital (2012), http://networkeddigital.com/2012/02/01/dyskurs_internetowy_vs_dyskurs_spoleczny/ (access: 03.11.2015)
Putnam, R. (2000), *Bowling Alone: The Collapse and Revival of American Community*, New York.
Smith, M. (1992), *Voices from the Well. The Logic of the Virtual Commons*, http://www.sscnet.ucla.edu/soc/csoc/papers/voices/Voices.htm (access: 03.11.2005).
Wellman, B. (2001), "Physical Place and Cyber Place. The Rise of Networked Individualism," *International Journal of Urban and Regional Research*, 25 (2), pp. 227–52, http://www.itu.dk/people/khhp/speciale/videnskabelige%20artikler /Wellman2001%20-%20%20personalized%20networking.pdf (access: 03.11.2005).

Aleksandra Wagner

THE MEDIA AS A SPACE OF DELIBERATION BASED ON THE EXAMPLE OF MEDIA DISCOURSE ON SELECTED ENERGY TOPICS — CONCLUSION

The analyses presented in this volume provide the foundations for attempting to diagnose the mainstream media discourse as a space for public deliberation. We perceive this space normatively, from the angle of the characteristics discussed above, such as inclusiveness, diversity of points of view, dialogicality, strength of argument, looking for the points of contact and mapping the differences between groups of actors, as well as their forming of coalitions and oppositions. The objective of this is to identify social problems and guidelines for their resolution, which then become the object of public policies. Important here is transparent presentation of interests, with priority given to the public interest – in the sense both of the good of the majority and of a beneficial resolution of problems for disadvantaged groups. The space of deliberation referring to media discourse is thus treated as a normative ideal of a symbolic space in which the discourses of various epistemic communities are present, visible to themselves and referring to one another. Moreover, these communities have the chance to become visible also to those who are not actively involved in them – viewers, readers, audiences in general. But this is not all. The polyphonic and intertextual space of this co-existence of discourses by its nature creates conditions for collective deliberation on issues of importance to society. The confrontation of various points of view is supposed to produce a better solution (than interest groups' initial proposals), but not to give the advantage to a specific point of view (e.g. through eristic processes) or make any one community dominant. At the same time, though, these normative criteria lead to critical analysis and evaluation of the communicative processes taking place in the media space.

Of course, the rift between the realm of ideal premises and the practice of how discourses function in the media is not meant to emphasise the pathologies of the latter, but to point to the need for and forms of action to reorganise this practice; to critically analyse not only the process of defining the goals and instruments for achieving it but also the norms that these processes will follow in the public sphere. The authors therefore do not treat media discourses as the only public discourses, but as those which are visible in the media space.

The many differences in the media discourses on the various topics are described in detail in the previous chapters. Yet certain similarities can also be seen. Energy issues are given prime importance in the media representations. Where the subject of energy occurs in the media, it is treated as an important subject, particularly for economic and political reasons. This claim to importance is expressed in the frequent publication of information on the front pages of newspapers, functioning as the main topic of a programme or statement (while energy issues are also covered in relation to other important subjects), and involving in the discussion people in high positions in state and business structures identified with power (decision makers). The leading actors in the discourse describe this subject as crucial to citizens, the economy and the country. The common good that is so significant in deliberation processes is defined here in terms of geopolitical interest (which large economic interests are to serve). Although the rivalry of global economies and struggle for the dynamic of economic growth demarcate the thinking on acquisition and use of energy, it is hard to speak of a global perspective, as all decisions are taken at a domestic level, where the primary interests are those of the state. The discourse is lacking a clearly outlined global perspective of perception of energy issues, for example their importance for the planet or inequalities on a global scale.

Despite the attributed and unquestionable "importance," these issues differ in terms of popularity. We can understand this in two ways. First, popularity refers to the frequency with which a given topic is covered in the media; this is decided by the dynamic of political and economic events. Plans, decisions, and meetings of key actors become a pretext for presenting and discussing energy issues. Hot topics in our period of analysis were the construction of a nuclear power station in Poland and the search for shale gas. Wind energy was discussed less frequently, and more in the local than the national media. This goes hand in hand with political priority being assigned to individual investments. Wind energy is the form least likely to be presented as of strategic importance for the state.

Second, popularity can refer to the way in which energy issues are presented to readers. Popular contents are presented in simplified form without the need for specialist knowledge or careful following of the subject, and are often embellished with sensation – like the corruption scandals over investments or tempestuous protests. They are usually addressed to the so-called "general reader," without specific profiling, whereas less popular contents are published with a specific target group in mind. We can thus observe that media addressing contents to people interested in economic issues (e.g. *Rzeczpospolita* or *Puls Biznesu*) are more likely to cover energy issues than media with a socio-cultural profile. It is also less common to present energy issues in terms associated with citizens' everyday lives: work, functioning of households, quality of life, local affairs. Perhaps the form of energy that comes closest to this everyday dimension is wind, which is rooted in the realities of communes and districts more than the others. Wind power is described in terms of neighbourhood, health and quality of life, but also of local tensions and conflicts, although even here these categories are simply present, rather than dominant.

The economisation of the discourse that is characteristic of presentation of energy issues is an element of power relations. It serves to achieve political interests, by strengthening or weakening the positions of those in power. This power is legitimised by specialist expert knowledge, which is to a great extent macroeconomic. It is interesting to note that the actors did not always treat the areas of ignorance and uncertainty that shone through in all the analysed topics as barriers to taking action. On the contrary, sometimes, as with the case of shale gas, knowledge gaps become a distinct impetus for action presented as the only way of securing practical knowledge. This kind of knowledge can then lead to economic calculations.

Topics of social consultations are very infrequent in the media discourses, while reflection on participatory ways of dealing with areas of uncertainty is essentially entirely absent. Not only do the media not consciously create discursive norms favouring deliberation, but they also fail to promote the very idea, to educate in the possibilities and tools for conducting it, only occasionally calling for broader consultations, rarely giving information about the processes of social dialogue – meetings taking place and the results thereof – and even more seldom of possibilities of participation.

Although the media discourses on energy issues are characterised by various degrees of inclusiveness and diversity of the positions expressed, studies conducted in other countries also point to a domination of the economic perspective. Despite the growing visibility of climate change and calls for a transition to a low-emissions economy, these discussions always take place within the current economic structures (Uusi-Rauva, Tienari 2008). They seem incapable either of initiating the radical changes that scientists deem necessary for solving the ecological crisis (Dryzek 1997; Prasad, Elmes 2005) or of effectively opening the communicative space to alternative perspectives and values.

In the Polish media, these structures model the discourse according to categories of profitability, economic risk, benefits and losses. They are represented by actors who are influential in a communicative sense and have high media visibility. The analyses show that other actors, such as those representing NGOs or informal citizens' groups, though present in the discourse, find it hard to occupy independent positions. Rather, they act as points of reference for the dominant actors. The asymmetry of these positions is plainly felt and legitimised by the (rather arbitrary) reference to the common good. Actors from within the system (representing the strong fields of politics and economics) often appear in the role of representatives of the state interest (equated with the general interest of citizens), whereas those from outside are depicted as representing the interests of minorities and individual groups, or even rival interests to the Polish state.

The economic perspective, expressed by the code profitable–unprofitable, is spliced with the political one, and it is this way of speaking and thinking about energy issues that is very much dominant in all the subject areas. Economic development, energy prices and costs of investments define the parameters of the discussion on Poland's energy future, at state level but also at the local level – voivodeships and districts. The very idea of development and civilisational progress is strongly equated with economic growth, as it is GDP growth that is expected to guarantee the prosperity and security of citizens. A slowdown in growth represents a threat for the future of Poles and places a question mark against their economic security. The alternative perception of progress referring to sustainable development, quality of life, and eco-development is marginal and confined to words. These ideas often appear as an element of image-based communication, but without being discussed more widely. They usually function either as slogans in the declarative statements of politicians and business leaders or as labels attached to movements contesting the dominant paradigm of thinking about the future of energy. In neither case are they accompanied by profound reflection, extended arguments or even an outline of space for debate. Interestingly, although the issues associated with aspects of climate change, CO_2 emissions and the EU's climate policy appear in all the topics, they do not constitute a fundamental point of reference for the main issue organising the discourses. Even with wind energy, with the strongest allusions to ecology, environmental protection and low-emissions technologies, dominant are local concerns associated with specific investment projects or the future of the districts. Research on the media discourse on wind energy in the USA, despite the increased significance and power of wind farms there after 2007, demonstrated a similar trend (Stephens et al. 2009).

The media discourse on energy in Poland is elite-driven and generally exclusive, accompanied by the belief that this is a difficult subject requiring specialist knowledge. In all three fields, the threshold of competences entitling actors to speak out was high, something underlined by those who do participate. Citizens are assigned positions of ignorance and lack of interest, which is also illustrated by the results of opinion polls. Mechanisms of exclusion are much more evident than those of inclusion. In all the subject areas, the same categories of actors are dominant (although the specific entities vary): politicians and business representatives, supported by experts, mostly from the field of economics. Institutional actors – states, ministries and government offices, and business organisations (banks, companies, consulting agencies) – play an important role in all three discourses. NGOs, political parties and research institutions appear in the background.

Whereas, as we have seen, certain groups of actors present in the discourse are clearly marginalised (NGOs, civic leaders and activists, local politicians, residents), many are entirely absent. If we compare the communicative activity in energy/environmental issues in Poland and Germany, for example, what is striking in the Polish media is the lack or very limited presence of consumer organisations, trade unions, schools and teachers, artists and social scientists (apart from economists).

Despite the differentiation of the discourses in many respects, as shown by the previous chapters, the media space is lacking radical discourses giving an alternative to the dominant paradigm. Even the internet space, which could become an area for developing and communicating different views and visions for energy, does not fulfil these expectations. The areas of internet communication that we analysed are not a deliberative space. Rather, they are characterised by similar trends to traditional media – press, radio, television – meaning above all dominance of the economic perspective, instrumental use of technological knowledge (scientific data supporting ideological goals), and a low level of dialogicality. What sets them apart is a higher level of dispersal of contents, their fragmentary nature and the fact that the contents which are often linked to other statements do not indicate which ones. They constitute a commentary, sometimes only loosely linked to substance. Of course, this does not mean that the internet does not provide possibilities of communication to groups or individuals contesting the dominant structures and perspectives. Yet those that it does offer are barely visible in the public space. Owing to capitalist mechanisms associated with marketing, market positioning, and access to costly communication technologies, professionalisation of network communication, strong, well-organised actors possessing economic capital, i.e. beneficiaries of the present system, gain much better conditions for organising the discursive space around themselves in a way that others can perceive. This is the first condition of having real influence on what happens in the communicative public space.

In their accounts of the individual subject areas explored in this book, the authors analysed in detail the resources used by actors to build and maintain their influential position, but also the mechanisms deciding on who is permitted a voice in the discourse and who is not. The next question is the claim to importance given to these discourses and assuring them a broader reach than one's own epistemic community. According to Giandomenico Majone, "the most important function both of public deliberation and of policy-making is defining the norms that determine when certain decisions are to be regarded as policy problems" (Majone 1989: 23–24). Furthermore, he argues that because uncertainty of the future is so ubiquitous in policy making, the values of those responsible for it are of great importance (Majone 1989: 26). When reality is characterised by a high level of variability and risk associated with making decisions, one of the mechanisms used to justify their course is reference to values. The criteria of suitability, pertinence and significance are therefore removed from the axionormative system. This explains the tendency of the actors in our analysed discourses to refer to values – development and progress, security, patriotism, freedom – although the semantic fields of these concepts prove to be varied (e.g. security). Use of this value (in various domains and contexts) constitutes the well-known strategy of securitisation of discourse, serving legitimisation of political actions and decisions (cf. Fischhendler et al. 2014).

Our analyses clearly pointed to certain blank spaces in the media discourses. The public sphere created in media communication is not representative of what goes on beyond its boundaries. Although it indicates the existence of controversies or conflict axes, it does not form a map of the diverse positions and views. The actors whose voices are heard occupy unequal positions, and the relations that exist between them can be described as relations of dominance and discrimination, if only because of the symbolic resources attributed to these positions (e.g. knowledge and ignorance, importance and unimportance etc.). Many arguments and standpoints articulated in the non-media space are not found in media sources, and some actors do not exist in it at all.

The authors of the analyses also point to the rational nature of the debates. This rationality is expressed, for example, in basing persuasive mechanisms on so-called hard numerical data, something that does not aid deliberation. Emotions, usually attributed to marginalised actors and confronted with the clinical reason of experts giving calculations, do not help with better mutual understanding, but rather with labelling behaviours and depreciating positions that contest the dominant economic-technocratic order. Rationality donning the mask of quantifiability is illusory. The data quoted, often based on estimates or documenting, for example, distributions of opinion, lacks any extended commentary to explain the specific details. It is also often presented fragmentarily. Statistical and other economic data is thrown around, and the actors presented the evidence constructed in this way as facts. Yet this evidence is always based on context, its meaning resulting from a concrete situation and needing to be framed appropriately (Majone 1989). An excellent example is data on the forecasts of shale gas resources in Poland. This data, presented as facts, varies hugely in the discourse. Measurable and objective figures can be used for subjective and ideological interpretations, and are also frequently a type of resource to which actors other than those citing them in a given situation (interview, programme) do not have access, which makes it difficult to discuss them.

The risks associated with planning future actions are also quantified. All the discourses we analysed are more prescriptive or proscriptive than descriptive – meaning that they more often refer to what will or should occur than to existing facts. In this way, the discourses construct visions of the future saddled with a high level of uncertainty (although the actors frequently colonialise this future, presenting it in a language of facts, rather than prognoses). One of the ways of reducing this uncertainty is transforming it into quantifiable risk, which is usually economic. In the other areas the future sometimes serves to put off troublesome problems, removing them from the agenda of current issues (e.g. solving the problem of radioactive waste or the environmental consequences of shale extraction technologies). In these cases, the mechanism of reduction of uncertainty is trust in the state, administrative services, science or the law. The actors who support a given investment assume that undertaking actions will in future bring solutions to controversial questions (we know what we do not know, and how to get the missing knowledge). Their opponents, meanwhile, point to the uncertainty additionally exacerbated by taking actions whose consequences are currently hard to predict (we do not know what we do not know). To refer to the concepts of futurisation and defuturisation in the sense coined by Niklas Luhmann (1976), we can state that in the analysed discourse on selected energy issues, the actors rather seek to narrow the options of the future to one desired scenario (defuturisation) than to "open the future" by permitting various scenarios to be constructed in order to discuss them further (futurisation). Despite the discrepancy in the preferences of the various groups of actors and their visions of the energy system, from the interpretation of the past (Poland's own and that of other countries) is derived a priority of technological and economic development common to everybody. Although the politicians stress that the various energy sources are complementary rather than mutually exclusive, the actors in the discourse often treat them as rivals.

To sum up the media discourses on energy issues, I would state that they are dominated by a positive attitude towards the technologies they discuss and solutions to energy questions. If this attitude is not enthusiastic, it is based on more or less directly expressed acceptance of the planned actions. Opposing positions and contesting discourses have considerably less media visibility. Furthermore, the dominant discourse in the media is limited in terms of analysis of social aspects taking into consideration the perspective of various groups of citizens. For example, the discourse contains scant mention of issues connected to inequalities – the participation of various groups of citizens in the risk and in the expected benefits, or the consequences of industrialisation of originally rural land. The economisation and tendency for the discourse to refer to state level means that problems remain abstract for the majority of consumers of the media, while the benefits are often expressed in the language of ideology. A pretext for covering energy issues is often given by political decisions or economic investments, and the statements of the main actors are then clearly used to persuade.

It is worth comparing this observation with the results of research on the attitude of European societies to various energy technologies (nuclear power or fracking), according to which Poles usually exhibit a higher level of acceptance than citizens of other countries (cf. Eurobarometer studies). The media discourses, which give precedence to business-political projects, take place at the macro level, and present energy issues as abstract problems for the average citizen, but in a persuasive and often ideological way, are of no small significance here.

The question we asked in this book about the character of the media space in the context of deliberation and the rules applying there demands an answer. The analyses that we have presented paint a picture far removed from a dialogical space searching for a broad and mature agreement. It might therefore seem that the mechanisms of exclusion and domination shown so clearly will lead to the perception of this space as an arena in which the individual interests and differing perspectives of actors clash. Yet the battle taking place here is seldom one in which the arms are the arguments of representatives of various worlds. While the main skirmish goes on at the fringes, it is only the strongest who flex their muscles in the arena itself. So it is the key actors of the economic and political sectors who dominate the media space. Despite the divergent interests (e.g. climate policy and economic objectives) or the mutual unpredictability of partners (on the one hand the instability of political decisions as an element of economic risk, and on the other the fluctuations of the economic situation), they form a kind of coalition symbolically supported by the cited experts from the circles of science and economic consulting. This is all fortified by such values as energy independence, stability of supplies and citizens' security. From time to time, from the crowd congregated outside the arena, another actor is summoned, who is not always au fait with the rules of the game. But the crowd view this actor, without the position strengthened by the symbolic resources of recognised knowledge and status, as weak and helpless, or alternatively agitated and aggressive, determinedly fighting for attention. In this sense, then, the media discourses are closer to the logic of Habermasian dramaturgical action than to communicative action.

Bibliography

Dryzek, J. S. (1997), *The Politics of the Earth. Environmental Discourses*, New York.

Fischhendler, I., Boymel, D., Boykoff, M. T. (2014), "How Competing Securitized Discourses over Land Appropriation Are Constructed: The Promotion of Solar Energy in the Israeli Desert," *Environmental Communication*.

Luhmann, N. (1976), "The Future Cannot Begin: Temporal Structures in Modern Society," *Social Research*, vol. 43, no. 1, pp. 130–52.

Majone, G. (1989), *Evidence, Argument and Persuasion in the Policy Process*, New Haven /London.

Prasad, P., Elmes, M. (2005), "In the Name of the Practical. Unearthing the Hegemony of Pragmatics in the Discourse of Environmental Management," *Journal of Management Studies*, 42 (4), pp. 845–67.

Stephens, J.C., Rand, G. M., Melnick, L. L. (2009), "Wind Energy in US Media. A Comparative State-Level Analysis of a Critical Climate Change Mitigation," *Technology Environmental Communication*, vol. 3, no. 2, July, pp. 168–90.

Uusi-Rauva, C., Tienari, J. (2008), *The EU Energy and Climate Package in the Media in January 2008. A Look at Intertextuality and Who Gets to Say How Things Stand*, http://www.vakki.net/publications/2009/VAKKI2009_Uusi-Rauva&Tienari.pdf (access: 26 February 2016).

APPENDICES

Appendix I

Table 1. List of analysed press title issues – corpus of texts

Year	Title	Issue
1986	Polityka	38
1986	Polityka	19
1986	Polityka	20
1986	Polityka	20
1986	Polityka	22
1986	Polityka	23
1986	Polityka	1
1986	Polityka	1
1988	Polityka	51
1989	Polityka	11
1989	Polityka	11
1989	Polityka	13
1985	Rzeczpospolita	47
1985	Rzeczpospolita	100
1986	Rzeczpospolita	196
1986	Rzeczpospolita	296
1986	Rzeczpospolita	111
1986	Rzeczpospolita	111
1986	Rzeczpospolita	113
1986	Rzeczpospolita	114
1986	Rzeczpospolita	109

Year	Title	Issue
1986	Rzeczpospolita	73
1987	Rzeczpospolita	289
1987	Rzeczpospolita	12
1988	Rzeczpospolita	61
1988	Rzeczpospolita	73
1989	Rzeczpospolita	39
1985	Trybuna Ludu	74
1986	Trybuna Ludu	173
1986	Trybuna Ludu	210
1986	Trybuna Ludu	257
1986	Trybuna Ludu	113
1986	Trybuna Ludu	113
1986	Trybuna Ludu	120
1987	Trybuna Ludu	265
1987	Trybuna Ludu	152
1987	Trybuna Ludu	80
1988	Trybuna Ludu	235
1988	Trybuna Ludu	271
1988	Trybuna Ludu	291
1989	Trybuna Ludu	131
1985	Tygodnik Powszechny	16
1985	Tygodnik Powszechny	20
1986	Tygodnik Powszechny	30
1986	Tygodnik Powszechny	20
1986	Tygodnik Powszechny	25
1987	Tygodnik Powszechny	46
1987	Tygodnik Powszechny	47
1987	Tygodnik Powszechny	47
1987	Tygodnik Powszechny	49
1987	Tygodnik Powszechny	49
1988	Tygodnik Powszechny	40
1985	Życie Warszawy	27
1985	Życie Warszawy	5
1985	Życie Warszawy	123
1985	Życie Warszawy	123
1985	Życie Warszawy	123
1986	Życie Warszawy	167
1986	Życie Warszawy	220
1986	Życie Warszawy	210
1986	Życie Warszawy	211

Year	Title	Issue
1986	Życie Warszawy	247
1986	Życie Warszawy	263
1986	Życie Warszawy	112,115
1986	Życie Warszawy	113
1986	Życie Warszawy	110
1986	Życie Warszawy	113
1986	Życie Warszawy	138
1986	Życie Warszawy	46
1987	Życie Warszawy	293
1987	Życie Warszawy	174
1987	Życie Warszawy	179
1987	Życie Warszawy	149
1989	Życie Warszawy	63
1989	Życie Warszawy	293

Rzeczpospolita

From January 1982 to 1989 the official Polish People's Republic government organ, national daily newspaper.

Życie Warszawy

National daily newspaper, published in 1944–2011 in Warsaw (publication suspended during martial law)

Polityka

National socio-political weekly, published in Warsaw since 1957. Previously expressed the views of moderately reform-minded Polish United Workers Party circles.

Tygodnik Powszechny

National Catholic socio-cultural weekly, published since 1945 in Krakow, taken over in 1953–1956 by the PAX Association (publication was suspended as *Tygodnik* refused to publish an obituary of Stalin). Regarded as the voice of the Catholic intelligentsia, maintaining independent thought to the extent permitted by the preventive censorship binding in the Polish People's Republic. Suspended during martial law, it was revived in 1982, becoming the only legal publication close to the opposition.

Trybuna Ludu

Politics and news daily, published in 1948–90 in Warsaw; Party Central Committee organ, formed by the merger of *Głos Ludu* (Polish Workers' Party) and *Robotnik* (Polish Socialist Party); propaganda instrument entirely subjugated to the Party. *Trybuna* had one of the highest circulations in the Polish People's Republic.

List of web portals monitored by Press Service

www.biznes.onet.pl
www.money.pl
www.cire.pl
www.bankier.pl
www.finanse.wp.pl
www.forsal.pl
www.wyborcza.pl
www.biznes.interia.pl
www.inwestycje.pl
www.gpwinfostrefa.pl
www.euro.bankier.pl
www.gielda.onet.pl
www.wiadomosci.gazeta.pl
www.wiadomosci.onet.pl
www.fakty.interia.pl
www.energetyka.wnp.pl
www.parkiet.com
www.biznes.gazetaprawna.pl
www.rp.pl
www.waluty.com.pl
www.nafta.wnp.pl
www.wprost.pl
www.wnp.pl
www.polskatimes.pl

www.gospodarka.gazeta.pl
www.gazetaprawna.pl
www.polskaradio.pl
www.tvn24.pl
www.wiadomosci.wp.pl
www.portfel.pl
www.fundi.pl
www.egospodarka.pl
www.tvp.info
www.wirtualnemedia.pl
www.finanse.egospodarka.pl
www.prnews.pl
www.finanse.wp.pl
www.portalmorski.pl
www.twoja-firma.pl
www.ipis.pl
www.naszdziennik.pl
www.news,oney.pl
www.wiaodmosci24.pl
www.banki.pl
www.budnet.pl
www.naukawpolsce.pl
www.wyborcza.biz

Unpublished reports prepared within the project "The Media as a Space of Deliberation..." used in the book:

Wit Hubert:
> *Selected Energy Topics in the Polish Internet Discourse. Research Report*

Maria Świątkiewicz-Mośny:
> *Selected Energy Topics in the Press Discourse. Research Report*
> *Wind Energy in the Press Discourse in the 1990s and 2007–2012*

Aleksandra Wagner:
> *Nuclear Energy in the 1980s Press Discourse. Content Analysis of Selected Press Titles. Research Report*
> *Nuclear Energy in the Press Discourse 2007–2012*
> *Shale Gas in the Press Discourse 2009–2012*
> *Selected Energy Topics in the Television and Radio Discourse. Research Report*

Technical Editor
Jadwiga Makowiec

Proofreader
Aneta Dzidek

Typesetter
Tomasz Pasteczka

Jagiellonian University Press
Editorial Offices: ul. Michałowskiego 9/2, 31-126 Kraków
Phone: +48 12-663-23-80, 12-663-23-82, Fax: +48 12-663-23-83